TOPSY

THE STARTLING STORY OF THE CROOKED-TAILED ELEPHANT, P. T. BARNUM, AND THE AMERICAN WIZARD, THOMAS EDISON

MICHAEL DALY

Atlantic Monthly Press
New York

All insert photos courtesy the Library of Congress, with the following
exceptions: Photo 4.3 ("Jumbo has fallen"): McCaddon Collection of the
Barnum and Bailey Circus. Manuscripts Division, Department of Rare Books
and Special Collections, Princeton University Library. Photo 5.1 (Adam
Forepaugh) and Photo 5.2 (Addie Forepaugh): Billy Rose Theatre Division,
The New York Public Library for the Performing Arts; Astor, Lenox and
Tilden Foundations. Photo 6.2 (The Fearless Frogman): Print Collection,
Miriam and Ira D. Wallach Division of Art, Prints and Photographs, The
New York Public Library; Astor, Lenox and Tilden Foundations.

Published simultaneously in Canada
Printed in the United States of America

FIRST EDITION

ISBN-13: 978-0-8021-1904-9

Atlantic Monthly Press
an imprint of Grove/Atlantic, Inc.
841 Broadway
New York, NY 10003

Distributed by Publishers Group West

www.groveatlantic.com

13 14 15 16   10 9 8 7 6 5 4 3 2 1

To the Daly girls: Dinah, Sinead, Bronagh, and, yes, Stella

CONTENTS

CONTENTS

TOPSY

THE 200-POUND BABY

The 200-pound baby thudded from womb to earth somewhere in an Asian forest on a date historical records list no more precisely than circa 1875. The first sounds she heard would have been the trumpeting and rumbling of the other elephants welcoming her into the world just as they each had been welcomed in their own first moments. She would have begun to learn even as she struggled out of whatever remained of the amniotic sac that she had been born into a uniquely caring society. This society's bonds only began with the mother who had remained standing during the birth and now gingerly stepped back to gaze upon her stirring newborn.

The others would have kept protective watch as the newest arrival awkwardly rose, the mother gently nudging the baby with a foot or giving a little hoist with her trunk, but only if it was needed. The baby would have rolled upright from her side and raised herself first on her forelegs, the two rear legs scrambling in earth wet with the cascade of fluids that had accompanied her arrival. She would have soon been up on all fours, and within minutes of her birth she would have been taking her first wobbly steps, her eyes huge and wide and pink-rimmed. The surrounding grown females would have stood ready to help the mother guide her baby between her forelegs, where she could begin to nurse. The baby would have suckled with her mouth, for it would be some days before she began to control an elephant's most distinctive appendage, her trunk, with its one hundred thousand muscles.

Among the myriad possible uses for the mother's trunk was giving her child a dusting of earth, perhaps to protect against biting insects and to dampen the scent that might attract predators hoping to snatch a vulnerable newborn. The whole group would have maintained a sunrise-to-sunrise vigilance against that threat as it waited for the baby's postnatal steps to become sure and strong enough for travel. A maternal shadow would have followed the baby as stagger became gambol.

The males in these extended family groups are driven off when they reach adolescence, usually to wander alone, sometimes in small "bachelor" groups. The other adults would all have been females, and they would have been as gentle as the mother in steering the baby back when she ventured too far, the sensory cells along the length of their trunks helping to gauge a touch that was gentle as well as firm, imparting a caress along with a nudge. These were *allomothers*, mothers in every way save when the baby sought to feed. There remained but one mother in the fullest sense as the baby's connections with the rest of the group branched out and deepened, caress by caress, touches so light as to prove the sensitivity of an elephant's skin despite its wrinkled thickness.

The usual wait would have been two days before the most senior female, the matriarch, gave the signal and began to move. The others would have followed, perhaps a dozen or more, any mothers with calves toward the front. The matriarch would have restricted the pace to that of the littlest one. The baby would have been not just *with* the group, but its immediate and collective priority.

Even so, the baby still would have been expected to walk unassisted through the forest, finding and developing her footing. The only time she would not have been moving on her own power was when the herd had to swim. The mother would then support the baby in front of her with her trunk as the herd moved tirelessly through the water, their buoyancy liberating them from an otherwise unrelenting demand of elephantine existence that the baby was still too small to know: gravity's translation of size to encumbrance. Elephants have been known to swim as long as six hours without touching bottom.

The perfection of their evolved design would have been demonstrated anew as they left the water and again became subject to gravity's pull. Elephants' footpads expand under their weight, reducing the depth they sink into wet earth. The footpads then contract as they are raised, breaking the mud's suction.

Back on dry land, another marvel of evolution would have made their tread appear to be considerably lighter than that of much smaller animals. The skeletal structure of their feet is angled in a way that has been compared to a platform shoe, so they walk on their toes, the weight spreading evenly toward the heel on a cushioning pad of fatty tissue. The pad is similar to the seismic tissue that whales and dolphins use to detect and receive sound waves in the sea and may enable elephants to detect vibrations in the ground. The footpads as well as the trunks contain Pacinian corpuscles, liquid capsules surrounded by layers of tissue and gel and containing nerve endings so sensitive to pressure as to enable these biggest of land beasts to detect the faintest of stirrings. This and similarly acute senses of hearing and smell compensate for relatively weak eyesight to such a degree that blind matriarchs have been said to lead a group successfully.

Along with their improbably light and sensitive tread came a gait by which the rear leg on one side moved up to land precisely in the print just made by the forefoot on that side and the same then happened on the other side, imparting a hint of what would in the next century come to be called a moonwalk. The group would have thus proceeded to a promising place to forage, their speed determined by the youngest, their direction by the oldest, who was necessarily the only female surviving from the time, as many as eight decades before, in which she had been born. Her position as matriarch was granted in recognition not of her physical supremacy over the others, but of wisdom distilled from the years she had followed her predecessor, the predecessor's wisdom derived from what her own predecessor had learned, it all going back generations with the promise of ever greater collective wisdom in the generations to come.

The group would have continually paused to feed, needing to do so some sixteen hours a day, each of the adults consuming some three hundred pounds of fodder. They likely would have paused during the midday heat, some of the adults keeping watch while others dozed standing up and the baby lay on her side, safe and secure. The group would then have moved as one with the newest member, on into the night and its rhythms of chirping insects and croaking frogs.

Had the baby been a male, he would have been destined to be banished in his early teens, perhaps to form a small group with other males, or to lead a solitary existence relieved by occasional encounters with females for breeding, a joining of just forty-five seconds. But the baby was a daughter seemingly destined to become a mother herself, then a grandmother, maybe even a matriarch who would pass on the ancient knowledge she was beginning to learn even now.

Meanwhile, the nursing baby would have consumed some three gallons a day, gaining as many as thirty pounds a week. She would have begun to master her trunk, siphoning up water to transfer it to her mouth and using the single sensitive little "finger" at the tip to feed herself samples of what her mother was eating.

When the forest up ahead suddenly erupted with shouts and gunshots, the baby would have ducked between her mother's legs. The clamor would have ceased as the matriarch led a retreat and the danger would have seemed to pass.

Tranquillity would have appeared to return to the forest, but the elephants would not have been able to travel more than six miles in any direction without again encountering the shockingly sudden noise and fire. They likely kept trying, particularly at night, when there would have seemed a better chance of slipping past. Each time it would have been the same.

In the mornings, the elephants might have sensed movement through the forest. Their fanning ears might have detected sounds of chopping and then of trees falling until evening, when there would again have been a furtive rustling in the surrounding undergrowth. The twin nostrils of their upraised trunks would have detected a scent foreign to the forest where they had harmoniously evolved over the ages, but they would not yet have understood the danger it signaled. The grown elephants might have leaned forward on a front foot to detect vibrations, what a scientist in a future time would term "listening with their feet."

After maybe a fortnight would have come the morning when the shouts and gunshots and fire erupted simultaneously from every direction but one, forcing the elephants to flee the lone way open to them. The group would have been driven to a fifty-yard space between two opposing walls made with felled trees. The elephants may have sensed danger ahead and balked at continuing, but the terror was now almost right upon them and they would have proceeded on, a gray and thundering storm, the matriarch still in the lead, but the wisdom born of centuries suddenly for naught.

The terror would have kept coming and the group would have kept fleeing, trumpeting shrilly not as the baby would have first heard them at her birth, but in total fear as the walls converged on either side of them. The baby would have found herself in a fast-moving and quickly thickening forest of huge legs. Even in such panicked circumstances, the bigger elephants would have remained so sure-footed and aware of where they stepped that the baby and the other little ones would have been in no danger of being trampled.

After one hundred yards, the walls would have narrowed to a gap not much wider than the space for a grown elephant and a calf. The space beyond would have suddenly opened up and it might have momentarily seemed to the group that it had escaped.

But the group was trapped within the twelve-foot walls of a kheddah, more felled trees lashed together with cane into an enclosing stockade. Any elephant who sought to test her strength against the wall would have first come to a trench four feet wide and four feet deep. And on the far side of the wall would have been men who fired guns and waved torches and jabbed with spears.

Elephants seeking to turn back would have found the four-yard gap had been closed with a reinforced gate as soon as they passed through. The baby would have been sheltered under the mother as the adults formed a protective circle, facing outward. Most likely, they would have just been left there for several days without food or water.

As the baby grew hungry, she would have discovered that captured mothers initially run dry of milk. Her plaintive cries and those of any other calves would likely have been joined by the adult elephants' signal of apprehension and uncertainty, made by rapping the end of the trunk on the ground while exhaling sharply, a sound a nineteenth-century catcher compared to "a large sheet of tin rapidly doubled."

When the captors deemed the time was right, the gate would have opened long enough to admit pairs of tame elephants called kookies. Each kookie would have had two men atop. One, a mahout, or tender, straddled the neck to guide the creature. The second, a roper, sat behind him.

The mahouts would have steered pairs of kookies so as to separate a grown elephant from the herd, squeezing in on either side. The two ropers would have slipped down, first slipping a rope hobble around the wild elephant's rear legs, then looping a rope around her neck. The captors then would have used the ropes and the power of the kookies to drag a captive out of the stockade and into the forest, where she would be tied to a tree. The captives who struggled would have been liable to be beaten and stuck with spears. The unmanageable ones, particularly any adult males who happened to be with the herd at the moment of capture, were sometimes killed right then and there.

When it came the mother's turn to be straddled and hobbled, the captors would not have needed to bother with the baby. She would have come along wherever the mother was dragged. No rope was required to retain a baby after the mother was tethered to a tree.

Either in the forest or after the extended march to a market town, the baby and the mother would have been forcibly separated. The mother would have been kept in restraints, for the captors otherwise would have had to kill her as the baby was pulled away, vainly struggling and screaming, ever more desperate as the distance between them grew.

Captors are known to have kept a baby moving in the desired direction and pace by placing her in a rope sling on a long pole with two men at each end, the baby low enough so her scrabbling feet touched the ground and relieved some of the weight.

Then would have come the long sea voyage, four months if direct to America, longer if first to an animal dealer in Germany, as was most likely in this instance. The baby probably would have been shipped to Hamburg along with at least some of the other captured elephants as a wholesale consignment intended for whatever buyers might express interest. A need for secrecy would have arisen only when the baby was purchased by a circus owner who was hatching a scheme that began with sneaking a baby elephant into America with no public notice. The arrival of any number of grown elephants was likely to attract attention, so the baby almost certainly traveled to New York alone, devoid of the company of her own kind, as she had never been, as she was never meant to be.

She traveled in her solitude either between decks or deep in the hold, a dark, dank dungeon that rose and fell, leaving the baby without even the security of her footing. The baby was probably kept in place during rough weather with a variation of what was employed with grown elephants: two iron ringbolts driven into the hull to tie the rear legs, and a teak bar installed at the front of the stall as a kind of handrail, only for a trunk.

"The beasts would themselves wrap their trunks around the wooden bar before them and hold fast, and in this position the waves might toss the vessel as much as they pleased but they couldn't throw the elephants off their feet," reported a captain of the era who transported elephants from Ceylon to New York.

If the baby was like most elephants, she got seasick. If she was like other baby elephants torn from their mothers, she cried out shrilly in her sleep, seeming to relive the trauma. She otherwise may have seemed to her captors to be mute, though she may have been sending out a rumbling long-distance call below the range of human hearing like the call whales send through the sea. She would have been calling out to the mother from whom she had been fully weaned nearly six years too early, the mother whom she would never see again.

The baby likely felt serious cold for the first time on the Atlantic. She almost certainly had enough control of her trunk to tuck it between her forelegs in the way of elephants when they are chilled. The country toward which she sailed had celebrated its one hundredth birthday in the heat of the summer just past but now was at the wintry start of a new year.

On finally reaching New York, the ship sailed past Coney Island on the port side and Staten Island on the starboard. Another elephant, Fanny, would make an astonishing swim across these waters a quarter century later in a bid to escape after being spooked by the ultimate fate of this same smuggled baby.

Just ahead lay the busiest harbor in the world. The Statue of Liberty was still nearly a decade from rising on a small island off to the left, and Ellis Island just beyond would not open until six years later. Human new arrivals were still being received directly on the tip of Manhattan at Castle Garden, which had served as the sandstone Fort Clinton during the War of 1812, then been converted into an entertainment arena whose many attractions had included the occasional circus and menagerie. It was now America's first immigration receiving center, with the primary purpose of protecting new arrivals from the swarms of sex traffickers, swindlers, and thieves who awaited each shipload. The inflow of immigrants had slackened after the Panic of 1873, which had been triggered largely by reckless speculation on railroads that reverberated into widespread bankruptcies and foreclosures. The economy was now rousing itself back into growth so prodigious that the dawn of America's second century had the glow of destiny. The Reconstruction Era was nearing an official end and in this new Gilded Age railway trackage was tripling, connecting boundless natural resources to burgeoning industry, goods to markets, supply to demand, all of it made more productive and efficient by an inventive spirit that would produce five hundred thousand new patents in twenty years. Coal production in those golden decades was increasing eightfold. Agricultural production was more than doubling even as society was being industrialized and urbanized. Business was being reshaped by the forces of incorporation and consolidation, changes that led to the rise of a small number of super-rich titans but also saw the overall per capita income increase to double that of Germany and France and higher by 50 percent than that of Great Britain. Those seeking to share in the prosperity were arriving in such record numbers that Castle Garden would process more than eight million immigrants before it was closed thirteen years hence. The demand for workers was so great that employers waited there to hire the able-bodied as soon as their arrival was duly recorded.

The ship carrying the baby elephant would have continued on to one of the port's cargo piers, which then handled more than half of America's international commerce. The newest arrival must have found the pier to be a disorienting assault of unfamiliar sights and sounds and smells and icy air. Other elephants had been met by reporters and clamoring crowds. This was the first to arrive in secrecy, hustled ashore, then transported by wagon, ferry, and wagon again to Philadelphia and the winter quarters of the Adam Forepaugh show, with considerable care taken to avoid any attention.

Forepaugh was a onetime butcher boy turned shady horse dealer who had found his present calling when he took part ownership of a circus that had failed to make good on a debt. He was now in a fierce and protracted struggle with P. T. Barnum for supremacy as the greatest showman in what was surely becoming the greatest of nations.

Both Forepaugh's show and Barnum's show were growing to a thousand performers, sideshow attractions, canvasmen, ticket takers, hawkers, teamsters, cooks, bill posters, and press agents, as well as trained horses, lions, and the perpetual favorite, elephants. Both had big tops so big they could hold huge crowds of those who worked in the factories and tilled the fields and labored in the mines and laid the railroad track. Both offered an escape from grinding drudgery into the fabulous, a brief reprieve so enticing that some employers simply called a circus day rather than try to press on with distracted and discontented workers. Both rewarded anyone who could fork over a modest fee with a three-ring extravaganza that was more than any one pair of eyes could take in. Both gave spectators a sense that it all arrived just for them, that it was all for them, that if their labors made other men into giants of industry and finance, then at least a giant of show business was coming to them, needing them, soliciting them. Both shows also imparted a sense of connectedness not just to the rest of the immediate crowd, but also to the crowds at all the other locales along the route, making the audience part of a popular culture that transcended differences in ethnic origin, that put everyone under one tent, that made them Americans.

But no matter if Forepaugh matched or even exceeded his rival in every other way, Barnum demonstrated an unmatched genius at capturing and manipulating the public's imagination. Barnum had made himself the patriot's patriot in the Centennial year just past. He had opened each performance with a salute by a battery of thirteen cannons representing the original colonies. A woman clad as the Goddess of

Liberty would appear, accompanied by a bald eagle and men costumed as Continental troops along with a chorus that sang the "Star-Spangled Banner" and then urged the audience to join it in a rousing rendition of "America." The show would conclude with fireworks.

"A Fourth of July celebration every day," Barnum later wrote of that season.

And there had been a promotional souvenir magazine called the *Barnum Centennial Advance Daily,* the front cover emblazoned with a photo of Barnum surrounded by American flags, as if he were central to the great celebration, which indeed he strove energetically to become. The back cover offered a depiction of the signing of the Declaration of Independence credited to the "Bureau of Engraving."

"Circulation 2,000,000," the magazine had announced on its cover before the actual circulation of the very first copy.

On his part, Forepaugh had renamed his circus the Great Centennial Show, but otherwise it remained too much the same, featuring creatures whose intended appeal was that they were exotic and not American. That had not served him well in a birthday year when things American were the most prized.

The poster that had accompanied the Forepaugh show's Fourth of July appearance in Grand Rapids, Michigan, was headlined "Our Nation's Centennial Jubilee," yet the center was absent of even a single star or stripe and was dominated by a drawing of a bellowing rhinoceros that Forepaugh had imported the previous February from the animal dealer in Hamburg. Forepaugh' procession into town had been dwarfed by the city's own parade, in which forty-one different groups passed under a seventy-foot-high arch. They had included a wildly costumed "crew" called the Horribles and Forepaugh had offered them a small fortune to admit him as a member so he would at least be part of the celebration if he could not marshal it. The Horribles had declined, though they had requested and received two of Forepaugh's elephants to draw an ambulance thereby made comic.

Whatever fireworks display Forepaugh may have planned for that night had been preempted by an elaborate spectacular long planned by the city. The thirty-four elements had included a representation of its own Goddess of Liberty as well as George Washington on horseback and an "emblematic piece in letters of fire" spelling out "Peace, Prosperity, Freedom, the Result of 100 Years." The final element, what the program had termed "the finest of the evening," had featured "flags and shields surmounted by 'Grand Rapids, July 4, 1876' and underneath 'Good Night.'"

After such a finale, only an anticlimax could come from a circus owner who had not been able even to buy his way into the Horribles. And that had been neither the first nor the last town where the Forepaugh show had been out of step with the patriotic passions of the Centennial year. The 1876 season had been the first and only season where Forepaugh lost money. He was now resolved to restore his good fortune and top his rival in the season to come with an all-American sensation.

Adam Forepaugh understood that the transformative event after arriving in this nation of immigrants was not securing a job or gaining citizenship. It was the birth of the first child on U.S. soil, a child not subject to *jus sanguinis*, nationality by bloodline, but *jus soli*, nationality by birthplace; not from but of, as American as anybody.

In early February of 1877, the newspapers received a copy of a breathless missive that Forepaugh had supposedly sent to one of his top assistants:

I sent you a short dispatch about our good luck this morning. It no doubt surprised you, but I am now able to give full particulars of the strange event. The performing elephant "Betsy" of the five which my son had in training in our winter quarters in Germantown made us all happy this morning by giving birth last night to the only baby elephant ever born on American soil. The mother is a mammoth beast, standing over 11 feet high and as docile as any I ever saw. The newcomer is only about 18 inches high, but a little beauty. It is male, and began walking just before noon. From its birth to that moment it lay as though sleeping and we were very much afraid it would not live, although it seemed healthy in every respect this afternoon. There is no doubt that we shall be able to keep it and put it on the road this summer. At the sight of this intruder, the other elephants seemed very uneasy and cross and bellowed and threw themselves wildly around, so it was about all we could do to prevent them from demolishing everything within reach. We had a conference of medical men at our winter quarters this afternoon to see this native American elephant and they were very much delighted. The little fellow takes quite naturally to the situation and will soon become a great pet. We shall put him in training as soon as practicable and next summer shall be able to present to the country a real marvel of wonder to the American public. Today I would not take $20,000 for the baby.

A. Forepaugh

News of the first American-born elephant generated all the excitement that Forepaugh sought. The bills posted in advance of performances now included, "A Beautiful Baby Elephant. The first ever born in captivity outside the Tropical Zone. To see this newborn infant nursing with its mouth and trunk is the rarest, queerest sight ever beheld."

Forepaugh's rival then sent a missive of his own to the newspapers:

I deem it a duty to warn the public against the fraud being perpetrated on them by one Adam Forepaugh in conspicuously advertising for exhibition and as the principal feature in his menagerie, a baby elephant, which he falsely claims was born in Philadelphia last winter. It is an established zoological fact that elephants do not breed in captivity and there never was [one] born on this side [of] the Atlantic. The one advertised by Adam Forepaugh is a small and inferior Asiatic elephant, exported from Singapore to Hamburg, and there offered to my agent, who declined to purchase it.

As conclusive evidence of the correctness of this statement, I will give $100,000 for either a baby or full-grown elephant born in America.

Your obedient servant,
P. T. Barnum

Forepaugh had said he would not take $20,000 for the baby and here was Barnum pledging five times that. The Barnum response also conveyed the reason he knew that Forepaugh could not even consider the offer. The animal dealer in Hamburg was Carl Hagenbeck, whom Barnum had met several years before, when he visited Hamburg and ordered $15,000 in animals, including elephants, giraffes, and a dozen ostriches. Hagenbeck subsequently also sold animals to Forepaugh, in particular elephants. Hagenbeck would later write:

My faithful friend Barnum sent me huge orders for elephants. Barnum and another American named Forepaugh were at this time serious competitors in the circus world, and the American public seemed to have an especial predilection for elephants. At all events, elephants were the chief attraction and the fact was very fortunate for me. . . . I was perpetually receiving fresh orders not only from Barnum but also from Forepaugh, for the rivals were continually endeavoring to out trump each other.

Forepaugh must have assumed that Hagenbeck would not risk alienating one of his two biggest customers by telling Barnum or anybody else the true origin of the baby elephant. Forepaugh clearly did not anticipate that one of Barnum's agents might have been offered the same baby. This also could have been just a cover story. Hagenbeck could have secretly tipped off his "faithful friend" Barnum about all his rival's purchases.

Whatever the case, Forepaugh now faced a big test of nerve over a little elephant. He backed down without a reply and abandoned his sensational claim. The subsequent ads listed a baby elephant among the other attractions but dropped any reference to the purportedly historic circumstances of the baby's birth. The exact details of her capture and transport would remain murky for the very reason that the fraud had required Forepaugh to sneak the creature into its supposed birthplace without notice. What is certain is Forepaugh's baby was born in the wild, most likely in Ceylon (now Sri Lanka), but perhaps in India or Burma or Malaysia.

And the baby boy was a baby girl.

She was back with a group, if not a family, joining five grown elephants as the Forepaugh show prepared for the start of the 1877 season in Philadelphia. The first step of her training would have been to teach the baby to respond to her name. Hers came from a character in Harriet Beecher Stowe's 1852 novel *Uncle Tom's Cabin,* a young slave girl snatched by "speculators" so soon after her birth that she has no memory of her mother.

"How old are you, Topsy?" another character asks the girl.
"Dun no, Missis," the girl says.

"Don't know how old you are? Didn't anybody ever tell you? Who
was your mother?"

"Never had none!" said the child, with another grin.

"Never had any mother? What do you mean? Where were you
born?"

"Never was born.... Never had no father nor mother, nor nothin'.
I was raised by a speculator, with lots of others...."

"Have you ever heard anything about God, Topsy? ... Do you know
who made you?"

"Nobody, as I knows on.... I spect I grow'd. Don't think nobody
never made me."

That line gave rise to the popular expression "grow'd like Topsy,"
which originally meant growing without particular intent or plan. It
also came to mean growing at a remarkable rate, as was the whole
country, as was the motherless baby elephant who grew a pound a
day, seven pounds a week, thirty pounds a month. She learned that
when "speculators" made a certain sound they meant her.

"Topsy!"

THE ELEPHANT

Eight decades before Topsy's secret offloading, a sailing ship named after the country that was three months shy of its twentieth birthday and just beginning its remarkable growth entered New York harbor after a long and perilous voyage from India. The junior officer who kept the *America*'s log on this thirteenth day of April in 1796 happened to be Nathaniel Hathorne, father of the novelist, who would add a *w* to his name, supposedly to distinguish himself from a predecessor who had been the hanging judge at the Salem witch trials. Hathorne's normally diminutive handwriting dramatically increased in scale as he recorded a hugely unusual passenger: "Elephant on board."

This first of such creatures to land on these shores had been acquired in Bengal by the captain, Jacob Crowninshield. He wrote of his purchase and of his accompanying expectations in a November 2, 1795, letter from India to two seafaring brothers: "We take home a fine young elephant two years old, at $450. It is almost as large as a very large ox, and I dare say we shall get it home safe. If so, it will bring at least $5000.00."

Crowninshield went on, "I suppose you will laugh at this scheme, but I do not mind that, will turn elephant driver. We have plenty of water at the Cape and St. Helena. This was my plan."

He noted that a third brother, who co-owned the *America* with him, had declined to go in on the elephant.

"If it succeeds, I ought to have the whole credit and honor, too."

The primary motive may have been profit, but there was more at work. He ended by saying, "Of course you know it will be a great thing to carry the first elephant to America."

The arrival was reported in the *New York Journal*: "The Ship *America*, Captain Jacob Crowninshield of Salem, Massachusetts, Commander and owner, has brought home an ELEPHANT from Bengal in perfect health. It is the first ever seen in America and is a great curiosity. It is a female, two years old."

Ten days later, the ELEPHANT was put on display at the corner of Broadway and Beaver Street in Manhattan. The New World had already seen its first African lion in 1720, first camel in 1721, first polar bear in 1733, first leopard in 1768, first jaguar in 1788, first orangutan in 1789, and first ostrich in 1794. None approached the elephant in size and novelty and impact.

This largest of land mammals was not caged or otherwise restrained and would have needed little effort to snuff out a beholder's life; it posed no immediate danger only because it so chose. It remained outwardly tranquil, as if nature were not ultimately just a fierce struggle for the survival of the fittest, as if there were something more in existence's grand scheme. Its big, extravagantly lashed eyes were neither piercing nor cringing, but simply watchful. Its size seemed less a weapon than a vantage, in the way a mountain is. Its serenity was that of a living peak risen above the fray.

And what made the creature all the more fascinating was the appendage the French had termed a *trompe*, or trumpet, becoming trunk in English. Absent this feature, the creature might have seemed like just some huge, big-eared cow. This proboscis unlike any other extended, reached, selected, retrieved with surprising dexterity and precision. The fingerlike digit at the end was clearly sensitive and all the more remarkable in contrast with the creature's brutish bulk. The inescapable impression from witnessing the trunk's workings was that it was guided by intelligence beyond that of all the other beasts, both common and exotic, with the possible exception of the more human-like simians.

The elephant was clearly a whole other concept of corporeal being and yet was our kin in sagacity, to a degree that was difficult to gauge. Here was an alien intelligence native to our own planet.

Here also was great commercial potential. Crowninshield got not only the glory, but also the gold, and double what he had anticipated. The *Journal and Patriotic Register* reported the sale of "an ELEPHANT" to an unnamed buyer in a back-pages brief, noting, "The animal is sold for $10,000, being supposed to be the greatest price ever given for an animal in Europe or America." The owner, identified in a subsequent report only as a "Welshman named Owen" quickly recouped the exorbitant expenditure with pay-per-glimpse exhibitions of what was given no name beyond simply "The Elephant."

After two months on exhibition in New York, The Elephant was walked untethered to Philadelphia, then America's biggest city. The curious flocked to High Street, where a look could be had for fifty cents (twenty-five cents for children) between dawn and dusk. The

Philadelphia Aurora reported on July 28, 1796, presuming the behemoth to be male, "There has just arrived from New York, in this city, on his way to Charleston, an elephant. He possesses the adroitness of the beaver, the intelligence of the ape and the fidelity of the dog. He is the largest of the quadrupeds; the earth trembles under his feet."

The report added an observation that would prove generally true for elephants through the years to come: "He has the power of tearing up the largest trees and yet is tractable to those who use him well."

The Elephant continued a long trek south, generally traveling at night to prevent any free glimpses, making periodic appearances on the way to wintering in Charleston. She was back in Philadelphia in the spring, when the city was visited by another new arrival in America by way of New York. Thomas Abthorpe Cooper was a promising young actor from England scheduled to make his Philadelphia debut at the Chestnut Street Theater. There was a problem as opening night for *Alexander the Great* approached.

"The seats were not taken," a contemporary theater historian named William Dunlap noted.

Cooper had a financial guarantee from the theater's manager no matter what the turnout, but his foremost concern was something other than money. "My fame, which is my deity," he wrote in a letter.

He then had an epiphany that, in a contemporary's words, "might save the manager and relieve him from the mortification of a beggarly house." He made his inspiration a reality with a sixty-dollar rental fee and an extra bill announcing, "In Act I, the Grand Triumphal Entry of Alexander into Babylon; in which will be introduced for this night only a Real Elephant, caparisoned as for war."

The show sold out, all two-thousand-plus seats taken.

"Those who had declined to take a seat to see and support the best tragedian that had yet played in America filled the house to overflowing to see the stage dishonored by an elephant," the historian Dunlap sniffed.

Cooper went on to the fame he so desired, described by some as America's first great actor. The bigger draw, The Elephant, proceeded north for a return engagement in New York, a stint behind a coffee shop in Providence, and then on to Boston.

"The most respectable Animal in the world," a broadside in Boston announced. "In size he [*sic*] surpasses all other terrestrial creatures; and by his intelligence, he makes as near an approach to man, as matter can approach spirit."

Experiments two centuries hence would indicate that elephants can recognize themselves in a mirror as distinct from others of their kind, a capacity shared only by humans after the age of two, as well as adult apes, though not monkeys, and occasionally dolphins. The keeper of The Elephant may have detected in those huge eyes the glint of the rare species whose members have a sense of self. The keeper certainly noted The Elephant's memory. The broadside reported that after being separated from her owner for ten weeks, The Elephant had recognized the man the moment he walked in the door and had cried out "till his [*sic*] Friend came within reach of his trunk, with which he caressed him, to the astonishment of all those who saw him."

The broadside also reported that The Elephant "eats 130 weight a day, and drinks all kinds of spirituous liquors."

"Some days he has drank 30 bottles of porter, drawing the corks with his trunk. He is so tame that he travels loose, and has never attempted to hurt any one."

There was one warning.

"The Elephant having destroyed many papers of consequence, it is recommended to visitors not come near him with such papers."

The original admission fee was fifty cents, but this was too much in Boston, even for "the greatest natural curiosity ever presented to the public." The price was cut to a quarter.

The Elephant went on to Salem, the hometown of Hathorne and Crowinshield. Those who paid the twenty-five cents there included Rev. William Bentley of Salem, who was widely regarded as one of the better of his species. Bentley was happy to turn over his pulpit to clerics of other faiths and supported education for all, African-Americans included. He spoke twenty-one languages and gave over half his minister's salary to needy parishioners. He was also extremely observant, as evidenced in his diary.

"Went to the Market House to see the Elephant," he wrote. "The crowd of spectators forbad me any but a general & superficial view of him. He was six feet, four inches high. Of large Volume, his skin black, as tho' lately oiled. A short hair was on every part, but not sufficient for a covering. His tail hung one third of his height, but without any long hairs at the end of it."

Bentley saw that the creature remained more independent than had been suggested: "His legs were still at command at the joints, but he could not be persuaded to lie down. The Keeper repeatedly mounted him but he persisted in shaking him off."

The Elephant had apparently been looking for something else when he destroyed the papers mentioned in the warning.

"Bread & Hay were given him and he took bread out of the pockets of the Spectators," Bentley observed.

Bentley also noted a feature that was widely either overlooked or ignored.

"We say *his* because the common language. It is a female & teats appeared just behind the forelegs."

Yet, as progressive and good-hearted as he was with his fellow humans, Bentley did not seem even to consider the trauma this young elephant must have suffered during capture and then transport across the sea and now, surrounded as she was by boisterous crowds. The Elephant may have been as close to man as matter can be to spirit, but she was still viewed as matter. Neither Bentley nor seemingly anyone else felt she warranted more concern and sympathy than cattle or sheep as she continued her perpetual tour of the curious.

The reception in the tiny South Carolina hamlet of Asheepo was noted by a British traveler named John Davis. He later wrote, "The inhabitants of every sex and age had gathered round. . . . I could not but admire the docility of the elephant, who in solemn majesty received the gifts of the children with his trunk."

Davis went into one of the hamlet's handful of log houses, where an elderly slave was squatted in front of a fire, evincing no interest in the creature.

"Well, old man, why don't you go out to look at the elephant?" Davis asked.

"He calf!" the slave replied.

The Elephant had grown two feet since her arrival in America, but she was still an Asian. She seemed therefore but a calf compared to the even bigger African elephants the slave had seen in his own land before he was snatched and transported and sold in much the same way as this traveling curiosity, though almost certainly with even less care and concern. The ultimate fate of this first elephant is unclear, though she did not likely live the fifty to seventy years typical in the wild. A captive probably would not have survived much more than half that time as stress and lack of exercise and poor diet took their toll.

* * *

The elderly man in the log house might have felt a stab of homesickness had he seen the second elephant to arrive in America. This big African had been acquired for a reported mere twenty dollars at an auction in London, a price at least partly attributable to the fact that elephants were nothing new to England, the first having been brought there in 43 AD by the Roman emperor Claudius, the second having been given by Louis IX of France to Henry III in 1255. The English king made the gift part of the Tower of London menagerie, but the elephant died two years later, reportedly from drinking too much wine. The European mainland had seen numerous elephants, two of them having gained considerable renown. The first, the male Hanno, had been given by King Manuel of Portugal to Pope Leo X in 1514 but died two years later after being administered a laxative mixed with gold, in keeping with his status. He was buried on the Vatican grounds, and the pope personally wrote his epitaph, which included "in my brutish breast they perceived human feelings." The second was the female Hansken, who toured the continent in the seventeenth century, performing such tricks as waving a flag and wielding a sword. Rembrandt made four chalk sketches of her in 1637.

The well-regarded American artist Edward Savage, known for his portraits of George Washington and Thomas Jefferson, acquired the further distinction of exhibiting what landed in 1804 in Boston as America's second elephant.

At one point, this new elephant was displayed in Manhattan at the Bull's Head Tavern, where Washington had assembled the troops for his triumphal entry into the city two decades before. The tavern was now owned by a former Hessian soldier turned butcher. Henry Astor was from the small German town of Waldorf and was an older brother of John Jacob Astor, who would become the richest man in America, its first multimillionaire.

Tens of thousands of cows, pigs, and lambs were herded each year from outlying farms to the pens surrounding this tavern on the Bowery, which was then the northern edge of the city. Prize cattle were sometimes paraded past the homes of the rich with a band leading the way and the elder Astor and other butchers coming behind, knives ready to fulfill orders. The best livestock were displayed in the pens adjoining the tavern while butchers and drovers bartered, drank, and gambled.

"A literal stock market," one writer would later note.

Amid the mooing and squealing and bleating and the accompanying great stink of the doomed stood the largest of the animals, one nobody contemplated butchering. This creature was too obviously sentient for simple slaughter, not to mention too rare and valuable, as a drover from the Westchester town of Somers proved when he bought the elephant for a reported $1,000.

Along with being a drover, Hachaliah "Hack" Bailey was a farmer, cattle merchant, land speculator, stage line manager, toll collector, postmaster, town inspector, school official, and militia officer. One problem his new acquisition presented was what to call her, for this was not The Elephant, only An elephant. The creature would require a name to distinguish her from the one who was still out there, touring.

Bailey named the elephant Old Bet in honor of his three-year-old daughter, Betsy. The sentimental moniker aside, the elephant was still first and foremost an investment. Bailey hedged his risk much in the way of investors in the other kind of stock market that would later arise in downtown Manhattan. He sold two shares of Old Bet for a total of $1,400 more than what the elephant had cost him, a sweet deal made sweeter by the prospect of a cut of the profits as one of the new partners took the elephant on tour.

The partner proved to be a bookkeeping precursor of modern movie studios, claiming that there had been no profits after expenses. Bailey responded by pointing a rifle at Old Bet.

"Do what you please with your half of that elephant, but I'm fairly determined to shoot my half," he reportedly said.

Bailey thus secured his due share of the profits and put them toward also acquiring a caged tiger named Nero. The tiger was exhibited along with Old Bet as part of a traveling menagerie that included a bear and some dogs that performed tricks. The menagerie began using canvas sidewalls to ward off prying, unpaying eyes.

As had her predecessor, Old Bet traveled in freebie-warding darkness. One group of scalawags is said to have scattered a trail of potato peels off the main road to a stack of firewood. A dark form appeared and the scalawags set the wood ablaze, figuring to save everybody a quarter with the bonfire's light. They beheld a horse covered with a blanket that had been sent ahead by Old Bet's owner.

Unlike her predecessor, Old Bet tolerated people on her back. Her acquiescence in this regard was put to a test when she crossed paths with a traveling troupe of trick riders and acrobats in June of 1812.

The first such troupe had been brought to America back in 1793 by John Bill Ricketts, a famed British rider who built a wooden amphitheater known as a circus in Philadelphia. Even with the inclusion of a rope walker and a clown, public interest soon waned and he moved on to New York and Boston and other cities, tearing down the old circus and building a new one at each new locale. He finally set out for the West Indies, where he was captured by pirates and subsequently drowned in a shipwreck in 1800.

After a lull of seven years, other circus troupes began to perform, including one starring Cayetano Mariotini, who was described by the

New York Clipper as morphing from "an incredibly fat fish woman in a huge bonnet and uncouth garments" into "an elegant cavalier" by peeling off layer after layer of clothing as he circled the ring standing astride two horses. On encountering Old Bet, Mariotini and his comrades prepared to make history by fitting a wooden platform on the elephant's back. Old Bet remained remarkably accommodating as the troupe formed a pyramid and executed various gymnastic stunts atop her in the first joint performance of a menagerie and a circus troupe.

After this performance, Cayetano and his troupe parted ways with Old Bet and continued on, reaching Ohio and doing good business with the help of a disapproving editorial in the Chillicothe *Weekly Recorder.* The newspaper opined, "The circus business is an unlawful calling, one that cannot be defended on scriptural ground. The performances are calculated to amuse the giddy and thoughtless and to excite the laughter of fools. There is no tendency to administer useful instruction, to regulate affections or restrain the inordinate passions of this audience."

Old Bet's separate way took her to Maine, where she was exhibited in a stable yard behind a Portland tavern. Twelve-year-old Neal Dow, future mayor and Civil War general, would recall, "It was a great wonder and the people thronged Portland from many miles around, on foot, on horseback and in every conceivable conveyance."

A prankster presented the elephant with some tobacco wrapped in paper. The resulting hilarity drew the attention of the keeper, whose experience with elephants could have been no more extensive than the time this one had been in America. He had learned enough to make a prediction regarding this apparently docile giant.

"[The keeper] asked what it was about and, upon being told, advised the man to get away from the place immediately because, as he said, the animal would be sure to resent it if opportunity offered and if he happened to pass within its reach would certainly kill him," Dow later wrote.

The man initially scoffed, recalled Dow, "but the keeper was so positive it would be dangerous for him to remain that he concluded to go."

The appearance passed without incident. Old Bet proceeded on to the small Maine town of Alfred, on July 24, 1816. She there encountered another tormentor, a farmer named Daniel Davis. He is said to have teased Old Bet either by giving her tobacco or by offering her something to eat or drink and then snatching it away, possibly an alcoholic beverage, for which this elephant had also developed a taste.

Old Bet is said to have reacted as the keeper would have predicted. Davis might have been seriously hurt or killed, but the keeper hustled him away before he suffered anything worse than a torn vest. The keeper no doubt indicated to Davis that he had brought it on himself and would not likely be so lucky if he ever came near Old Bet again.

Various accounts hold that Davis argued with Bailey or felt the show had fleeced the locals or was outraged that it was violating the Sabbath. The twentieth-century writer James Agee would suggest Davis and his fellow farmers had believed Old Bet to be "the reincarnation of Behemoth."

Most probably, Davis had imbibed a little liquor himself, further fuel to the fury of a tormentor who has met his comeuppance. He proved to be considerably more unpredictable than a tormented elephant, for nobody expected him to fetch a rifle and lie in wait. Davis shot Old Bet dead as she was led out of town.

"Ah! noble, generous, high minded intelligent animal, justly classed among the wonderful works of God!" read a letter to a newspaper from an Alfred resident before the shooter had been publicly identified. "Thou hadst past from the banks of the Ganges, to the shores of the new world, to gratify the just and laudable curiosity of mankind; to display the wonders of creation, and lead man to adore the maker and former of all things. And here thou hast come to fall by the hand of a miserable unknown caitiff, who only lives to disgrace his species."

Hack Bailey put his loss at $30,000, but even an elephant of such value was the legal equivalent of a cow and Davis spent only two days in the town jail. The public outcry nonetheless exceeded what would have accompanied the shooting of most humans. Popular interest reconfirmed, Bailey soon acquired another elephant, a female Asian he named Lil Bet.

To set this third elephant in America apart from its predecessors, Bailey decided to teach her some tricks of her own beyond Old Bet's ability to uncork bottles of stout, which was apparently self-taught. Lil Bet was billed as "the learned elephant," able to bow and sit and stand on two legs and carry her keeper in her trunk.

That should have been enough, but Bailey hyped Lil Bet as not just learned but bulletproof, a claim that demonstrated a surprising lapse in his understanding of his own species. A group of boys may have decided to put the boast to the test as the elephant came to a bridge in Chepachet, Rhode Island. Or they simply may have been looking to replicate the sensation that accompanied Old Bet's killing. Lil Bet's demise meant that two of the first three elephants in America had been shot to death.

In the meantime, Bailey had further extended his résumé to include innkeeper as he capitalized on the Old Bet killing by building the Elephant Hotel in his hometown of Somers, New York. He erected a granite pillar topped by a gilded figure of an elephant out front as a monument to the murdered Old Bet.

The three-story redbrick hotel became a gathering place for other sons of Somers inspired to operate either a traveling menagerie or a circus. The circus men included Joshua Purdy Brown, a cousin of Hack Bailey, who elaborated upon the canvas sidewalls used by the menageries to prevent free looks. Brown's circus is believed to have been the first to perform under a tent, this in 1825. His "pavilion" made the move from city to city easier and considerably less expensive than with the traditional wood structure. Brown was further able to stop along the way at small towns, where the potential audience had never warranted the cost and effort of a wooden venue. There were enough customers to fill a tent for a one-day stand, making for more revenue and less travel time between stops. Other showmen recognized the advantage; more and more tent shows formed and took to the road.

Menageries had already been visiting both cities and towns for some time. One run by another Somers man encountered Brown's circus in South Carolina in 1832. The two joined to become the first combination to travel together.

Back at the Elephant Hotel, the major circus and menagerie operators formed the Zoological Institute, whose avowed purpose was "to more generally diffuse and promote the knowledge of natural history and gratify rational curiosity." The more practical function was as a cartel that set routes and schedules among existing shows and kept out interlopers. The 135 signatories became known as the Flatfoots because, in the words of a local historian, "they put their foot down flat against any competition bringing a show into the eastern territory."

The hotel's grand ballroom was the scene of elegant soirees where eligible and hopeful young women mixed with showmen who were described by a newspaper as being "rich as grand Turks," but who "set more value on a trained horse or elephant than the attentions of lovely women."

Just two years after its formation, the Zoological Institute fell victim to a national financial calamity. The Panic of 1837—just like the Panic of 1873 to come—was the bursting of an economic bubble born of speculation so feverish it exceeded seemingly boundless opportunity. The ever-prescient Hack Bailey had sold the Elephant Hotel the year before and moved down to Virginia, establishing winter quarters for traveling shows at what is now called Bailey's Crossroads. He returned to Somers, "the cradle of the American circus," at the end of his life and was buried in the town cemetery. An obelisk marking his grave is chiseled with three watchwords: "Enterprise, Perseverance, Integrity." The first two were embraced by his successors with considerably more fervor than the third.

THREE

BARNUM

During his time in Connecticut, Hack Bailey occasionally visited the town of Bethel and stopped into a general store, where there was a boy behind the counter named Phineas Taylor Barnum. The brief encounters made real all the tales young Barnum had heard of the first great elephant entrepreneur. Barnum would later speak of Bailey as a kind of father figure, describing his actual father as "a man of many endeavors but few successes" who ran a failing hotel and a failing livery stable as well as a failing store.

Barnum's maternal grandfather, also named Phineas Taylor, had imparted to the boy an early lesson in myth and deception. The grandfather expressed his appreciation for having the child named after him by announcing at the christening that he was deeding his grandson a five-acre parcel called Ivy Island. The grandfather would often declare that this made young Barnum the richest child in town, and the family encouraged the boy to consider himself landed gentry as he grew older. The father again and again asked him how it felt to have such wealth. The boy was ten when he got his first look at his estate.

"I saw nothing but a few stunted ivies and straggling trees," Barnum would recall in an autobiography. "The truth flashed upon me. I had been the laughing-stock of the family and neighborhood for years. My valuable Ivy Island was an almost inaccessible, worthless bit of barren land, and while I stood deploring my sudden downfall, a huge black snake (one of my tenants) approached me with upraised head. I gave one shriek and rushed for the bridge."

Further lessons in deception came at the store from suppliers who would stick stones and rubbish into bundles of cloth that were billed as pure linen or deliver loads of grain that were several bushels short. Young Barnum also learned all he wanted to know about routine drudgery, which he happily if briefly escaped at age twelve, when a drover hired him to help herd some cattle down to New York.

Barnum stayed at the same Bull's Head Tavern where Old Bet had been displayed. He put his wages toward some firecrackers and a toy gun that fired a wooden stick, store-bought toys being considerably less common in this time before leisure came of age. He employed these purchases in what might be viewed as his first Manhattan show. He got one blow from the bartender after he fired a wooden stick at him and another from the proprietor after he startled some customers with the firecrackers.

Barnum then returned to the failing store his father was running along with the other failing enterprises. The father's very health failed and he died at the age of forty-eight. His son had to borrow money to buy shoes for the funeral.

"At fifteen, he began the world not only penniless but barefooted," an early biographer noted.

Barnum went to work in an uncle's store, where he briefly managed to boost profits with a lottery in which the top few prizes were cash, the lesser and much more numerous prizes items that had been slow to sell. He went on to run an unsuccessful rooming house and to start a newspaper called the *Herald of Freedom*, which folded after he was jailed and fined for libel. He seemed destined to be too much like his father as he proceeded on through a series of unspectacular business ventures.

He had not forgotten Bailey's example, but even if he had had the price of an elephant, the creatures were no longer such wonders that one in itself seemed likely to generate even a modest fortune. He then heard that the owner of a very different and considerably less pricey traveling exhibit was looking to sell.

The exhibit in question was Joice Heth, who was being presented as the 161-year-old nurse of George Washington. She was a human being, but an African-American one and therefore subject in slave states to being bought and sold no differently than an elephant, only cheaper. Her Kentucky owner had begun to see her value decrease as measured by the audience she drew, but he still wanted $3,000. Barnum bargained the price down to $1,000. He only had $500, but he managed to borrow the balance. He soon repaid it thanks to the powers of hype and advertising he had discovered while running a newspaper.

"The Greatest Natural and National Curiosity in the World" proclaimed the posters and ads.

One pamphlet read, "JOICE HETH is unquestionably the most astonishing and interesting curiosity in the World! She was the slave of Augustine Washington, (the father of Gen. Washington,) and was the first person who put clothes on the unconscious infant, who, in after days, led our heroic fathers on to glory, to victory, and freedom."

Barnum clearly saw no irony in that invocation of freedom. The pamphlet went on, "To use her own language when speaking of the illustrious Father of his Country, 'she raised him.' JOICE HETH was born in the year 1674, and has, consequently, now arrived at the astonishing AGE OF 161 YEARS."

Barnum began by exhibiting her in New York, describing himself as "proprietor of the negress" even though slavery had been abolished in that state seven years before. He raked in as much as $1,500 a week as he moved on to such venues as the Barnum Hotel, the still struggling inn his mother was now running in Bridgeport, Connecticut. Crowds kept coming to see a woman who, by Barnum's own description,

from age or disease or both, was unable to change her position; she could move one arm at will, but her lower limbs could not be straightened; her left arm lay across her breast and she could not remove it; the fingers of her left hand were drawn down so as nearly to close it, and were fixed; the nails on that hand were almost four inches long and extended above her wrist; the nails on her large toes had grown to the thickness of a quarter of an inch; her head was covered with a thick bush of grey hair; but she was toothless and totally blind, and her eyes had sunk so deeply in the sockets as to have disappeared altogether.

Barnum added, "Nevertheless she was pert and sociable, and would talk as long as people would converse with her. She was quite garrulous about her protégé, 'dear little George,' at whose birth she declared she was present."

Heth, of course, received no more share than would Old Bet of the proceeds, which began to decline after seven months. Barnum provided an early example of his particular genius when he planted a letter in a Boston newspaper signed only "A Visitor" stating that the exhibit was "a humbug," but the truth was "vastly more interesting."

"The fact is, Joice Heth is not a human being," the letter went on. "What purports to be a remarkably old woman, is simply a curiously constructed automaton, made up of whalebone, India-rubber, and numerous springs that are ingeniously put together, and made to move at the slightest touch according to the will of the operator."

Ticket sales surged as people flocked to see for themselves whether, as one writer later suggested, Heth was "a fake or a fake fake." Barnum had recouped his investment many times over when she died, but he did not stop there. He announced a public autopsy and 1,500 people paid fifty cents each to squeeze into the City Saloon in Manhattan and watch prominent surgeon Dr. David Rogers dissect her. Rogers determined that she had not been much more than eighty, or half the age advertised. Barnum shrugged and arranged for an article in the *New York Herald* that suggested this was not really Heth at all, that she was still alive and out there somewhere.

Barnum then took on an Italian acrobat and tightrope walker named Antonio, whom he rechristened Vivalla. Barnum actually had to pay this person, and the twelve dollars a week was barely offset by the modest audiences as they traveled from city to city. Barnum had to pawn his watch and chain in Washington, D.C., just to secure enough funds to move on. He was nearing a crisis when he opened at the Walnut Theater in Philadelphia.

"And now, that instinct . . . which can arouse a community and make it patronize, provided the article offered is worthy of patronage —an instinct which served me strangely in later years, astonishing the public and surprising me, came to my relief," Barnum later wrote.

"And the help, curiously enough, appeared in the shape of an emphatic hiss from the pit!"

The hiss proved to originate from a performer named Roberts, who afterward told Barnum that he could easily match Vivalla's feats and then some.

"I at once published a card in Vivalla's name, offering $1,000 to any one who would publicly perform Vivalla's feats at such place as should be designated," Barnum recalled.

Barnum got Roberts to accept the challenge very publicly, with the secret understanding that the actual recompense was to be only thirty dollars.

"A great trial of skill between Roberts and Vivalla was duly announced by posters and through the press," Barnum recalled. "Meanwhile, they rehearsed privately to see what tricks each could perform, and the 'business' was completely arranged."

Barnum found that rivalry could be as big a draw as curiosity, with each performer attracting passionate partisans.

"Public excitement was at fever heat, and on the night of the trial the pit and upper boxes were crowded to the full," Barnum later wrote. "The 'contest' between the performers was eager, and each had his party in the house. So far as I could learn, no one complained that he did not get all he paid for on that occasion. I engaged Roberts for a month and his subsequent 'contests' with Vivalla amused the public and put money in my purse."

Barnum teamed up with Aaron Turner's Traveling circus and toured from city to town. He was doing well enough to buy a new black suit, and he was striding around Annapolis in it on the day before a show when Turner pointed him out to some locals.

"I think it very singular you permit that rascal to march your streets in open day," Turner reportedly said. "It wouldn't be allowed in Rhode

Island, and I suppose that is the reason the black-coated scoundrel has come down this way."

Turner then told them the man in black was the Reverend E. K. Avery, an infamous Rhode Island murderer of a defenseless young woman. A mob roughly seized Barnum and was preparing to lynch him when Turner admitted that he had only been jesting.

"My dear Mr. Barnum," Turner is said to have told his partner afterward, "it was all for our good. Remember, all we need to insure success is notoriety. You will see that this will be noised all about town as a trick played by one of the circus managers upon the other, and our pavilion will be crammed to-morrow night."

The engagement was indeed sold out, but Barnum had soured on Turner. Barnum took his $1,200 cut and struck out on his own with Vivalla, along with a black entertainer named James Sandford and several musicians. Sandford abruptly left the show as they reached Camden, South Carolina, and Barnum sought to live up to the advance advertising by singing "plantation melodies" with a blackened face.

He was in blackface on another night when there was a commotion between two white men and he reflexively sought to mediate. One of the parties pointed a pistol at Barnum's head and demanded to know how he dared to speak to whites that way. Barnum quickly rolled up his sleeve.

"I am as white as you!" he exclaimed.

Barnum took as a new partner Henry Hawley, famed both as a magician and as America's most ingenious liar. Hawley had a standard response when one of his tall tales was challenged: "It's just as true as anything I have told you tonight."

Barnum returned to New York with more than double the $1,200 he made with Turner but declared himself "thoroughly disgusted" with life on the road. He placed an advertisement in the newspaper offering to invest $2,500 in a worthwhile venture and the many who responded included inventors, saloon keepers, pawnbrokers, lottery operators, even a counterfeiter who wanted to put the money into paper, ink, and dyes for "a safe and rich harvest."

In keeping with a resolution to become a more conventional businessman, Barnum decided on a German immigrant who sold waterproof paste, bear grease, and cologne. Any profits from the joint venture disappeared with the German when he skipped back to Europe.

"A good-looking, plausible, promising—scamp," Barnum later said.

In the meanwhile, Barnum chanced to meet John Diamond, a teenage dancer who was among the first to combine the styles of the freed slaves and the Irish immigrants consigned to mutual squalor in the notorious Five Points slum in lower Manhattan. Diamond performed this "break-down dancing" in blackface, his visage smeared with burnt cork, a wooly wig on his head. He joined the percussive, lightning footwork of Irish step dancing and the full-body dance of Africa.

Barnum signed a deal with Diamond's father and mother and hired an agent to take the teen on tour. Barnum remained behind in New York where he and his wife had two daughters, a two-year-old and a newborn. He sought to be a non-traveling showman by leasing the Vauxhall Gardens saloon, but proceeds were so meager he had to abandon it after just three months and join Diamond on the road.

"I dreaded resuming the life of an itinerant showman, but funds were low, I had a family to care for, and as nothing better presented, I made up my mind to endure the vexations and uncertainties of a tour," he later wrote.

Barnum traveled with Diamond to Troy, Buffalo, Toronto, Detroit, Chicago, and St. Louis. Great dancing did not translate into great profits and Barnum was barely covering his expenses when they arrived in New Orleans. He had just one hundred dollars, and, after a fortnight, that dwindled to the point that he had to put up his previously pawned and redeemed pocket watch as security for his dining bill. He then mounted a variation on the "contests" between Vivalla and Roberts. The poster read: "Challenge: Master Diamond, who delineates the Ethiopian character superior to any other white person, hereby challenges any person in the world to a trial of skill at Negro dancing in all its varieties for a wager from \$200 to \$1,000."

Barnum cleared as much as \$500 in a single night, but he and Diamond soon had a falling out. The dancer continued on his own and Barnum felt doubly betrayed when one of his associates set off with a fourteen-year-old orphan he had taken under his wing. The orphan was now foisted on the public as "Master Diamond."

Barnum had the associate jailed. The associate thereupon arranged for the man who had sold Joice Heth to file a complaint that Barnum had never given him a quantity of brandy that was supposedly part of the price. Barnum was himself briefly jailed and he returned to New York, in his words, "resolved once more that I would never again be an itinerant showman."

He began to buy and sell illustrated Bibles but was not ready to give up being a showman altogether. He again rented the Vauxhall Gardens saloon, using his brother-in-law's name so as not to alienate Bible buyers. He searched for a new "break down" star in Five Points and found a spectacularly talented teenage dancer named William Henry Lane. Known as Juba, Lane had started out at ten dancing for coins on a street corner and now was faster and more stylish and more original and simply just better than Diamond or anybody else. There was only one problem: Juba was actually black.

"There was not an audience in America that would not have resented in very energetic fashion, the insult of being asked to look at the dancing of a real Negro," the British writer Thomas Low Nichols later noted. "To any man but [Barnum] this would have been an insuperable obstacle."

Barnum applied burnt cork to Juba's face and pulled a wooly wig over his close-cropped hair. Juba became the first black man to appear in blackface.

"Had it been suspected that the seeming counterfeit was the genuine article, the New York Vauxhall would have blazed with indignation," Nichols wrote.

Barnum billed the new dancer as Master John Diamond and staged "contests" just as he had in New Orleans with the original Diamond. A letter appeared in the *Sunday Flash* making the scandalous accusation that Barnum's new blackface dancer was a fake fake:

> The boy is fifteen or sixteen years of age; his name is "Juba"; and to do him justice, he is a very fair dancer. He is of harmless and inoffensive disposition, and is not, I sincerely believe, aware of the meanness and audacity of the swindle to which he is presently a party. As to the wagers which the bills daily blazon forth, they are like the rest of his business—all a cheat. Not one dollar is ever bet or staked, and the pretended judges who aid in the farce, are mere *blowers*.

The letter was unsigned, but the author was quite possibly Barnum himself in a variation on the letter that suggested Joice Heth was actually an automaton. The scandal almost certainly filled seats in the Vauxhall Gardens and generated the nineteenth-century equivalent of buzz.

Almack's was a low-ceilinged basement tavern and bordello owned by a black man and his mulatto wife on Orange Street in Five Points. The visitors there in 1842 included Charles Dickens, who wrote in

American Notes of watching Juba, the teen he called "the greatest dancer known," take the floor.

"In what walk of life, or dance of life, does man ever get such stimulating applause as thunders about him, when, having danced his partner off her feet, and himself too, he finishes by leaping gloriously on the bar-counter?" Dickens wrote.

The passage brought fame to both the dancer and the saloon. Juba was able to perform outside Five Points without burnt cork and a wig. Almack's became Dickens' Place. It added an elephant to its attractions, though elephants had lost so much of their novelty that the creature drew nary a mention in the press.

Barnum, in the meantime, had again found the Vauxhall venture too expensive to continue, and the Bibles were not bringing in what he had hoped. He garnered a few extra dollars writing freelance advertising copy for the Bowery Amphitheater, originally built by the Flatfoot circus and menagerie cartel.

"I was at the bottom rung of fortune's ladder," Barnum would recall.

He was still Barnum, which meant a simple lack of money did not stop him from putting in a bid when he heard the American Museum on Broadway was for sale. He may have felt fate was at work, for this collection of curiosities included the stuffed remains of Old Bet.

The price was still $15,000—or about $15,000 more than he had.

"What will you buy it with?" a friend supposedly inquired.

"With brass," Barnum replied, "for silver and gold have I none."

Barnum convinced the owner that while he had but a pittance to put down, he would make the museum such a success he would quickly pay off the purchase price. He thereupon embarked to make good on his word, adding entertainments and a constantly changing host of exhibits. He ventured the inverse of blackface with "Madagascar albinos," described in the museum guide as possessing "features being so decidedly Ethiopian as to preclude the possibility of doubt as to their being purely African," making them "beyond all doubt, white negroes." He also had Dora Dawron, the "double-voiced vocalist, who sings with equal cue and effect a loud-and-manly tenor and a delicate-and-feminine soprano while dressed one half as a man, one half as a lady, and changing to the audience simultaneously with the change of voice." Other exhibits included a model of Niagara Falls "with real water."

The buildup to his first big attraction began with three letters to New York newspapers spaced about ten days apart, the first post-marked Montgomery, Alabama, the second Charleston, South Carolina, and the third Washington, D.C. The letters were signed by different individuals, but each reported that a Dr. J. Griffin, naturalist with the British Lyceum of Natural History, had passed through that locale with a genuine mermaid that had been found off the "Feejee Islands" and preserved in China. The third letter expressed the hope that the New York newspapers would clamor for Griffin to accord the city the opportunity to see the "great curiosity" before he sailed home to England.

Several days later, Dr. J. Griffin checked into a top Philadelphia hotel. The afternoon before he was to depart for New York, he offered the proprietor a glimpse of the mermaid. The hotelier was not discouraged from summoning any newspaper editors he happened to know.

"The Philadelphia press aided the press of New York in awakening a wide-reaching and increasing curiosity to see the mermaid," Barnum later wrote.

Curiosity yet again became coin as crowds paid to see the "Feejee Mermaid," which, in a woodcut Barnum gave the newspapers, looked very much like the creature of myth, but in person looked very much like a mummified monkey's head and torso sewn to the bottom half of a large fish. Barnum subsequently acknowledged in his autobiography that he wrote the seemingly far-flung letters and sent them to friends with instructions on when to mail them to the New York newspapers. He further acknowledged that there was no British Lyceum and that Griffin was in fact Levi Lyman.

"Who was my employee in the case of Joice Heth," Barnum added.

The museum's biggest human attraction was also its smallest, having stopped growing when he stood only twenty-five inches. Charles Sherwood Stratton was just shy of his fifth birthday when his distant cousin Barnum brought him and his mother from their Connecticut home to New York.

"Mrs. Stratton was greatly surprised to see her son announced on my Museum bills as General Tom Thumb," Barnum later wrote.

Barnum informed the public that his new marvel was eleven years old and from England, the name having been taken from British folklore. The fictitious honorific was ironic, but it also intuitively played on the diminutive figure's appeal, a fascination as intense as that inspired by an elephant, and not entirely unrelated.

Just as the biggest of land animals allowed its beholders to imagine a natural order not predicated on ferocious struggle, the smallest of generals mocked a social order ruled by stature and macho supremacy. Barnum noted that the boy possessed a "keen sense of the ludicrous," which he displayed with precocious aplomb, cracking jokes and imitating such iconic half pints as Napoleon and Cupid.

Tom Thumb was a sensation and would end up responsible for 20 million of the 82 million tickets Barnum would sell in his various enterprises in his lifetime. Relatively scant interest was generated by Vantile Mack, the Giant Baby, described in the museum guide as "only 7 years old, yet weighed 257 pounds, measured 61 inches round the chest, and just one yard round the thigh; the largest child of his age ever known." Others of the less popular human extremes at the museum included the Arabian Giant and the towering Very Thin Man, who seemed more like typical specimens of their species as they engaged in an increasingly vituperative rivalry. They finally prepared to do battle, one grabbing a supposed Crusader sword, the other a war club that, by Barnum's account, "might have been the one that killed Captain Cook." Barnum voiced outrage that they would even think of engaging in mortal combat without due preparations.

"It must be duly advertised," he declared, leaving the giants laughing and peace restored.

To the usual bombast of his advertising ("mammon is ever caught with glare") Barnum added a slyer tactic, which began with hiring a man who had come in off the street asking for a handout. Barnum instead presented the man with five bricks.

At Barnum's secret instruction, the man set down four of the bricks on as many corners in the surrounding streets. The man then quickly strode from spot to spot, at each solemnly exchanging the brick in his hand for the one on the sidewalk, remaining resolutely mute.

"You must seem to be as deaf as a post," Barnum would recall telling the man. "Wear a serious countenance; answer no questions; pay no attention to anyone; but attend faithfully to the work, and at the end of every hour, by St. Paul's clock, show this ticket at the Museum door, enter, walking solemnly through every hall in the building."

He was then to exit the building and repeat it all over again. This kept up for several days, with more and more people noticing the man and following him. Barnum enlisted the intervention of a policeman, who declared the growing crowd a hazard and escorted the "brick man" away. That generated even more public attention for Barnum's Great American Museum. He festooned the building with flags and banners and placed atop the roof New York's first "Drummond lights," cylinders of lime turned incandescent by intense flame, the result subsequently known as "limelight" when used in theaters.

So many people were now arriving at the entrance beneath the limelight beacons that Barnum too often suffered the agony of being unable to accommodate people who had cash in hand. He became particularly distressed on St. Patrick's Day, when a large number of Irish patrons brought their dinners with the intention of making not just a day but an evening of it as well rather than passing through and making room for others. He enlisted a workman to paint and hang a sign that had a pointing finger and read: "THIS WAY TO THE EGRESS."

Just as he hoped, a good number of the customers assumed that an egress must be some kind of exotic animal. Barnum's account of the ploy would mildly mock the accents of the crowd and play off a current expression, "seeing the elephant," which had come to mean seeing the world's remarkable sights: "The throng began to pour down the back-stairs only to find that the 'Aigress' was the elephant, and that the elephant was all out o'doors, or so much of it as began with Ann Street."

Barnum was soon prosperous enough to follow his childhood idol Hack Bailey into the actual elephant business, thanks to proceeds from the museum as well as a lucrative European tour with Tom Thumb and a wildly successful American tour with the opera singer Jenny Lind, "the Swedish nightingale," who was welcomed to New York by a Barnum-drummed crowd of thirty thousand.

But as had been demonstrated at Dickens' Place, so many people had at this point literally seen an elephant that presenting just one was not likely to draw much attention. Barnum entered into a partnership with Seth B. Howes, who had started out in the business at age eleven, tending to Lil Bet as Hachaliah Bailey took her on tour. With Howes, Barnum now sought to outdo his childhood hero Bailey and acquire a herd.

THE ELEPHANTINE
EXPEDITION

In May of 1850, Barnum and Howes chartered the ship *Regatta* and dispatched a representative on what they termed an "elephantine expedition" to the island nation off the coast of India then called Ceylon, now Sri Lanka. The representative arrived hoping to purchase from temples and government officials enough elephants to create a sensation back in America. He discovered that the government was in turmoil due to a particularly arrogant British governor and that monsoons had washed out so many roads that every available elephant had been pressed into service to clear and repair them.

The representative enlisted a guide and ventured from the coast into the interior jungles where the elephants were living wild. The local kings had long prohibited the killing of elephants on pain of the transgressor's own death, but that had changed with British rule. British officers considered it fine sport to shoot such a large creature. They were not just after ivory like the poachers who would in the next century hunt elephants into near extinction, particularly in Africa, where both genders have tusks. They killed Asian females with equal zest even though they are tuskless. The record holder was Major Thomas Rogers, a colonial administrator and district judge said to have killed more than fourteen hundred elephants during an eleven-year period ending in 1845, when he was struck by lightning, celestial electricity that many locals viewed as divine justice.

Barnum's sole aim was to capture, and to that end his representative followed the long-standing local strategy involving a kheddah, almost certainly the same method that would be employed to capture baby Topsy.

As with Topsy's herd twenty-five years later, the elephants must have either not caught the scent or not sensed a serious threat when the trackers crept up, careful to remain upwind and hidden. Otherwise, the elephants would have retreated deeper into the forest by the time the hundred catchers arrived. The catchers had done their stealthy best to go undetected as they split into two groups, filing off to the right and to the left. Each group posted a pair of catchers every fifty yards or so as they formed a circle six to eight miles in diameter around the herd. The "surround" was completed with a light bamboo fence, not designed to contain the elephants but to mark any place they broke out and to indicate which catcher should be held responsible.

If any of the herd approached the perimeter, the pickets drove them back with shouts and gunshots and flaming torches, just as they later would with Topsy. Such encounters occurred more often at night, so it was during the day one picket from each pair slipped inside the surrounded area to help construct a stockade that was near an established path but well hidden by foliage and close to water. The stockade workers rejoined their partners at night to man the perimeter, then returned to their labors in the morning.

After maybe a fortnight, the stockade was done. The pickets spent one last night in pairs on the perimeter. One of each pair remained behind to maintain the surround while the others began to close in, shouting and brandishing torches and firing guns in the air as they drove the elephants into the trap.

When it was all over, the Barnum expedition marched nine newly captured elephants to the port of Point de Galle, one a calf, the others fully grown if not exactly giants of their species. The elephants were understandably nervous when loaded upon a tippy lighter that was to ferry them two at a time to the *Regatta*. One male broke free of his restraining ropes and bolted, scattering a crowd of onlookers.

Eventually, the male was brought back. He, like the others, calmed once the lighter pulled away from the dock and further fuss would only have made the footing more unsteady. Elephants seemed to be creatures with some sense of when struggle became self-defeating.

The elephants did become resistant again when the lighter was alongside the ship and they were fitted with a harness, an outsize version of the kind used to load horses, with multiple belly bands. A line rose to a wooden block and tackle that had been affixed to a reinforced yardarm or boom.

The elephants quieted once more when their feet left the lighter's deck and they were hoisted up over the gunwale with the help of a windlass, human ingenuity prevailing over their massive bulk. Creatures who had never been off the ground since they thudded upon it at birth and who had always walked supreme felt themselves airborne and helpless as they were swung over the open loading hatch. They were lowered into the hold and fussed only briefly, any resistance being met by the stringencies of a mahout who had been brought along.

The long sea voyage took them down through the horse latitudes, zones of scant wind where becalmed ships were said to sometimes become so short of water they had to let horses aboard perish. The *Regatta* had plenty of water, even with each of the elephants drinking as many as fifty gallons a day in addition to eating as much as three hundred pounds of food a day, but it still lost one of the younger captives to unspecified causes as it passed the Cape of Good Hope. The crew hoisted it overboard and into the sea. The remaining elephants survived being squeezed into the hold for the four-month, twelve-thousand-mile trip, without drawing a fresh breath or taking a free step.

"They behaved really well during the passage, accommodating themselves to their straitened quarters and hard fare with a patient philosophy worthy of general imitation," an observer reported.

A Barnum-size crowd was waiting to welcome the ship when it returned, almost exactly a year after it had departed. The new arrivals were joined by two elephants leased for the day to make an even ten adults. The augmented herd was harnessed in pairs to a painted wagon billed as the Great Car of Juggernaut.

The real Car of Jagannath, in India, was a gigantic wagon forty-five feet tall and thirty-five feet square with seven-foot wheels. It was brought out once a year for a great festival in which the figure of Jagannath, or Lord of the Universe, was (and still is) transported from the main temple in Puri to his "summer home" less than a mile away. The Car was (and is) drawn through deep sand with ropes by thousands of the Hindu faithful.

Barnum's car was about the size that might have been used to carry dry goods in his clerk days, but painted and affixed with carved elephants and figures of supposed Hindu gods. He likely was inspired by James Raymond, a menagerie impresario from upstate New York who had been a founder of the Flatfeet and who in the 1840s owned five of the six elephants then in America, the biggest herd the nation had ever seen until now. Raymond had introduced the bandwagon and had four of the elephants pull it as the musicians played. He had become disconsolate and left the business after three of the four died, apparently succumbing to the inexpert care and brutalities of their handlers.

Within hours of landing in New York, Barnum's elephants pulled the car up boisterous Broadway past Irving House. In one of the hotel's front windows, Jenny Lind, the Swedish Nightingale, stood in review, back in America for a second Barnum-sponsored appearance.

The showman paired Tom Thumb with the calf elephant and sent them on the road along with the eight surviving grown captives, a lion tamer, an armless man, and wax figures of all thirteen U.S. presidents. Barnum himself stayed behind, saying he had "neither time nor inclination to manage such a concern." He could send his name on tour without personally suffering the travails of the road. And he was busy with his museum as well as something even bigger. He had developed plans to build a utopian city for "the New Man" on farmland he had purchased across the Pequonnock River from Bridgeport, Connecticut.

Meanwhile, the show's day-to-day operations were overseen by Howes, who, since his childhood days with Lil Bet, had become known as "the father of the American circus," credited with erecting the first billboard and with being the first to use paste rather than tacks to put up posters. He was better at advertising than delivering, if what was billed as Barnum's Asiatic Caravan, Museum and Menagerie was any indication. One of the early stops was Princeton, New Jersey, and local college boys drawn by the preshow hype were apparently less than wowed; even a whole herd of elephants was no longer enough to impress. The students expressed their overall disappointment by pushing the Car of Juggernaut into the nearest body of water.

The car was looking a little worse for wear when the show subsequently arrived in Brooklyn. A writer for the *Brooklyn Eagle* opined, "The Great Car of Juggernaut is a complete sham, being a wagon of the plainest ordinary construction and painted outside in the most irregular manner; the Hindoo deities or what is meant to represent them and figures of elephants ... being intermingled which shows the artist's beautiful ignorance of his subject."

The writer noted that the procession was two short of the advertised ten elephants, the two rentals having been returned. He described the museum part of the show as "one of the most disreputable, shabby affairs in existence." The wax presidents, he said, bore "not the slightest resemblance to the living reality."

If the herd of huge beasts elicited only a yawn, the writer did find the diminutive Tom Thumb to be "worth the whole price of admission ... quite a well bred little fellow, very well proportioned and as accomplished as a Parisian dandy." The article concluded that "with the exception of Tom and the feats of the man without arms, it could not be compared with many similar exhibitions that are in the country."

The ensuing reviews were even worse, but the show was always a day ahead of publication and it generated a handsome profit.

In New York, Barnum was distracted by yet another project, this one involving the British inventor of what was purported to be and what the showman actually believed to be a revolutionary fire extinguisher. Barnum opened an office on Broadway and soon sold $180,000 worth of Fire Annihilators, with the promise of a full refund should an upcoming public demonstration not prove completely satisfactory.

In the last days of 1851, Barnum erected a fifteen-foot-square wooden structure, rising one story and a loft, on a vacant patch of what is now Manhattan's Upper East Side. A sizable crowd gathered as the structure was stocked with combustible material just after sundown. An assistant was preparing to set it alight when there came a cry.

"Don't! Don't! Let me out! Don't burn me up!"

The voice seemed to be coming from the loft and an officer clambered up, finding nothing. Barnum gave the signal to go ahead, but the voice came again.

"Will you burn a fellow alive? Let me out!"

Another check found the loft empty and the crowd began to grumble that it was all just another Barnum stunt.

"Humbug!" a man called out.

"Joice Heth!" called out another.

"Mermaid!" called another, referring to the Feejee fake.

"Have a little patience, gentlemen, and we'll proceed!" Barnum said.

As the assistant finally set the fire, a whole litany of sounds seemed to emanate from the building, not just voices but also the squeal of panicked pigs. Barnum had a sudden suspicion and scanned the crowd, spotting his friend the noted ventriloquist and magician, Signor Blitz. The mystery was solved, but in the chaos the annihilator was not applied until the fire had grown beyond the ability of any such device to extinguish it. Barnum honored his money-back guarantee, though he remained convinced the fire annihilator actually did annihilate fire. He announced the lesson learned.

"Real merit does not always succeed as well as humbug," he said.

He still had the traveling show, whose name he changed in the second season to P. T. Barnum's Grand Colossal Museum and Menagerie. The abysmal reviews and reputation then finally began to catch up with it and the net proceeds declined accordingly, prompting a hike in the price of admission from twenty-five cents to thirty cents in the North, fifty cents in the South. That produced a corresponding rise in dissatisfaction, and customers in Lynchburg, Virginia, rioted against this overcharging Northern show. The circus workers who witnessed the start of the trouble shouted what had become the traditional cry whenever conflict with locals threatened to turn physical.

"Hey Rube!"

The longtime circus hand George Conklin would later write, "This was the S.O.S. call of the circus, and everyone who could leave what he was doing would grab a stake and rush into the fracas. The town gang was always the loser. If it had not been, the circus could not have stayed on the road long. Black eyes, bloody noses, bruised heads and broken bones were common. Often there were more serious injuries and sometimes a man was killed. Very often, men connected with the circus were arrested, but they were seldom convicted, for in such a rough-and-tumble fight it was almost impossible to tell which man inflicted a particular injury and the authorities usually got the wrong one."

However poorly the Lynchburg toughs fared, they critically injured three circus men and trashed much of the equipment and trappings. The ticket wagon was demolished.

The net profit fell from $71,000 in 1852 to $48,547 in 1853 to just $6,000 in 1854. The last show of the season was back in Brooklyn and Barnum decided to close it down. He sold Howes his share of the assets save for a single elephant.

In the Connecticut city of Bridgeport, train passengers riding through on the way to and from New York beheld the novel sight of an elephant pulling a plow. The stunt was timed to the train schedules and the only crop Barnum reaped was publicity, boosting both his American

Museum and East Bridgeport, the dream city he was continuing to build. He was decent enough to warn away farmers who wrote inquiring about the benefits of elephant plowing.

"I began to be alarmed lest some one should buy an elephant," Barnum later wrote. "I accordingly had a general letter printed, which I mailed to all my anxious inquirers. It was headed 'strictly confidential.'"

The letter advised that the high cost of purchasing an elephant was compounded by the onerous cost of feeding one, which far exceeded its value as a working farm animal.

"He could not earn even half his living," Barnum wrote.

The recipients apparently honored the confidentiality of the letter, for word of it did not seem to reach the newspapers. Barnum naturally did nothing to dispel the continued enthusiasm of the reporters who delivered firsthand accounts of his elephant plowing.

"Newspaper reporters came from far and near, and wrote glowing accounts of the elephantine performances," Barnum later wrote. "One of them, taking a political view of the matter, stated that the elephant's sagacity showed that he knew more than did any laborer on the farm, and yet, shameful to say, he was not allowed to vote. Another said that Barnum's elephant built all the stone wall on the farm; made all the rail fences; planted corn with his trunk, and covered it with his foot; washed my windows and sprinkled the walks and lawns, by taking water from the fountain-basin with his trunk; carried all the children to school, and put them to bed at night, tucking them up with his trunk; fed the pigs; picked fruit from branches that could not otherwise be reached; turned the fanning mill and corn-sheller; drew the mowing machine, and turned and cocked the hay with his trunk; carried and brought my letters to and from the post-office (it was a male elephant); and did all the chores about the house, including milking the cows, and bringing in eggs."

Images of the plowing elephant appeared in newspapers across the country and beyond the sea as Barnum repeated the scene for passing trains.

"Heads were out every window," Barnum wrote.

A farmer friend named Gideon Thompson asked to see for himself "how the big animal worked."

"I knew him to be a shrewd, sharp man and a good farmer, and I tried to excuse myself, as I did not wish to be too closely questioned," Barnum later wrote. "Indeed, for the same reason, I made it a point at all times to avoid being present when the plowing was going on. But the old farmer was a particular friend and he refused to take 'no' for an answer; so I went with him 'to see the elephant.'"

Several gawkers were present when Barnum and the farmer Thompson arrived. The farmer watched silently for fifteen minutes and then strode into the field, sinking nearly to his knees in the oft-plowed earth.

"What is your object, sir, in bringing that great Asiatic animal on to a New England farm?" the farmer asked by Barnum's account.

"To plow," Barnum replied.

"Don't talk to me about plowing!" the farmer said. "The ground is so soft I thought I should go through and come out in China. No, sir! You can't 'humbug me.'"

Thompson offered an expense versus efficiency appraisal of the elephant.

"He can't draw so much as two pair of my oxen can, and he costs more than a dozen pair," the farmer declared.

"You are mistaken," Barnum said. "That elephant is a powerful animal. He can draw more than forty yoke of oxen, and he pays me well for bringing him here."

"Forty yoke of oxen!" the farmer exclaimed. "I don't want to tell you I doubt your word, but I would just like to know what he can draw."

"He can draw the attention of twenty millions of American citizens to Barnum's Museum," Barnum said.

Among the draws at the museum were the conjoined twins Chang and Eng Bunker from Siam, all the more spectacular for fathering twenty-two children by a pair of sisters. And there was What-Is-It?, also known as Zip the Pinhead, a young New Jersey microcephalic dressed in animal skins and displayed in a cage as having been captured "in the interior of Africa in a perfectly natural state, roving about like a monkey or Orang Outang." He was billed as "the connecting link between man and monkey."

And there was Josephine Boisdechene Clofullia, who festooned her six-inch beard with a diamond supposedly presented to her by Napoleon III after he learned she was styling her whiskers in the same manner as his own. She became front-page news when a man filed a lawsuit against the museum, seeking to recoup his twenty-five-cent admission along with damages on the grounds that the bearded woman was not a woman at all. The case went to trial and three doctors testified that they had examined her and that she was indeed a woman. Barnum prevailed, as he knew he would when he orchestrated the suit, which packed the museum with people anxious to judge for themselves.

Barnum was on the way to becoming America's first millionaire showman, ensconced in a Bridgeport mansion he dubbed Iranistan, said to be the grandest private residence in America. His dream city appeared to get a big boost when the seemingly profitable Jerome Clock Company offered to relocate from New Haven to East Bridgeport and bring with it as many as a thousand workers. Barnum had only to provide certain financial guarantees to get the company through a slow period. He agreed after being shown records indicating that Jerome had nearly half a million dollars in reserves and nearly $200,000 in anticipated revenue.

"I had 'East Bridgeport on the Brain,'" Barnum later wrote. "Whoever approached me with a project that looked to the advancement of my new city touched my weak side and found in me an eager listener. The serpent that beguiled me was any plausible proposition that promised prosperity to East Bridgeport."

The "Prince of Humbug" himself became the victim of an audacious scam in which his guarantees were used to acquire company debts on his behalf, or rather to his detriment. The Jerome Company was in fact imploding and Barnum found himself owing more than half a million dollars. His dream city was never to be and he was left bankrupt at the age of forty-six.

"The gods visible again," a humbug-hating Ralph Waldo Emerson said of Barnum's apparent ruin.

Barnum had to give up Iranistan and board his family with a farmer in Westhampton on Long Island. He managed to pay the farmer only after he came upon a dead whale while strolling the beach. He transported the whale to Manhattan, where it was put on exhibit at the museum he had kept from creditors by "selling" the contents to two friends for a dollar. The friends gave him a cut of the modest profits brought in by a deceased creature presented as nothing more than itself.

Barnum retained a surplus of audacity and America's most famous bankrupt went on tour giving lectures on "The Art of Money Getting, or Success in Life."

Money he got, adding the lecture proceeds to tickets sales for tours by Tom Thumb and Jenny Lind, who both stepped forward to assist the showman in his hour of need. He reassumed official ownership of the New York museum in March of 1860 and, in a measure of how far he had quickly come from using a dead whale to pay off a farmer, he now acquired two living belugas, one fifteen feet, the other twenty. He installed them in a water tank in the museum basement.

"As it is very doubtful whether these wonderful creatures can be kept alive more than a few days, the public will see the importance of seizing the first moment to see them," a broadsheet announced.

The public responded accordingly, as did the newspapers, an article noting of the beluga duo, "A long-continued intimacy has endeared them to each other, and they go about quite like a pair of whispering lovers, blowing off their mutual admiration in a very emphatic manner."

One did indeed die, and a Barnum paean declared, "May both whales meet again in the open seas of immortality!"

A less likely love was presented by an exhibit that proved to be a big hit in a time when tensions were growing between the Northern and Southern states and partisan strife loomed. The museum guidebook described it thus:

THE HAPPY FAMILY. A miscellaneous collection of beasts and birds (upwards of sixty in number), living together harmoniously in one large cage, each of them being the mortal enemy of every other, but contentedly playing and frolicking together, without injury or discord. . . . The family comprises 8 doves, 4 owls, 10 rats, 2 cats, 2 dogs, 1 hawk, 3 rabbits, 1 rooster, 8 Guinea Pigs, 1 Raccoon, 2 Cavas, 1 Cuba Rat, 3 Ant Eaters, 7 Monkeys, 2 Woodchucks, 1 Opossum, 1 Armadilla, &c., &c.

Barnum had imported the Happy Family after seeing it in England and perhaps not even he knew how the exhibitor maintained such an improbable truce. Some observers guessed he selected creatures with particularly docile temperaments. Others figured the animals were intimidated with harsh treatment after hours and kept so overfed they did not contemplate eating each other.

Whatever the secret, the Happy Family offered a vision of harmony that was hugely popular. This same benevolent side of nature was suggested by the largest of land mammals, but the onetime part owner of nine elephants appeared to have lost faith in their money-getting potential. Barnum left Howes to make a solo attempt with a traveling circus. Howes then sold all but two of the herd to which he had taken full title, a male and a female.

The male was already named Romeo. Howes renamed the female Juliet and presented them at his new Franconies Hippodrome, a nineteenth-century version of the ancient Greek horse racing venue. Howes's hope was to entice people to the show rather than have it travel to them, but even with these largest of lovers the Hippodrome shut after two seasons. The star-crossed elephants were sold off separately. Romeo was on his way to becoming known as America's first "bad" or, in the parlance of the show world, "ugly" elephant.

FIVE

UGLY

Romeo was same big male who had demonstrated his high spirits and feisty temperament early on by going "rogue" on the dock in Ceylon after being captured by the Barnum expedition. The mahout who helped subdue him had clearly not endeared himself to the elephant during the long ordeal at sea. The elephant killed him shortly after arriving in America, perhaps the first such death here, one bit of unprecedented drama that Barnum kept from the newspapers.

At that point the elephant was named Canada, but it was changed to Romeo after he killed a keeper in Canada. A press agent subsequently sought to explain simultaneously one elephant's apparent disappearance and another elephant's ill temper by saying that Romeo had sought to save Canada during an accident on a bridge, holding on to the unlucky elephant for an hour before his strength gave out. The press agent said Canada had fallen to his death and Romeo had been left emotionally traumatized.

In truth, Romeo's sometimes murderous disposition was almost certainly a result of the brutality he suffered at the hands of his successive keepers. The prevailing philosophy among American trainers was based on fear and pain. The trainers generally operated with the belief that elephants needed to be physically intimidated from the start and mercilessly punished if they failed to obey, beaten without stop until they gave a cry of surrender. Orders often were accompanied by a jab with the sharp point of an ankus, popularly known as an elephant hook or bull hook, a wood-handled metal crook with a spike on the end. Elephants supposedly did not really feel it because their hide was so thick, even though their constant nuzzling and stroking of each other would seem proof of their skin's sensitivity.

A similar approach was taken to the children who were "adopted" by early circuses from what the *New York Times* described as "almshouses [and] degraded parents, in whom the love of rum had extinguished all sparks of parental affection, and who would be consoled by a few dollars for the loss of their too-often unwelcome urchins." The paper reported that one apprentice recalled he "was seldom spoken to without both an oath and a blow, and that the lithe lash of the heavy wagon-whip cracked about his ears all day, from the time it woke him from his sleep in the all-too-early morning to the hour it sent him tingling and revengeful to his wretched bunk at night." Another former circus child recalled "nothing but blows, oaths and kicks from morning till night, to which was added also no inconsiderable amount of wholesome starvation."

Elephants cost considerably more than a child to acquire, but often-times fared even worse because their size convinced their abusers that they could take more and needed more to get the intended message. The result with Romeo (not to be confused with a different elephant of the same name who arrived from India in 1832) was that he killed another keeper in Missouri and yet another in Florida. He was termed "the most dangerous animal of its kind" and "the worst elephant in America."

A press agent might have tried to turn that fearsome reputation to financial advantage had the public found danger to be part of an elephant's appeal, as it did with the snarling lions and tigers. But elephants were viewed as wise, above the fray, possessing an actual overview, a manifestation of a utopian benevolence such as had made the Happy Family exhibit at the Barnum Museum such a success.

"It is astonishing to think how docile these huge creatures are, when it is remembered that but a brief time since they were running wild in the jungle," *Gleason's Pictorial Drawing-Room Companion* remarked.

Lions were considered only to be acting in accordance with their nature when they mauled to death three members of a circus band that had been positioned atop the cage when its roof collapsed. An elephant who turned violent was considered an aberration, a rogue, bad, regardless of what may have triggered the rage. There were no bad cats, but there were bad elephants just as there were bad people.

The badness was assumed to originate in the captive rather than in the captors. Such "ugly" elephants were said to "deserve" punishment, even more of the brutality that had given rise to the behavior in the first place. They were thought to need to have the badness beaten out of them, to be taught a lesson, to be completely subjugated.

The philosophy sometimes produced the desired result in the short term, but it ultimately succeeded only in making a "bad" elephant worse, an even uglier reflection of the abuser. His reputation aside, Romeo seemed sufficiently subdued at the time of the Hippodrome's closing that a circus called the Mabie Menagerie and Show did not hesitate to buy him. He did apparently become more troublesome as the show hit the road and the owners sent for a tall, raw-boned trainer from Ohio who had a growing reputation for being able to handle even the most difficult elephants.

"When all other means failed with elephants, there was but one thing to do, 'Send for Craven,'" noted circus chronicler C. G. Startevent.

Stewart Craven had been sixteen years old in 1849, when Isaac Van Amburgh's menagerie performed near his Ohio home. Van Amburgh had become famous for daring to step into a cage with an array of big cats, including a lion, a tiger, and a leopard. He was forthright about his methods, saying, "They believe I have the power to tear every one of them to pieces if they do not act as I say. I tell them so and have frequently enforced it with a crowbar." He answered any fainthearted critics by citing the Bible, specifically, Genesis 1:26: "And God said, let us make mankind in our image and likeness; and let them have dominion over the fish of the sea, the birds of the air, all the cattle, all the earth, and all the creatures that crawl on the earth." He reinforced the biblical justification by dressing in a toga and sandals as he imagined King David had during his encounter with the lion. His signature stunt was having the lion lie down with the lamb as in the Book of Isaiah and even having a nine-year-old come in as a stand-in as the little child who shall lead them.

Young Craven joined the show as it continued on and proved able to juggle while he rode on the tusks of the elephant Tippo Saib, appearing as an authentic marvel in such venues as Niblo's Garden in New York, where Barnum had first exhibited Joice Heth. His fellow trainers were more impressed to see him ride standing atop a moving elephant, for they knew that the loose skin there accorded what one protégé termed "footing about as secure as water." They were no doubt doubly amazed when he went up on one foot and just kept riding along, a figure of absolute self-assurance, triumphant with the elephant rather than over it. He clearly had an innate sense of balance, but he just as clearly had developed a sense of how an elephant would move from instant to instant. Here seemed to be not so much subjugation as comprehension.

Craven further demonstrated and developed his abilities as he trained the elephants Anthony and Cleopatra for an extended appearance at the Broadway Theater in New York. He now received the most serious challenge of his burgeoning career when the Mabie show, the current owner of Romeo, sent for him to come be its head elephant trainer.

The show was touring the South and Craven caught up with it in Jackson, Mississippi. He entered the tent as a paying customer.

"That was the first time I saw Romeo," Craven would recall. "I walked past the elephants and as soon as Romeo saw me he spotted me. He knew at once I was an elephant man. He threw up his head and then smelt me all over. I paid no attention to him, but walked on. Instead of turning to the next person and looking for apples, Romeo followed me as far as his chain would let him and kept his head turned toward me until I left the tent."

Craven did not announce himself to the manager until the next day, after he had followed the show to the town of Raymond.

"Before this, I wanted to keep incognito and take a look at the elephants," Craven said. "The man who had the elephants before was . . . a low, drunken brute. When he heard that I was to replace him, he was terribly mad."

The man stormed off and Craven took charge.

"As soon as I saw the elephants, I saw something was wrong. The man had gone away without fastening Romeo securely. The chain around his leg was only fastened to a light stake."

Craven ducked under the rope that had been stretched as a perimeter to keep back passersby. Craven began by petting Romeo, seeking to make a connection with the already notorious elephant before moving to secure the chain. Romeo made clear that he preferred not to be bothered.

"He took me up with his trunk and set me gently outside the rope."

The question of the chain remained and Craven again ducked under the rope.

"This time, he picked me up and threw me at least twenty feet, and if he could have followed me he surely would have killed me."

The chain held for the moment, but that could have changed in a deadly instant as Romeo strained after this elephant man. Craven sought to drive Romeo back, his immediate and reflexive goal now not to comprehend but to subdue, as if he were just any other trainer.

"Then he began to fight me."

Craven had not yet learned to consider the source of the fury. He simply responded in the usual way, answering force with force.

"We got the other elephants out of the road and began to beat Romeo with clubs and poles. He had about twenty-five feet of chain, and, of course, we could not get very near him. He rushed after us as far as his chain would let him, and we kept out of his road, punching him with poles all the time. Sometimes he got hold of the clubs we threw at him and then we all stampeded. He threw those clubs back with force enough to cut a man in two. We fought him all night, but could make no headway at all, except to aggravate him."

With the dawn came an urgency.

"The show moved on, and I was bound to follow with Romeo."

Craven and his assistants managed to fasten the chain to the three other elephants.

"Then we let them loose. I was already on horseback and led the way. As soon as Romeo saw me, he came for me, pulling the other elephants with him. He kept me going at a lively pace."

Craven headed into a patch of woods, with Romeo coming right after him. The assistants fastened a second chain to the one on Romeo and secured that to a tree. They then used the other elephants to pull, according Romeo less and less slack.

"By this means, we got Romeo's leg so held that he could not move it an inch. He was fighting as well as he could, however, all the time."

They set nooses on the ground and yanked them tight when Romeo stepped into them during his continuing struggles.

"Then we had him by all four legs."

They now used the other elephants to pull Romeo's legs out from under him, chancing upon a method that had been used in India for centuries and would become known as "taking" an elephant.

"And down he went."

Craven and the men again set upon him with the clubs.

"He fought and fought and gouged a big hole in the ground with his head."

Finally there came the sound Craven was waiting to hear.

"He soon gave up and halloed enough. When you hear an elephant cry that way, you know he's subdued. It's a very peculiar cry, and once you hear it you know it again. It's just like a man that's whipped."

He apparently meant a man who has reached his limit, though the whipping of slaves was common enough in the Southern states where the show was touring. He distinguished himself to some degree from other trainers, and from slave overseers, by not administering one blow more than he considered necessary. Enough was indeed enough, at least as he figured it at that time.

"Well, Romeo halloed, and just as soon as we could get the chains off, he was free. But he was so exhausted that he could not get up, and we had to help him. We fastened a chain around his head and made the other elephants pull him to his feet, and he was as docile as a lamb. We had no more trouble with him for a year afterward."

The show was in Cotton Gin, Texas, when Romeo expressed his particular displeasure with an assistant whom Craven himself described as "an ignorant fellow." Romeo knocked the assistant through a fence and the man escaped serious injury only by zigzagging around the posts. The assistant sought his revenge after Romeo was tied up, but the elephant seemed determined not to give him any satisfaction.

"He beat that elephant until [Romeo] was badly used up, but [Romeo] would not give in. It is remarkable what ill will Romeo had for that fellow. . . . The man I'm talking about would not go near the elephant after that and that was the wisest thing he ever did in his life, for Romeo would surely have killed him at the first chance. . . . Once an elephant gets spite against a man, he never forgets it."

Indelible in Craven's own memory was an occurrence while the show was making a winter visit to Chicago. Craven had gone out for the evening when Romeo turned on one of his keepers, knocking the man down. The keeper managed to flee outside and Romeo proceeded to wreck the interior of the building where he and a new elephant renamed Juliet were quartered.

"After doing as much damage as he could inside, he broke down the doors and marched into the streets of Chicago."

Juliet followed. The circus began an urgent search for Craven.

"They had at least fifty people rushing around town hunting for me. In the meantime, Romeo was causing the greatest excitement. A large crowd had collected and the elephant was rushing them through the streets."

The gawkers managed to escape injury by scampering up onto the boarded sidewalks, which were elevated eighteen inches above the street.

"The elephant was afraid to get on the boards. As soon as everybody appeared on the streets, however, Romeo went for them and drove them to the sidewalks. In this way he kept the streets clear."

The small army of frantic searchers was unable to find Craven, who was at the theater.

"I got back to the hotel around eleven o'clock and then heard about Romeo and went to look for him. I first found Juliet—she had got out, too—and got her home without any trouble. Then I went for Romeo."

The continuing uproar made Romeo easy to find. Craven studied the elephant for a moment before calling out his name.

"He threw up his head and didn't know where the sound came from. I called again and then he saw me. I cried, 'Come here!'"

Come he did.

"He came as a flash of lightning and as he came I went."

Craven dashed into the building where the elephants were being quartered and ducked into a dressing room just inside the entrance, which was elevated like the sidewalks, only higher.

"Old Romeo came in and stood in the entrance and there he stayed looking for me. He was frantic, and if he could have got me would have killed me sure."

Craven contrived to make Romeo literally chill.

"I got around the building and opened all the windows and doors, so as to make it as cool as possible—it was bitter weather—and thus freeze Romeo into going into his stall. But the fever was on him bad and that wouldn't work."

Craven ducked back into the elevated dressing room and sought to cool the situation more figuratively.

"I fooled around making as much noise as possible, but appearing to be unconcerned. . . . After a while, I handed an ear of corn to him from the dressing room, and he put it in his mouth, but would not eat."

Craven waited for a time and casually made another offering.

"At last he did eat a piece of bread and then I spoke to him. I told him to go into his stall. He hesitated a minute and then walked in. I knew he was all right and I followed and soon had the chain around his foot."

The crisis was resolved without Craven inflicting even a single blow.

"And that was the end of that trouble."

The show proceeded on to its winter quarters in Delvan, Wisconsin. The season done, Craven returned to Chicago, after having a financial disagreement with the parsimonious management. He arrived to find three urgent telegrams awaiting, asking him to return as quickly as possible. The true urgency of the situation became clear after he telegraphed back, demanding considerable remuneration.

"I got an answer right away accepting my terms and I went. It appears that as soon as Romeo found I had gone he got frantic and no one would go near him. He was all right when he saw me and stayed all right until spring."

Romeo and Juliet were lodged in an extension to the barn. The warming weather brought a group of curious women who asked to see the elephants drink. Craven obliged by setting Romeo and Juliet loose. The elephants stepped from the shadows into the sunshine.

"As soon as Romeo got into the light I saw he had a spell on."

The spell was not the result of any immediate provocation and was most likely a condition that had not afflicted The Elephant or Old Bet or Lil Bet or any other females. The condition is musth, from the Persian word *mast,* meaning intoxicated, which aptly describes this state of hormonal and emotional upheaval that periodically visits male elephants, generally between the ages of sixteen and sixty, most often in the winter, for periods ranging from two weeks to five months, peaking for a period of forty-five to sixty days. The onset is often signaled by spreading of the ears and widening of the eyes, which begin to roll and glare. The temporal glands roughly midway between the eye and the ear swell and are thought to cause maddening pain as they press upon the eyes. Ducts at the bottom edges of the glands begin to ooze a dark, gooey substance that seeps down toward the mouth. Urine runs along the inside of the rear legs. The level of testosterone in the blood spikes by as much as sixty times and the elephant becomes wildly aggressive.

The exact purpose of musth remains a mystery, perhaps because it may not serve any current purpose. Some scientists believe it is an evolutionary vestige dating back to the time of woolly mammoths, whose herds are thought to have included grown males. Musth among the mammoths could have served to signal a readiness to contest other males for dominance and demonstrate to females the robustness of a suitable mate.

The matriarchy of the elephant herd may have been an instance of social evolution outpacing the biological. One theory proposes that musth among elephants does function at least partly to prevent inbreeding by making its subject so wildly aggressive as to take on even dominant males who might otherwise monopolize the available and willing females. Adherents of this view caution that being in musth is not the male equivalent of being in estrus, or heat. The bulls so affected are often tumescent but do not evidence a heightened sex drive so much as a general fury.

At the approach of a male in musth, the adult females of a herd have been observed forming a protective circle. Musth may, if nothing else, confirm the wisdom of exiling grown males. Craven certainly knew what to do with his visitors when he saw Romeo in this condition.

"I can tell you, I got those ladies out of sight as quick as they could go. Juliet went to the trough and drank, but Romeo stood still, shaking his head. I went within a half dozen steps of him and said, 'Romeo, come here.' And he did come."

Craven dashed into the barn just as he had into the building in Chicago, but instead of food he took up a shotgun loaded with buckshot, not deadly for an elephant, but definitely stinging. Craven stepped into the doorway and Romeo started toward him. Craven called out the command for stop.

"Det!"

Romeo kept coming. Craven fired into his trunk. Romeo turned away and began wrecking fences and scattering hay mounds.

"Well to make it short, I had two days and three nights with him. I would go out with the gun, and when he came for me and would not stop when I called, I fired into his trunk."

On the fourth day, Craven ventured once more into Romeo's view and ducked into an extension next to the barn. Romeo charged after Craven and over some planks that were then raised with ropes, uncovering a pit that had been dug just inside the entrance deep enough to prevent the elephant from exiting the way he entered. The gun in Craven's hands dissuaded the elephant from making an elephant-size hole of the man-size hole that the trainer had cut in the far wall so he could slip out.

"Det!"

Stop Romeo did. Craven and his helpers soon had nooses around the trapped elephant's feet and they pulled his legs out from under him as they had on their earlier encounter with him. Craven's own testosterone must have been up for he did something he had never done before.

"It was the first and only time I burnt an elephant. . . . An inch bar of hot iron was pressed against his body . . ."

Craven knew the actual sensitivity of an elephant's rough-looking skin; the burning bar must have been agony itself.

". . . but he did not move."

Craven reached a conclusion.

"I saw that it would do no good and stopped."

Craven then proceeded as he had on other days, as if he had learned nothing.

"We beat him with clubs until he halloed. He gave up pretty soon and we took the chains off at once. Romeo was all right again."

Craven used a knife to dig the shot out of Romeo's trunk, trying to tell himself that it did no more real harm than bee stings. Craven did not consider until later that the elephant retained the memories of the gun and of the clubs and of the searing bar of iron, memories that joined those of other beatings, that would fuel other rampages, turning hormone-triggered fury into absolute rage. The ultimate outcome would lead Craven to a conclusion that would set him apart from his fellow elephant men. But this was still several years away as the Mabie show returned to the road.

That winter, the circus again toured the South. A typical newspaper notice in the *Yazoo City Democrat* accompanied its arrival in that Mississippi town in December of 1859: "Monsieur Craven will introduce those highly trained elephants, Romeo and Juliet, who have been received with unbounded demonstrations of applause wherever they have been exhibited. Truly they have to be seen to be appreciated."

Less welcome visitors to this part of the country included those who opposed selling and subjugating humans no differently than animals. The newspaper reported that a "live abolitionist" had been given "pretty plain ocular evidence" that he was not wanted. He was described as "five feet five or six inches high, with light hair, [and] only one eye."

"In his travels, let every man greet him with a kick Northwards," the paper advised, passing on another journal's "witty" remark that "If such men come into our midst and groan inwardly over the tortures of the slave, we should relieve them of their suppressed sobs, and make them groan outright."

An ad in the *Democrat* offered for sale "four of the best negro dogs in the state" whose usefulness in tracking down runaway slaves would be confirmed by "any planter or overseer on Silver Creek." A news item headlined simply "Hanged" reported, "The negro woman Eliza, who has been for some time under sentence of death for the burning of the gin house of Mrs. McCann, was hung on Friday."

The newspaper proved not completely jaded as it reported on one sort of spectacle that consistently outdrew even Craven's elephants.

"As is customary in Christian countries, a large crowd was present to witness the horrid spectacle of strangling a human being, bound hand and foot," the paper pointedly added. "To our astonishment, white women were there, who looked with apparent unconcern upon the scene. After death, the body was given over for dissection."

SIX

THE WAR BETWEEN
THE STATES, THE BATTLE OF
THE DWARFS

In the meantime, Romeo's original Juliet had been acquired by a clown, raconteur, and social commentator who had become the nation's first pop celebrity. Dan Rice had been born Daniel McClaren in New York, but he now went by the name of a clown who had been renowned in Ireland in his father's time. The Dan Rice of these shores had become one of the most famous men in America, blending wisecracks and wisdom, songs and soliloquies, dancing and diatribes, pratfalls and poetry. He was a prime precursor of the stand-up comics of later years, in particular those who were also social critics. He sported a goatee but no mustache, sometimes wore clownish stars and stripes, other times a top hat, all of which were said by some to have been combined by the cartoonist Thomas Nast into the model for his famous drawing of Uncle Sam.

Rice had started out with a trained pig named Sybil. He now rechristened the elephant formerly known as Juliet as Lalla Rookh, after a popular quartet of narrative poems by Thomas Moore. Rice nonetheless did not expect that an elephant would in itself be much more of an attraction than his pig. He sought to further his new acquisition's appeal by preceding her arrival with posters announcing that Lalla Rookh would perform a headstand.

Rice must have figured the audience would have already paid when it became clear that no such trick was forthcoming. He would later report that one town, apparently Ellicottville, New York, proved to have little tolerance for humbug. Rice would write that the local magistrate hauled him into court on charges of "obtaining money under false pretenses." Rice naturally sought to extricate himself with more humbug.

"I explained that it was all a mistake of my advertising agents, who had inadvertently pasted the elephant pictures upside down on the fences, so that they looked like those of a pachyderm standing on its head," Rice later wrote. "Strange to say, this story didn't go down."

He tried a more successful tack.

"Then I assured the court that my elephant could and would stand on its head, but as it was a female, innate modesty led it to decline to make such a spectacle of itself save under cover of darkness. Of course then I was honorably discharged."

In August of 1860, Dan Rice discovered that there was one actual circumstance by which a single elephant could still draw a considerable audience, rivaling even executions. He announced that Juliet, now Lalla Rookh, would "take the water" and swim the Ohio River from the Kentucky shore to Cincinnati. A crowd of fifteen thousand gathered on the Cincinnati side, another three thousand on the opposite bank, their differences in politics and allegiance momentarily forgotten, the only subject of contention whether or not the event would actually take place.

The stunt was scheduled for 9:00 a.m., and at the appointed hour the crowds along the Ohio saw the celebrated Dan Rice appear. The simple sight of him often caused a sensation just in itself. One young man had written to a newspaper some time before saying he had been at an Illinois hotel where Abraham Lincoln was supposed to visit, but had decided that he would rather go to the circus to see Rice. The writer arrived to find that Lincoln himself had come to see the renowned clown.

Yet, as Rice now boarded a skiff, all eyes were not on him but on the elephant being led to the river's edge. A reporter who watched her approach through the muggy heat of this already oppressive summer morning noted that she flapped her ears "quite majestically," though likely he did not know this is a way elephants cool themselves, lowering their body temperature by as much as five degrees. She was called "her aquatic majesty" and, in a double play on words, "her elephantship."

The skiff bearing Rice started for the opposite shore and the moment of truth arrived. Lalla Rookh thrilled all in attendance by plunging right in. Her keeper, C. W. Noyes, boarded a second skiff to escort her while Rice's craft led the way.

But rather than traverse, Lalla Rookh began to cavort, splashing and spraying as she might had she been back with her herd in her native land. The keeper afforded the scribes opportunities to offer various euphemisms for beating an elephant.

"The exertions of her keeper ... brought her back to a sense of propriety," wrote one.

Rice had proceeded ahead and stood on the far shore toward which Lalla Rookh was prodded. Several boatloads of gawkers had taken to the river, and when they came too close, the elephant turned to chase them away. They rowed away so quickly that "they would have put even the famous Harvard boat club to the blush," as one reporter wrote.

The keeper renewed his "exertions" and Lalla Rookh resumed the prescribed course, amazing the crowd as she sank so deep that only the tip of her extended trunk broke the surface; Aristotle had written of elephants doing this two millennia before. A pathologist who autopsied an elephant who perished in a fire in early-seventeenth-century Dublin had noted tissue connecting the lungs directly to the diaphragm and other tissue sheathing what was simply the pleural cavity on other mammals, a unique construction that allowed elephants to draw water through their trunks and further protected them from the pressure generated by such snorkeling.

When Lalla Rookh veered off course, the keeper corrected her via whatever bit of her he could reach. She began to disappear completely, suddenly free of her tormentors. She would remain submerged for so long that the spectators would become alarmed, worried that she had drowned. She would then suddenly surge to the surface with such force that half her body exploded from the water, a sight so exciting as to make the spectators forget Rice altogether.

The keeper would be on her and down she would go again, free once more until that last desperate instant when the need for air overcame the desire for freedom and she had to burst back into captivity. She eventually reached the shore, to cheers from the crowd. The *Commercial Advertiser* noted that city's more worldly citizens "are generally supposed to have 'seen the elephant' under every possible aspect."

"Now they have seen the aquatic one, their education may be considered complete," the paper concluded.

In those brief underwater escapes, Lalla Rookh had apparently stayed a moment too long. She had water in her lungs and the condition developed into a fatal infection. Rice was left with just himself and an equestrienne he dubbed Ella Zoyara. A rider of the same name for another show had caused a sensation when she turned out to be really a he costumed as a she. Rice encouraged speculation that this was the case with his Zoyara, then announced that his she really was a she, another of the show world's fake fakes. The bogus controversy generated enough ticket sales that the she was dubbed a "dam-sell" by the *Variety* of its time, the *New York Clipper*.

His various successes with deception led Rice to risk one that would eventually lead to his downfall, to him being simply damned. He had been in his native New York the previous year for the debut of northerner Dan Emmett's song "Dixie," performed by the Dan Bryant Minstrels in blackface. The song had become a huge hit, dubbed by the *New York Clipper* to be "one of the most popular compositions ever produced . . . sung, whistled, and played in every quarter of the globe." It gave the South the antebellum equivalent of buzz, but frictions with the North were already keeping many shows above the Mason-Dixon line. Dan Rice's Great Show now headed down the Mississippi River aboard the *James Raymond*, a side paddle steamboat named after the New York menagerie impresario.

Rice was in Memphis when Lincoln was elected and one bit of news that followed the event would have caught the attention of any circus hand. King Mongkut of Siam had offered America the means to overcome its woeful lack of a native elephant population.

"Elephants, being animals of great size and strength, can bear burdens through uncleared woods and matted jungles where no carriage and cart roads have yet been made," the king noted in a diplomatic missive addressed to Lincoln's predecessor but arriving after the new president had assumed office.

Mongkut, who would achieve Broadway fame via Rodgers and Hammerstein's musical *The King and I,* offered to provide young male and female elephants "one or two pairs at a time."

"When they arrive in America, do not let them be taken to a cold climate out of the registers of the sun's declination," the king advised. "Let them, with all haste, be turned out to run wild in some jungle suitable for them, not confining them any length of time."

He concluded, "If these means can be done, we trust that the elephants will propagate their species hereafter in the continent of America."

Lincoln diplomatically declined, writing, "I appreciate most highly Your Majesty's tender of good offices in forwarding to this Government a stock from which a supply of elephants might be raised on our own soil. This Government would not hesitate to avail itself of so generous an offer if the object were one which could be made practically useful in the present condition of the United States. Our political jurisdiction, however, does not reach a latitude so low as to favor the multiplication of the elephant, and steam on land, as well as on water, has been our best and most efficient agent of transportation in internal commerce."

Lincoln's political jurisdiction seemed in imminent danger of shrinking to only its colder latitudes, as his 1860 election was leading to the secession of the Southern states and therefore war. That specter and the accompanying rowdiness of the crowds further deterred most Northern shows from venturing South.

Rice figured he was one showman who could span all such divisions. He counted Lincoln among his myriad acquaintances, but he was also friendly with Jefferson Davis, to whom he had presented a silver-fobbed rabbit's foot for good luck. Rice continued south, making his first visit in six years to New Orleans.

But Rice was not some elephant who could please folks of all political leanings simply by splashing around. He was known for his oratory, which meant he was expected to orate when his show opened to a sellout crowd of 1,800 on December 10, 1860. He gave the speech of a star whose perpetual aim was to please his audience.

"The South has been aggrieved and she knows it, and the whole civilized world knows it, but none more seriously than those who have attempted to deprive her of her rights," he said.

Rice was still appearing in New Orleans in January, when the Louisiana legislature voted to secede. He needed only hear the church bells and cannons to gauge the popular sentiment and he adjusted his performances accordingly. A local paper opined that "Dan is Southern, feels it, talks it, acts it." He continued to pack the house night after night.

Rice had started back north, leaving the South to get by on the few circuses it could call its own, when the first shots were fired on Fort Sumter. The outbreak of war made it all the more imperative and all the more difficult for him to adjust his espoused sentiments to his more northerly audiences. He was apparently assuming that what had happened in New Orleans would stay in New Orleans when he gave a speech in Erie County, Pennsylvania, to a militia regiment as it headed off to fight.

"Annihilate treason!" he told the 83rd Pennsylvania Volunteers.

A report of his remarks in Pennsylvania reached New Orleans, where he was branded the Chameleon Clown. Reports of his earlier remarks in the South, in turn, caught up with him as he opened in Philadelphia. Audiences greeted him with loud hissing and barrages of rotten eggs. The onetime star needed police protection.

Up in New York, Barnum had remained consistently pro-Union, prompting the *Clipper* to accuse him of "trying the patriotic dodge."

He festooned his American Museum with the Stars and Stripes and began admitting African-Americans. He hosted a female Union spy who seems to have been actually genuine and he staged the play *The Hero of Fort Sumter*, even though the really big draws were the museum's many other attractions that offered New Yorkers a diversion from the conflict.

Business became bigger than ever as the brutal realities of the fighting grew increasingly apparent. People then wanted to think and talk of almost anything else.

As a result, Barnum was well on the way back from financial ruin. He was so encouraged that he decided to expand and sent a traveling sampling of his museum to Washington, D.C. The union's military brass were now joined by General Tom Thumb as well as a newer feature of similarly small stature, Commodore Nutt, known as $300,000 Nutt for the sum Barnum supposedly paid him to tour. A more accurate nickname would have been $15-a-Week Nutt.

The Cremorne Garden Circus was already exhibiting in Washington with a dwarf of its own, Commodore Foote, not to be confused with either the actual naval officer or the actual general with that surname. The Cremorne show took out a newspaper ad, issuing a challenge to "place Commodore NUTT and Commodore FOOTE together on a platform in some respectable building in this city, and let the public determine which is the smaller of the two."

The Cremorne show also proposed having an impartial committee judge the respective range of knowledge and artistic abilities of Nutt and Foote, with any proceeds from the event going to the Soldiers' Aid Association. Barnum took out an immediate ad in response:

The only reply Mr. Barnum thinks necessary to make to the challenge contained in the morning's paper is that he will not aid in a newspaper warfare for the purpose of giving notoriety to an itinerant adventurer. . . . The ladies and gentlemen who daily and nightly throng Mr. Barnum's establishment declare that never within their memory has been seen any "man in miniature" worthy of being named or thought of, or who will in the slightest degree compare with these symmetrical, intelligent, and talented little gentlemen—Commodore Nutt and General Tom Thumb, and, furthermore, that they never before witnessed in any one establishment such a vast and amusing concentration of talent and novelty as are to be seen at Barnum's Museum, Circus and Menagerie.

Barnum issued a challenge of his own:

With regard to the proposed donation to the Soldiers' Aid Association, Mr. Barnum has already paid thousands of dollars to aid the war for the Union, and he agrees that the services of Commodore Nutt, General Tom Thumb, or any other attraction which he has control of, are at the FREE disposal of the Soldiers' Aid Association whenever they hold a fair or exhibition where they may be of use to them. And Mr. B. will also present one thousand dollars to this Association whenever the showman alluded to will give five hundred dollars, after having paid up his unfortunate employees.

The exchange was dubbed the Battle of the Dwarfs and provided welcome merriment in a week when Union forces crossed the Potomac from Washington into Virginia. Lincoln would remain dissatisfied with the real generals until Ulysses S. Grant caught his attention. Grant was the son of a circus fan who would walk entire days to see one. Young Grant had gone to several as a boy and at the age of eleven answered a ringside challenge for boys to try for a five-dollar prize by riding a trick pony that had been trained to throw its rider. Grant managed to hang on and become the first ever to walk off with the prize, demonstrating a tenacity that would distinguish him during what was becoming a horror beyond imagining.

Back in New York, Barnum offered further diversion from the War Between the States with the wedding of his general, Tom Thumb, and the diminutive Lavinnia Warren at Grace Church on Broadway. The event was followed by a "honeymoon" reception hosted by President Lincoln at the White House.

The wedding photographer was Mathew Brady, who had a studio across Broadway from Barnum's Museum. Brady also photographed Barnum himself, as well as such other museum stars as the Bearded Lady, the Living Skeleton, the Siamese Twins, the Leopard Child, and the Pinhead, though none of the animals. He printed the photos of the celebrity performers on *cartes de visite*, cards that were collected and traded, precursors of baseball cards.

Brady became a celebrity himself with the photographs he and his assistants took of the Civil War, whose many battles included one in Lynchburg, where the locals had rioted over the admission price at Barnum's circus a decade before. The stark battlefield photographs gave many civilians their first sense of the enormity of the carnage that eventually claimed more than 600,000 lives. The expression "see the elephant" now came to mean witnessing combat, the bloodiest extreme of human experience.

SEVEN

4-PAW

Five days after the war's end and by chance the very day Lincoln was assassinated, the elephant Romeo passed into the possession of a new owner.

The entire Mabie menagerie was purchased by Adam Forbach, who had started out as a butcher boy in Philadelphia. He had been earning four dollars a month, board included, which was very generous for that time, but he hungered for greater glory and ran away from home, heading west. He eventually came to Cincinnati, where he reverted to supporting himself the only way he knew how, working for a butcher with the handy name of John Butcher. Forbach's restless desire for more prompted him to walk to Dayton and he there secured employment with another butcher, who had a sideline trading horses that were marginally more valuable alive than dead. Forbach had at least broadened his knowledge when he relinquished any instant hope of a more glamorous existence and returned home to Philadelphia.

He had enough innate business sense and little enough business principles that he saw an immediate opportunity when the Civil War caused a shortage of horses. He began buying superannuated nags from Philadelphia's horse-drawn tram companies and briefly stashing them on an island in the Schuylkill River. He then sold the same sorry creatures back to the same companies as fresh horses.

As the war dragged on, Forbach branched out, buying and selling as many as 10,000 horses in a year as he supplied the military as well as private companies. He established a "veterinary hospital" to work his usual scam on a grander scale, resulting in Union cavalrymen riding into battle on newly purchased mounts that had previously been declared unfit.

Forbach also sold forty-four horses for $9,000 to John "Pogey" O'Brien, whose circus was known for traveling with a band of particularly brazen and energetic pickpockets and swindlers. O'Brien liked to sport a double-breasted velvet vest with two rows of diamond-encrusted buttons and a gold watch chain from which hung a golden elephant charm with rubies for eyes and a diamond set in the trunk, but he failed to keep up the payments on the horses. He may have been distracted from business when his famously attractive daughter eloped with a sideshow attraction who had no arms or legs.

Forbach caught up with the delinquent O'Brien's circus in Pittsburgh, hoping to collect. The two became partners instead, the thirty-four-year-old Forbach proving to be an early example of a businessman smitten by show business.

From the start, Forbach was determined to make the show more than just another traveling circus and himself more than just another showman. He ventured a variation on his scam of hyping broken-down horses as new mounts and announced that he had retained Dan Rice for $1,000 a week, as if the clown were still the biggest star in

America and not struggling in the continued disgrace of having played both sides in the Civil War. The actual salary was likely just a fraction of that but Rice was happy to go along with the fiction, making his own effort to resurrect his image by building a war memorial in his hometown of Girard, Pennsylvania.

On his part, Forbach changed his name to Forepaugh, which he sometimes styled as 4-Paw, and joined his new partner in acquiring the ten animals of the Mabie menagerie. These included not just Romeo, but the elephant Annie, aka the new Juliet. Craven continued on as trainer. Romeo remained manageable as the New Dan Rice Menagerie braved the travails of the road.

The easiest part was the show itself. The hard work in a circus began as the evening performance was ending around 10:00 p.m. Crews would have already begun packing and as the audience departed they took down the tents and rolled up the canvas and packed the seat planks along with the poles and stakes and theatrical props and hundreds of other items, all by the light of pitch pine torches or outsize cotton balls soaked in alcohol. They then grabbed a couple of hours' sleep, roused around 2:00 a.m. by the watchman. They wolfed down an early breakfast and set out in two wagon "trains." The baggage train was faster and proceeded first at maybe eight miles an hour with the tents and equipment, led through the darkness on unmarked roads by a "boss hostler" on horseback who followed written directions such as "turn at red house" that would have been much more helpful in daylight. They would place some brush or a fence rail across the wrong turns at intersections to direct the slower cage train coming behind at maybe four miles per hour with the menagerie and the performers and the band. The worse the road, the worse the weather, the earlier they left. They had no waterproofs to ward off the rain and stripped off their shirts and stashed them in a box under the wagon so as to have dry clothes at the show. No matter how hard it rained, no matter how muddy the road became, a circus kept going.

"Rain meant mud and mud meant trouble," George Conklin would write of his time as a young circus driver. "Almost always some of them got in so deep that the rest of the train had to stop and pull them out."

Then on they would go, the drivers calling out "whoa up!" in the darkness if they had to stop. Drivers regularly dozed off, with predictable results.

"Everything seemed to conspire together to make the desire to sleep irresistible; the previous lack of it, the time, the quiet and darkness of night, the sounds of the train itself—jangling of harness and chains, chuckle and rumble of wheels, and rhythmic tread of horses' feet," Conklin would recall.

The tread of the elephants was preternaturally quiet given the animals' size; they walked on tiptoe as always, sure-footed thanks to the support of their thick footpads and an improbable sense of balance. They seemed tireless, ambling at around four miles per hour, the average speed of the cage train, much the same pace as if they were traveling in the forest, free of stakes and tethers, away from the roaring crowds and the brutal trainer. These were a Romeo and a Juliet brought together by force rather than love, a Juliet who should have been with a herd of females, a Romeo who should have been on his own since adolescence. Their every muted step away from the previous performance was a step toward more of the same at the next, but in between they were as close to free as they were likely ever to be again.

The show's perpetual goal on the road was for the elephants and the caged animals to arrive at the next destination in time to parade through the middle of town. The baggage train would have arrived far enough in advance to set up the tents. The exhausted workmen would sprawl around the perimeter of the big top during the shows, keeping a half-open eye out for kids trying to sneak in under the canvas while the elephants and other animals performed along with the acrobats and clowns.

Elephants see best in dim light such as that in a deep forest, but humans require brightness and the show did its best with a source that had been in use for centuries, nearly as long as elephants have been taken captive. Candles were stuck with melted wax atop the wagon wheels in the menagerie tent. The big top was lit with five "chandeliers," boards holding three hundred candles each, but the illumination was still chancy.

"At best the light was dim, flickering, and uncertain, but it was seldom that it was at its best, for often there were draughts sucking and drawing through the tent, making the candles flare up and smoke, or perhaps blowing out all on one side of the 'chandelier' while they were smoking on the other," Conklin remembered.

The show packed up by torchlight and the candles were lit again at the next stop. O'Brien continued to cadge extra income by selling "privileges"—not just the rights to peddle candy and lemonade on circus grounds, but also the rights of pickpockets, swindlers, and gamblers to work the show and move with it from town to town. The crooks included "Monday men," who specialized in stealing the wash off the clotheslines of the townspeople while they were at the parade or the show. O'Brien even employed a "fixer," who traveled a day ahead, visiting the local authorities.

"And by a generous use of blarney and money endeavored to secure immunity from police interference," Conklin wrote. "If his efforts were successful, and in those days they nearly always were, the town was said to be 'fixed' or 'safe.'"

O'Brien further accommodated the pickpockets by arranging for an announcement as the crowd waited for the ticket wagon to open.

"Ladies and gentlemen, we warn you to look out for pickpockets. This show does its best to keep them away, but sometimes they do get on the grounds. We don't want to have any of you lose your money while coming to our show, so we tell you about them and give you a chance to look out."

The invariable reflex was to check and make sure you still had your wallet, whose exact location the pickpockets duly noted.

"They in turn got busy," Conklin noted.

What the pickpockets did not get, the three-card monte dealers and magic elixir peddlers sought. The customer who reached the ticket wagon then faced a master shortchange artist whose skill in his chosen field matched that of any of the performers inside.

All told, enough of the ill-gotten gains ended up in Forepaugh's left vest pocket that he was as enthusiastically crooked as O'Brien.

The 1866 season ended in Philadelphia, where Romeo again suffered a "spell," charging into the street and chasing after the citizenry and generally causing havoc. Craven hurried to the scene and called to him. Romeo pursued Craven back into the quarters as before, but this time the elephant's rage was so all-consuming that he went after Juliet, knocking her down. Craven grabbed the shotgun as Romeo seemed poised to hit Juliet again and maybe kill her.

"I fired, and instead of hitting his trunk, the shot went into one of his eyes," Craven later said.

The owners could not have been pleased that Romeo was left partly blind, but they no doubt would have been considerably more displeased by the publicity that would have attended the news that Romeo had killed Juliet.

* * *

In the meantime, there had been a falling-out between Forepaugh and O'Brien. The owners dissolved their partnership and set up rival shows, with winter quarters across the street from each other in Philadelphia. O'Brien took the latest Juliet. Forepaugh took Romeo, and whatever separation pain the elephants suffered it did not seem to be of a Shakespearean magnitude.

Forepaugh also kept Dan Rice, continuing to "pay" the clown $1,000 a week. Forepaugh replaced any animals whose natural life span had been prematurely punctuated by the rigors of circus life. And he bought enough new ones to create a second show of his own.

"Forepaugh, despite of the many contributions he has made to the zoological cemetery in Philadelphia, intends to run two shows," reported the *New York Clipper*.

The new "Forepaugh's Circus and Menagerie" headed west with Romeo and twenty cages of animals. The Rice show stayed east, with dwindling profits reflecting his continued decline in popularity. Rice's latest and ultimate victim of fast-talking fakery was himself. He seemed to believe he really was a $1000-a-week star and when his old act was met with a yawn he decided he was meant for what he termed "higher things." He became increasingly cutting in his monologues. And he was further hampered by the increased size of the new big top, which forced the spectators in the farther reaches to strain to hear what then made them regret the effort.

Some wags on the show hung a "Dan Rice for President" banner as a goof, but he took it seriously and announced his candidacy. The leading candidate, the precocious circus contestant turned victorious general Ulysses Grant, was not concerned.

* * *

The next season, Forepaugh decided to field just one show, under no name but his own. He positioned himself during the performances either by the ticket wagon or at the main entrance to the big top, keeping a keen eye on attendance. He declared he would plow back his profits into making the Forepaugh show ever grander and at least in this regard he was as good as his word, adding ever more bandwagons and performers and animals. He became the first showman to have a separate tent just for the menagerie, where the animals could be admired between appearances in the ring.

In all other regards, Forepaugh was notoriously tightfisted, often "redcrossing" his employees, shortchanging their pay envelopes, then blaming a subordinate if they dared challenge him.

"It was a common question among his men, 'How much are you short this week?'" Conklin would recall.

Forepaugh chose to save a few more dollars by replacing Craven with a fellow named John Trowolla, who had little experience with elephants but would double as a trainer and ringmaster for forty dollars a week. Trowolla's view of Romeo was reflected in a newspaper account of a lawsuit he subsequently filed alleging that Forepaugh had unfairly fired him, replacing him with somebody who worked even cheaper.

"Mr. Trowolla being sworn testified that Mr. Forepaugh employed him to take charge of an immense, strong and ferocious elephant named Romeo."

Forepaugh took the stand, insisting that Trowolla had asked to be relieved of his duties. Forepaugh did confirm that he had hired a new trainer at twenty-five dollars a week. The new trainer, William "Canada Bill" Williams, had been such a big believer in the primacy of force he was termed an "elephant killer." And if he had not actually killed one, it was not for lack of effort. The outcome had been what Craven and indeed Old Bet's keeper might have predicted.

"Witness then engaged the elephant killer Williams and he took charge of Romeo and had no trouble with him from that time forth until the animal killed him," the newspaper reported.

Whether due to musth or mistreatment or both, Romeo remained so enraged for months after the latest killing that his minders had to feed and water him through a hole in the roof of the splintered stall where he was chained. He took particular dislike to certain people and threw stones at them with his trunk when they were within range. Residents surrounding the Forepaugh show's winter quarters outside Philadelphia expressed concern that he might escape and go on a rampage.

"Mr. Forepaugh states that Romeo cost him $40,000 and of course he is anxious to have such a valuable piece of property brought to terms," the *Philadelphia Ledger* reported.

That was actually just $2,000 less than the cost of the entire Mabie menagerie, but Romeo did represent a considerable investment. He would also constitute a considerable loss if this star attraction stayed chained in a stall when the show resumed touring. The first show of the 1868 season was just days away when Forepaugh suffered an expense he had sought to avoid while under the impression that handling an elephant required no more expertise than handling a big horse.

"In the spring, I was sent for to conquer him," Craven later said.

Romeo's rage only increased when he beheld Craven with his one good eye. Craven proceeded to bring him down as before, lassoing the legs and drawing them out, this time with block and tackle and the pulling power of gawkers who were enlisted to assist.

But Craven had not yet come to understand that he needed only to keep the elephant restrained until the "spell" passed.

"We got him down and began to punish him. It took us all Saturday and Sunday night and until Monday morning before he halloed."

The *Philadelphia Inquirer* reported that the elephant would be appearing with the rest of the show as it began its season the following Wednesday.

"Our citizens need have no apprehension of danger, as Romeo, like Richard the Third, is 'himself again,'" the paper noted.

Forepaugh saw no need to continue paying Craven now the crisis had passed, and the trainer departed. Forepaugh's brother, George, took charge of Romeo and the elephant remained generally docile through the season.

The show was in its winter quarters near Connersville, Indiana, when Adam Forepaugh purchased a female elephant, the latest to be named Lalla Rookh. The new arrival was secured with ropes a distance from Romeo. She managed to pull out the stakes during the night and the elephants were standing contentedly side by side when George Forepaugh arrived the next morning. The trainer separated them again.

Romeo made his displeasure known by grabbing George Forepaugh with his trunk and tossing him against a wall. The trainer summoned a posse of circus men and locals. Romeo ripped a wood beam from the rafters overhead and threw it at them with what a reporter termed "tolerable aim and direction."

George Forepaugh stayed completely out of Romeo's range for five days while Romeo went without food or water, to no apparent effect. The men finally ventured to follow Craven's example, using ropes to draw Romeo's legs out from under him. Romeo lay tied on the ground as the Forepaugh brother stepped up with a bull hook. Forepaugh drove the spike into the elephant's flank.

"Speak!" Forepaugh commanded.

Romeo responded by striking Forepaugh with his trunk. The other men beat Romeo for hour after hour with iron rods, spelling each other. Forepaugh jabbed with the spike again and again. The elephant finally gave that cry of surrender.

"A child can now drive him with a rye straw," George Forepaugh declared.

Or so it seemed until 1872, when, after four years of George Fore-paugh, Romeo suddenly seized the trainer with his trunk and tossed him into the air. Romeo was "taken" again, this time with added vengeance, suffering significant injuries to his legs. There was little if any public outcry about what one reporter called "day long docilizing treatments." The *New York Times* did suggest that the elephant was becoming more trouble than he was worth.

"Romeo has outlived his usefulness," the paper said.

Forepaugh sought to explain the elephant's ill humor by saying that Romeo was still grieving the tragic death of his lover. Juliet was said to have died back in the winter of 1864, when the ground had been too frozen for burial. Poor Romeo's prior owner was supposed to have cruelly forced him to drag her body onto a frozen lake, where it would submerge under its own weight come spring.

None of this was true, but the tale of tragic love might have made Romeo a big draw for years to come had cruelty not been compounded by ignorance and neglect. His keepers were baffled as he became lame and then seriously ill that June during a stop in Chicago.

"His disease was in the forefeet, which, for some unknown cause, had become affected with inflammation, resulting in acute pain and general debilitation of the system, the effect of which had been noticed by a rapid wasting of the flesh," a reporter explained.

His keepers apparently were unaware that an elephant's feet need regular care, particularly if chained for long periods in a pestilential slurry of mud, urine, and dung.

The fissures in the footpads that serve as a kind of natural tire tread to prevent slipping can deepen to where they become painful and prone to infection. And the toenails can crack and become infected during long sedentary periods if not properly maintained.

In Romeo's case, the injuries from the latest "taking" could not have helped matters. The infection spread up his forelegs and a Chicago surgeon from the city medical college operated, removing from his feet numerous small bones that had become necrotic. The elephant lost several gallons of blood, but the big threat remained the infection, which was unchecked.

Two days after the operation, on June 5, 1872, Romeo died. One newspaper article was headlined "Obituary Extraordinary," another "The Mighty Dead," this one reporting, "Chicago . . . was the scene of an event the occurrence of which will excite interest in almost every city, town, or village in America, being no less than the death of the celebrated performing elephant 'Romeo,' the largest and most valuable of his species ever brought to this country, and more famous than any who have gone before him."

Romeo was reported to have killed four keepers besides Williams. The *New York Times* spoke of him as if he were human, saying, "He had many friends in various parts of the country, and his death will no doubt be sincerely mourned, notwithstanding the recollection of his crimes."

Forepaugh accorded Romeo a celebrity's send-off. The elephant lay in state in the menagerie tent and a band played Pleyel's "Hymn" and Handel's "Dead March" from *Saul*. Thousands filed past.

"Many shedding tears over the dead old hero," the *New York Clipper* noted.

The reporter observed, "The least affected person in the assemblage was Adam Forepaugh."

Either on the advice of a press agent or at his own prompting, Forepaugh subsequently played the heartbroken owner, one article reporting "a quiver in his voice" and a "suspicious turn of the head," as if to hide welling tears.

Craven grieved from afar.

"Romeo was a fine fellow," Craven said. "He was the greatest elephant of his day."

And the trainer's thoughts were not of Romeo's supposed crimes but of the crimes perpetrated against him. Craven understood that the final excesses by the Forepaughs had been preceded by more than two decades of brutality to which he himself had been party, an escalating cycle of subjugation and rebellion, of must and musth. He was coming to believe that it need never have been at all.

"I knew Romeo well, and if he had been properly handled, he never would have become so bad," Craven said. "If he had been handled right from the first he would have been the biggest card in this business today."

Craven took the outcome as proof of the wrong way to train and keep an elephant. Craven was formulating the right way, deciding that his initial sense when he managed to ride one-footed atop an elephant had been correct, that it was better to understand than to dominate. He had learned that a blow inflicted was a blow remembered, that a hallo of surrender was accompanied by smoldering rage. He now understood that when his own rage drove him to apply a hot iron bar it not only *did no good*, it did bad, made bad, the bad that was then ascribed to Romeo.

In pondering such questions of good and bad, Craven was not reaching an ethical opinion. He had not made a primarily moral decision not to be cruel. He was simply acting on what he had come to understand about both elephants and humans, the humans including himself. The result was an elephant training and tending system requiring meticulous patience and unflagging attention to what was most effective at that specific moment with that specific creature. The underlying principle should not have been revolutionary.

"Kindness," Craven said. "But you still must be firm. As a general rule kindness will go further than punishment."

At the core of Craven's evolved approach was a respect for the elephant along with an assumption that the animal was basically good-natured and willing to do what was required. Craven made a statement that set him apart in the circus world.

"If there were no bad keepers, there would be no bad elephants," he said.

Around this time, Craven was retained by Howes' Great London Show to train five elephants who had been captured in Ceylon by a nephew of Barnum's partner in the original elephantine expedition there two decades before. Craven soon had them performing such novel tricks as forming a five-elephant "living pyramid" on pedestals of various heights. The feat was widely viewed as all the more remarkable because the elephants were just a few months out of the jungle, but that very fact may well have been part of the reason he was able to accomplish it so quickly. The scant time since their capture also marked the relatively brief period they had been liable to mistreatment. And they had not known Craven before his epiphany. There were no memories of prior brutalities on his part to dilute the power of kindness. The pachyderm pyramid could be viewed as a monument to that power.

Craven would later remark to a reporter that elephants subjected to harsh circumstances "never felt really well and fully themselves." Two of the new captives—a female named Hebe whom Craven affectionately called Babe and likely the male Mandarin—now felt so well and fully themselves that they mated, possibly the first such coupling of elephants on American shores.

EIGHT

THE FIRE, THE PLOWING ELEPHANT, THE PANIC, AND THE "DUSKY ATTENDANT"

P. T. Barnum's prodigious money getting had been interrupted when the great American Museum burned down in July of 1865, an added cruel twist to the Fire Annihilator saga. This blaze three months after the end of the Civil War was described as the establishment's final spectacle, drawing thirty thousand gawkers, Barnum's biggest crowd yet. Police shot the living animals that managed to escape the flames. The stuffed creatures consumed by the fire included Old Bet.

Barnum opened a new museum at another location in Manhattan, the exhibits including an anaconda that ate small mammals live. The spectacle drew a protest from Henry Bergh, a shipping heir and the founder of the American Society for the Prevention of Cruelty to Animals.

"I assert, without fear of contradiction, that any person who can commit an atrocity such as the one I complain of, is semi-barbarian in his instincts," Bergh declared.

Bergh had been roused to social action originally by witnessing the cruel treatment of horses on the streets of New York City, in particular horses that drew wagons and carriages. He subsequently campaigned to end dog fighting, cock fighting, and rat baiting. He conceived of the use of clay pigeons rather than actual birds for skeet shooting. He had even sought kinder treatment for the sea turtles on display at the Fulton Fish Market, enlisting the noted Harvard zoologist Louis Agassiz to declare that the creatures were indeed capable of feeling pain and thirst as they were left lying on their backs, prevented from escaping by ropes tied to holes punched in their flippers.

Barnum himself now sought Agassiz's opinion, enlisting the scientist to write a letter to Bergh saying the snake would eat only live prey and would otherwise likely starve to death. Agassiz wondered if Bergh "would object to eating lobster salad because the lobsters were boiled alive, or refuse oysters because they were cooked alive, or raw oysters because they must be swallowed alive." Bergh could hardly challenge the very expert he had once cited.

The question became moot when Barnum's new museum also burned down in 1868. Barnum had in the meantime gone into politics and gotten himself elected to the Connecticut state legislature, where the man who had once essentially purchased "George Washington's nurse" became a leading voice in favor of black suffrage, declaring that "without regard to color or condition, all men are equally children of the common Father" and that "a human soul . . . is not to be trifled with."

In his own very particular soul, Barnum was still a showman. He did not need much convincing when a Wisconsin circus operator named

W. C. Coup said the time had come for him to quit the statehouse for the big top and present the world with what would soon be billed as "The Greatest Show on Earth," not to be confused with Dan Rice's Great Show.

P. T. Barnum's Grand Touring Museum Menagerie, Caravan and Hippodrome prepared to hit the road in 1871, starting on Fulton Street in Brooklyn. The procession, which the *New York Clipper* promised would be "the most gorgeous ever witnessed in this country," concluded with a sight already familiar to railroad passengers who passed through Bridgeport, Connecticut.

"At the close of the procession, Barnum's historical plowing elephant will give a free exhibition of his plowing, with other exhibitions portraying the wonderful sagacity of this animal," the *Clipper* announced.

The procession proved to include a number of cages that had not yet been painted, while others were said to be "still upon the ocean." But the show was something new and therefore worthy of hyping, no doubt with considerable encouragement from Barnum.

"The whole procession, though far from complete, we decided [to be] one of the finest things of the kind ever seen in this county," the *Clipper* reported.

As the spinmaster Barnum headed north, the *Clipper* ran a letter "from a correspondent" speaking of "vast crowds that flocked from every direction." The show at Waterville, Maine, was described as a scene "which has never been equaled in this or any other country." The crowd was said to be so large that Barnum had to run continuous shows from day into night to accommodate everybody.

In the meantime, Forepaugh started the season on Sixth Street in Washington, D.C., with all his wagons painted, and considerably more animals and performers than his new rival had.

"The street procession was quite attractive, although there was no special feature," the *Clipper* yawned.

In virtually all regards save perhaps press agents, the Forepaugh show was at least the Barnum show's equal. Forepaugh was determined to surpass his rival to the point that his undeniable superiority would overcome Barnum's celebrity. Barnum may have been hoping to lull Forepaugh into easing up when he visited the other man's show shortly after the start of the 1873 season. Barnum was so gracious as to make it seem he was just being gracious.

"I have come all the way from New York solely to see Mr. Forepaugh's famous show, and I have been amply repaid for so doing," Barnum told the newspapers. "It is novel, varied, and interesting and I say without hesitation that the exhibition cannot be surpassed by any menagerie in the country—not even by myself."

Of course that did not stop Barnum from subsequently saying that his own show "by far surpassed any attempt ever made with a traveling exhibition in any country." He reported that "such a combination of curiosities and marvelous performers" was costing him $5,000 a day.

"I suppose there is a limit beyond which it would be fatal to go, in catering for public instruction and amusement, but I have never yet found that limit," he said. "My experience is that the more and the better a manager will provide for the public, the more liberally they will respond."

Barnum's publicity getting seemed to make Forepaugh only more determined to best him. Forepaugh kept on building up his show even as the newly reunited country was hit by the Panic of 1873. This was an unprecedented financial crisis whose contributing factors included the publicity getting of George Armstrong Custer, one of those real generals forever seeking to prove how big they are, how high they tower over lesser mortals.

The individual who played the most significant role in triggering the panic was Philadelphia banker Jay Cooke, who during the Civil War had risen to prominence as the self-anointed "God's chosen instrument" who arranged and managed the mammoth bond sales, totaling some $1.5 billion, that bankrolled the Union side. He had naturally made himself a tidy profit. He had also made it possible for Forepaugh and other profiteers to amass their initial fortunes. He was now widely expected to be appointed secretary of the Treasury when Grant became president. Cooke had, after all, privately assisted Grant in achieving a measure of financial comfort. And Cooke's brother was one of Grant's poker buddies.

Grant instead appointed a dry goods tycoon, A. T. Stewart, who had to withdraw his name because the law precluded an active merchant from holding the post. The job then went to a Massachusetts politician and early advocate of black suffrage, George Boutwell.

Cooke needed something else for which he could be an instrument of God, and just being the head of the country's leading financial firm—Jay Cooke and Company—was apparently not enough. Cooke embarked on a project that had the right ring of destiny: the construction of a second transcontinental railway, this one up through the territories where Lewis and Clark had ventured. He now began bankrolling a Northern Pacific Railroad from the Great Lakes to Puget Sound, undeterred by a warning from the tycoon Cornelius Vanderbilt about the folly of building a rail line "from nowhere to nowhere."

The proposed line ran through lands in the Montana territory that had been granted by treaty to the Sioux, and Cooke sought to preempt any trouble by hosting a tribal delegation headed by

Chief Spotted Tail at his opulent mansion outside Philadelphia. The feast ended with ice cream molded in the shape of various animals. The entertainment was Barnum's pal Signor Blitz, ventriloquist and magician extraordinaire. Blitz's signature trick was "bullet catching," where a bullet was marked by a member of the audience, then loaded into a pistol and fired at Blitz, who then seemingly caught it in his mouth.

The Cooke financial expedition of 1874 was bigger than either the Forepaugh show or the Barnum show as it embarked to survey the proposed rail route, with 275 wagons and a military escort comprising fifteen companies of infantry and ten of cavalry and a contingent of seventy-five Indian scouts. Custer, there as the commander of the Seventh Cavalry, was working hard to make himself a legend as they ventured into what was termed hostile Indian territory.

The complication was that the hostiles were not demonstrating adequate hostility, though the scouts did come upon a trio of Sioux and manage to scalp two of them. Custer rode ahead of the main column and eventually spotted and gave chase to a half dozen Sioux. They sought the urgent support of a larger group whom Custer decided had been lying in ambush. He did battle with an estimated three hundred warriors, followed by a second fight with an estimated five hundred warriors he came upon the next day. The dispatch that appeared in the newspapers dramatically reported that his horse had been shot out from under him, but his unit suffered only one fatality while killing forty of the enemy.

All that made for exciting reading, but it also made for nervous investors, who were already unsettled by an economic downturn in Europe and a growing sense that the frenzy of postwar railroad building had exceeded the actual need. Cooke had unexpected difficulty selling the bonds needed to finance his construction and reached a crisis point when the banks demanded $1 million in immediate payment. He defaulted.

The response to the sudden collapse of the country's leading financial firm led to a panic that gave the resulting crisis its name. The New York Stock Exchange closed for ten days. The Panic of 1873 deepened into a prolonged depression and over the next two years 89 of America's 364 railroads went bust. Some eighteen thousand businesses closed. Unemployment reached 14 percent. The wages of those who had jobs were cut by almost half. Thousands of homes were foreclosed.

But if people had fewer coins in their pockets, they were more in need of escaping their worries. Barnum leased a large roofless structure on Madison Square in Manhattan that had served as the main depot for the Harlem and New York Railroad until 1871, when its owner moved operations uptown to his new Grand Central Station. Now, in 1874, Barnum arrayed plank seats around a large ring. He named the new venue Barnum's Monster Classical and Geological Hippodrome.

On his part, Forepaugh was prosperous enough to buy more elephants, so that by 1875 he had five, as well as an 8,600-pound rhinoceros and "the largest and finest living giraffe in America."

The caged rhino was paralyzed after it fell through a bridge in upstate New York and was transported to a hotel, where it succumbed to injuries and the hotelier demanded full payment before releasing the body to be skinned. The giraffe died the same day, October 13, 1875, after catching a chill to which its long neck was believed to have made it especially vulnerable. The double loss put all the more premium on the elephants and during the winter break leading to the 1876 season Forepaugh suffered the further expense of retaining Craven to train his herd.

As evidenced by its posters, the trainer advertised as "Prof. Craven" had still been with the Great London Show in the 1875 season that had just ended. He had apparently remained after it passed into the ownership of a banker named James Kelly and a showman named Henry Barnum, who claimed to be a distant relative of the famous P. T. This other Barnum proved to possess none of his supposed kinsman's genius for showmanship. That had become clear after the elephant Hebe appeared to become seriously ill as the Great London Show was traveling by rail from Omaha to Kansas City on Sunday, May 29, 1875. The circus had paused to drop Hebe off in St. Joseph, Missouri, where it was scheduled to return for a performance later in the week. The developments on Monday, June 30, had been reported in the Tuesday edition of the *St. Joseph Morning Herald*.

"St. Joseph has the honor of having born within its limits the first baby elephant ever born in the United States," the paper had announced. "All day yesterday, crowds flocked down to see the wee chap, and probably they will increase in number today."

The paper had added that "the elephantress and her baby" were expected to be put on display that Wednesday, when the circus returned to St. Joseph. The Wednesday paper had a front-page message from Henry Barnum.

"Kiss the baby for me. I have named it 'Joe,' in honor of fair St. Joseph."

But the next morning's paper had made no mention of the baby. Even an article about the circus's performance in St. Joseph had said only, "Instead of 5 performing elephants, there were but four. The fifth was taken sick on Monday."

On June 12, the *New York Clipper* had reported, "A baby elephant was ushered into the world at St. Joseph, Mo. on May 31. Its mother travels with Howes' London Circus." But that was it and all the show-biz paper of record subsequently said was, "The elephant with Howes' London Circus, which had been ill, has recovered and rejoined the show."

If the birth had been a hoax, the circus would not likely have chosen a venue so small as St. Joseph and certainly would have contrived to present the public with something more than the absence of an adult female. The only plausible explanation is that the baby died sometime between its birth on Monday and the circus's return on Wednesday.

There were no newspaper stories about little Joe's gallant fight for life or his mother's elephantine grief, as there almost certainly would have been if P. T. Barnum had been involved. What could have been a sensation or at least a drama passed without notice and Henry Barnum continued on his way to going bust.

When Craven now rejoined the Forepaugh show, he may have brought news of that first and ill-fated birth of an elephant in America. Or word may already have reached the show. Either way, Forepaugh does not seem to have harbored any hopes that the trainer would arrange a coupling of his elephants with more lasting results. The incident could have been taken by Forepaugh as more proof of the popularly held notion that successfully breeding elephants in captivity was impossible.

What Forepaugh did want Craven to do was teach his elephants tricks such as he had taught the Howes elephants. Craven used kindness augmented by the hoisting powers of blocks and tackle to teach his latest pupils a series of feats culminating in a pyramid that Forepaugh would tout as unique, unequaled by Barnum.

As the start of the 1876 season neared, Forepaugh asked Craven to travel with the show. The trainer demanded a hefty sum that

Forepaugh would have dismissed out of hand had he a ready alternative. The showman stalled.

"I am very busy now, wait till I get my show open," Forepaugh reportedly told Craven.

Meanwhile, Forepaugh's press agent prepared to put out a story involving the showman's son and only child, fifteen-year-old Adam Jr., known as Addie. The boy was said to have shown an early passion for elephants, concealing himself in the hay room and peering through a knot in the wall to watch Craven—identified in the account only as "a well known trainer"—at work. Addie supposedly learned of the trainer's financial demands and suggested to his father that he be allowed to take over training and managing the elephants. The son supposedly revealed that he had not only secretly studied the trainer's technique, but convinced a circus worker to assist him in putting the elephants through routines of his own in the early morning hours.

"Pop, I can do it," Addie is supposed to have told his father.

The "well known trainer" was still on hand for the season's first show, in the Forepaugh hometown of Philadelphia. Forepaugh afterward had the elephants brought back into the empty big top. Addie supposedly demonstrated what he had learned. The elder Forepaugh was reportedly so impressed that when the well-known trainer renewed his salary demand that night, the owner dismissed him and put his son in charge.

Craven would later dispel the myth of the boy peering through the knothole, offering a less enticing though charitable version, telling an interviewer, "Young Forepaugh is a smart trainer and will make a good one in time. He got his first instruction from me."

The article made no mention of another teenager, one who truly had paid close attention to Craven's methods. Moses "Eph" Thompson had joined Forepaugh's show when it passed through his hometown of Ypsilanti, Michigan, three years before, in May of 1873, just as he was turning fourteen. He had been tending the elephants but was African-American and had been mentioned in the press only as an unnamed "dusky attendant" and a "Negro tender."

Out of public view, Thompson demonstrated the smarts and instincts that would make him one of the greats. He likely was a major reason the elder Forepaugh felt able to let the high-priced Craven go in a Centennial year when his rival was sure to out-Barnum himself. Forepaugh was so famously cheap that he was known to lie to his employees about being unable to obtain butter in town and then rejoice in the cook tent at what he was saving by not serving any at the meal. He could only have been delighted to spare himself the expense of Craven while hyping his Addie as a boy wonder.

Meanwhile, the black and therefore underpaid Thompson almost certainly did most, if not all, of any subsequent training. That explains why everybody was barred from the facility where the elephants were housed and instructed, save for Thompson and Addie, the latter billed by his father's show as "the youngest elephant trainer and performer in the world."

As Forepaugh made ready for the new 1876 season, his native city and home base was making far grander preparations for the nation's one hundredth birthday. Philadelphia had been named the official site of America's Centennial celebration and it would be hosting the country's first world's fair, rivaling those held in France and England with more than two hundred buildings spread over forty-nine acres. More than ten million people, or 20 percent of the country's population, would be coming for what was to be less a commemoration of America's glorious past than an exposition of a glorious present and a glimpse of a boundless future. The most popular attraction promised to be Machinery Hall, where President Ulysses Grant and the emperor of Brazil, Dom

Pedro II, would each turn a valve setting in motion a huge steam engine designed by inventor George Corliss. That would, in turn, drive eight miles of shafting and animate hundreds of machines with what was then America's most promising form of power, the steam that propelled the railroads and enabled factories to be built beyond any ready source of hydropower.

"The American multitude rejoiced at its own success and the triumph of the great American inventor," a newspaper would say of the moment when a crowd of 186,000 cheered the moment the huge engine was set in motion.

The plans that would have mattered most to Forepaugh were those of Barnum as described in January 1876 in the *New York Times*.

"With the advent of the Centennial Year, the great showman P. T. Barnum announces his intention to organize and exhibit the most colossal show ever collected," the *Times* said. "He says he is about to produce the culminating show combination of his lifetime, and will exhibit them in the Centennial year to the greatest multitude of civilians and strangers that has ever on any one occasion or celebration been drawn together in the World's history."

Forepaugh remained determined to best him. Forepaugh had the new elephant tricks and he got a replacement rhinoceros from Hamburg and just before the Fourth of July his show would begin erecting two big tops to Barnum's one. But perhaps because of the exciting innovations of the exposition back in Philadelphia as well as his own fixation on fielding a show that outdid Barnum, Forepaugh failed to understand—as his rival so dramatically did—that the Centennial season was different, that it was a moment in history whose overriding passion was old-fashioned patriotism.

The result was Forepaugh's first losing season. Forepaugh decided upon a scheme for the season ahead to rouse the patriotic fervor that had been so manifest in Grand Rapids and all the other towns and cities. The inspiration for the scheme may well have been the little-noticed birth and presumptive death of the baby elephant Joe in St. Joseph. It would have been only natural for a true showman to ponder what he could do with such an event, particularly if an American-born baby survived. And, as Joe's birth had received so little notice, another baby could certainly be presented as the first.

Forepaugh most likely set the scheme in motion by buying the baby animal that would come to be called Topsy from the dealer in Hamburg, only now ensuring that his new purchase did not reach public notice, as had his replacement rhinoceros when it arrived in New York the previous February. He could hardly pass off the baby elephant due to arrive on this coming February—in 1877—as the first one to be born in America if anybody were to report seeing it come off a ship from some foreign land before its supposed birth date.

Forepaugh succeeded in getting the baby into the country and to the show's winter quarters undetected. He might even have pulled off the ruse, and Topsy might have gone down in history as the first American-born elephant, had he thought to use an animal dealer other than the same one used by Barnum. Forepaugh no doubt understood that when Barnum then offered $100,000 for an American-born elephant, he did so only because he knew the baby's true origin and would not have to pay. What Forepaugh apparently failed to consider was that this same German animal dealer had a close personal relationship with Barnum. Forepaugh backed down so quickly it almost seemed he had learned never to humbug a humbugger.

CROOKED TALE,
CROOKED TAIL

Little Topsy had been smuggled in with the intention of making her the biggest of draws, but as the 1877 season commenced she was reduced to fourth billing. The first again went to the replacement rhinoceros, the second to "the only living male hippopotamus in this country."

"It sweats blood!" the poster said of the hippo.

Below that were the six trained adult elephants. Only then, in smaller type and prefaced by "Let the Ladies and Little Ones see it," came what had been Forepaugh's great hope.

"There was born on the first of February, 1877 in our Great Menagerie a Beautiful Baby Elephant."

Forepaugh stuck by the lie just enough to save face but not so stridently as to draw another challenge from Barnum. The poster made no clamorous claims about the elephant being the first born in America. It only asserted in even smaller print underneath that the baby was "the first and only ever born in captivity outside the tropical zone."

The top of the poster announced that Forepaugh would at least be catching up with the Barnum show in traveling by rail rather than by wagon: "Three Separate Railway Trains! The World has never seen its equal."

Forepaugh had contracted with an Ohio firm to build thirty-seven railroad cars, but they were not completed at the season's start and the show had to set off from Philadelphia in wagons for the first weeks. The baby walked along with five grown elephants through deepest night and, in the illusory freedom between towns, she almost could have been moving through darkness with her herd before the traumas of the capture and the ship. Only, her mother and aunts were gone and the herd's pace was set not by the baby but by the captors.

At the start of summer, the railroad cars were ready, each forty-two feet long, only two of them sleeping coaches, those largely reserved for management and performers. Laborers were to sleep where they could, the elephant tenders squeezed into a coffin-tight loft above their charges, but surely still finding this mode of travel considerably more comfortable than the wagons. Not so the elephants themselves, who no longer had those unfettered nighttime treks. They instead stood crammed together hour after hour, jolted, jarred, and jangled.

Forepaugh had just started actually following his rival onto the rails when the continuing economic downturn after the Panic of 1873 prompted the railroad companies to cut their workers' wages. The result was the Great Railroad Strike of 1877, beginning on July 14 in West Virginia and soon shutting down two-thirds of the nation's trackage. The strike turned violent, claiming more than one hundred lives.

Forepaugh was delayed nine days between shows in Clinton, Iowa, and Milwaukee, Wisconsin, then another nine days between shows in

Dubuque, Iowa, and Fremont, Nebraska, eternities by circus standards. He let go the majority of his performers and resolved to head west with a stripped-down show, away from the epicenter of the strike as well as the worst of the economic depression.

Forepaugh had kept the baby elephant who was growing at the pound-a-day rate that earned her the name Topsy, translating to eighteen pounds during the two delays and another twenty-one pounds during a three-week ride west on the decade-old transcontinental railway.

The train stopped in the broiling summer heat for two shows in Wyoming and another two in Utah, where the Union Pacific Railroad and the Central Pacific Railroad had been joined with a golden spike driven by Leland Stanford, the hammer and the spike wired so that each impact translated into a click on the telegraph system, the first event transmitted instantly and nationwide, ending with Morse code for the single word DONE.

The East and West Coasts were now joined into one great nation and the arrival on these tracks of even a stripped-down version of the Forepaugh show caused great excitement. The show represented another kind of national wealth, another kind of reward as it made four stops in Nevada, which was nearing the end of a gold and silver rush that had produced $700 million in precious metals. The parade drew a large and diverse crowd in Reno, then a booming mining town and long before it became dependent on divorce and gambling.

"Not a few red men and a sprinkling of Chinamen completed the throng that lined our streets yesterday—and all because 4-Paw's big 'horse opera' was here," the *Nevada State Journal* reported, employing a phrase that would later be applied to Western serial movies. "When a circus ceases to draw, then comes the millennium, sure."

The five stops in California included a twelve-day stand in San Francisco. The show wintered in nearby Hayward. The baby was now two, around the age for her training to extend beyond responding to her name.

Topsy's schooling would no doubt have been predicated on blows and jabs had young Addie Forepaugh been the primary trainer as he was touted. He may never have actually studied Craven's methods enough to discern the underlying principle and its effectiveness. He also may have simply enjoyed wielding the bull hook. He was by his own declaration an energetic practitioner of the traditional philosophy predicated on pain and fear.

But the secret trainer was a true student of Craven. And the knowledge of how slaves of his parents' generation had suffered may have made Eph Thompson all the more receptive to a radical philosophy based on gentleness.

With the avowedly brutal Addie taking the credit, but the gentle Thompson most likely doing the actual training, the motivating principles would have been praise and rewards as Topsy learned that "Mile up" meant to move forward quickly, "Tail up!" meant to use her trunk to hold the tail of the elephant ahead of her in a procession, and "Det!" meant to stop.

In the meantime, Topsy continued to grow like Topsy, a big toddler more than a baby as the 1878 season kicked off in Hayward with two rainy days at the end of March. The show undertook the longest "jump" of the season, 410 miles to San Bernardino made longer by a broken wheel on one of the sleeping cars. They no sooner finished the show there than they took down the 145-foot round top and the 80-foot menagerie tent and packed everything aboard the train again for an 84-mile jump to Anaheim. Next came the 27-mile jump to Los Angeles and the 167-mile jump to Bakersfield and so it went, six days a week for twenty-eight weeks, the shortest jump just a mile, the total distance traveled 9,048 miles. Topsy and the other elephants never walked much more than the distance from the train to the show grounds. Except when they were performing or parading, they were tethered either in the menagerie tent or aboard the rumbling, rattling train.

The official "route book" documenting the season's progress reported that the sideshow featured a bearded lady as well as the Smallest Man Alive and an "educated hog." The main program began with the "grand opening pageant," which included Topsy as well as the five grown elephants, along with "camels, comic masqueraders, and mounted knights and ladies." Then came "exercises with cannonballs" and the "principal act of polite equestrians," followed by Hector the riding canine, an educated Turkish stallion, and the Boneless Wonder, as well as the Enchanted Barrel, spun and flipped by Louis Leslie, "the equilibrist king and foot juggler of America." There were also various acrobats and clowns, riding acts, and a woman who walked a stretch of telegraph wire, and the act that made the circus the circus, the act Topsy would soon join, "the wonderful school of highly educated performing elephants, five in number, introduced by their trainer, Master Addie Forepaugh." A highlight of the season came on May 3 in Colfax, California, when an acrobat bounded off a springboard to manage a double somersault over the quintet of grown elephants.

The route book makes no explicit reference to Topsy, though a poster did mention midway down a "Baby Elephant 'Chicago,'" the temporary name change apparently intended to drum up business in the biggest scheduled stop in the Midwest. The birthplace was again given as Germantown, Pennsylvania, but the birth date was for some reason changed from February 1 to February 22 of 1877, even though this was nearly three weeks after the elder Forepaugh had announced the birth. The high hopes that had accompanied that scheme were now dashed, but with the depression ending and Barnum presenting no direct competition on Forepaugh's chosen route, the show prospered as it headed east.

Forepaugh invested his continuing profits into rebuilding his show with the perpetual goal of making it greater than the one that billed itself "The Greatest." He acquired four more elephants for a total of ten by the start of the 1879 season. His show seemed anyone's equal or more as it opened in Louisville, Kentucky, and proceeded through that state, then Indiana, Illinois, and Michigan, arriving in Flint on the Fourth of July.

The Flint appearance should have been all the more memorable for coinciding with the nation's 103rd birthday, but Forepaugh had been preceded into the city the month before by a show that displayed a new marvel, one that spoke of a future that was brighter than what was immediately foreseen at the Centennial fair just three years past. Whatever marvels appeared in the Forepaugh big top were illuminated only by the usual candles, whereas Cooper & Bailey's Great London Circus had become the first to go electric, employing the super-bright arc lights developed by Ohio inventor Charles Brush.

This Fourth of July was also the thirty-second birthday of the Cooper & Bailey show's dominant partner, and, with the help of the light generated by the arc between two electrodes, his life was promising to become another great American success story. James Anthony Bailey had been born James Anthony McGuiness in Michigan. He had been orphaned as a young child and consigned to a cruel guardian.

"On the slightest provocation I was whipped," Bailey would later say. "I was kept working so hard that I was always late at school, so I was continually being whipped by the teacher and kept after school. Then for being late coming home, I was whipped again. I stood that until I was nearly thirteen years old."

Barefoot and with no possessions other than a jackknife with a broken blade, he had begun walking.

"I remember well now the morning that I started down the country road, determined never to return except as my own master," he later said.

By his own account, he had been working as a $3.25-a-month farm-hand, "very hard work for a small boy," when a circus passed through. He had joined the other local boys in posting bills in exchange for a ticket and had met an advance agent named Fred Harrison Bailey, nephew of Hack Bailey of the earliest days of elephants in America. The agent had been impressed enough by the boy to take him on as a kind of apprentice.

The boy had assumed his mentor's surname and as James Bailey had become an advance agent himself at sixteen. He had been barely into his twenties when he invested his savings in the Hemmings, Cooper & Whitby circus. Whitby had been fatally shot during a fracas at the entrance to the big top during a performance in Louisiana, and Bailey had bought his interest. Richard Hemmings had then departed and the circus had gone to Australia as Cooper & Bailey. The trip had been a financial disappointment, but Cooper & Bailey was still able to acquire the Great London Show upon its return. Its luck took a turn toward golden when it chanced to pass through Cleveland that April just as the inventor Brush was demonstrating his new sensation by lighting the city's central square. The event was accompanied by band music and an artillery salute and a roaring crowd right out of a showman's dream.

Cooper & Bailey continued on, having acquired exclusive rights to the Brush system. And with electricity provided by a steam-driven generator, the show was able to re-create the excitement inside its big top in Flint, dazzling the audience even before the first act took to the ring. The Cooper & Bailey 1879 route book noted of electric light, "It was thought at first it would prove a failure, but its success as a special feature of the show has been too great to require further comment."

However superior the Forepaugh show was the following month, the relative dimness of candles was more suited to the eyesight of elephants than that of humans. Forepaugh had been outdone by a rival show that had seemed a minor worry. And with the rights to the Brush system taken, the best Forepaugh could do was contract a Detroit engineer to provide an inferior arc lamp system for the following season.

Meanwhile, Forepaugh had the engineer hoist a sample up one of the center poles during a two-day stand in Detroit, so his show could at least join the ranks of those that had exhibited an electric light.

Onetime Forepaugh partner Dan Rice was touring the same part of the country with a much more modest show that traveled by steamboat. He responded to the Cooper & Bailey sensation with a variation of an old ploy by which a circus would precede a rival's route with posters and flyers saying the other show was carrying a deadly contagion. Rice's circulars began:

> The public are now by this information made aware that a show called Cooper & Bailey's Great London Circus . . . have for an attraction the Electric Light. It draws many people to see it regardless of what danger they are rushing into. I regard it as a duty that I owe to the public to inform them what I know about it.

The circular went on to say that some time before, Rice had himself introduced an electric light produced by a man named Lamon Rosel, who seems to have been entirely fictitious.

He in a short time died from the effects of the chemicals that he created the light with. Many of my troupe took sick and one member, James O'Connell, who had weak lungs, died in a short space of time after the light was introduced; we could not account for it for a long time, but hearing so many complaining that the lights affected their eyes, caused many to grow sick and others to complain of dizziness in the head, I gave up the continuance of the scheme, although it was very attractive.

Years went—at last one Edison appears as the inventor of the new and powerful light. The London Show gets the exclusive right of using it for a time with their show.

The circular was referring to the great Thomas Alva Edison, the homeschooled genius who boasted of having read every nonfiction tome in the Detroit Public Library as a lad and who had begun his experiments in a railroad mail car while he worked as a twelve-year-old "train boy" hawking snacks and a newspaper he published himself. He had gone largely deaf around that time, perhaps as a result of scarlet fever as a younger child or because of persistent ear infections. He would initially attribute the hearing loss to being boxed in the ears by a conductor. He would later say the conductor hoisted him by his ears. He would insist that he was grateful for the result because it "saved me from small talk" and freed him to think. His ponderings had produced inventions ranging from a rat paralyzer that electrocuted rodents to a stock ticker to a phonograph by which this hearing-impaired inventor allowed the world to preserve and listen to sounds. But in fact he had nothing to do with Brush or the system acquired by Cooper & Bailey's Great London Circus.

Rice may have assumed otherwise after an April article in the *New York Herald* headlined "The Triumph of the Electric Light" reported that Edison had developed a revolutionary incandescent bulb. The Edison report was itself a bit of showman humbug, for the inventor had announced his discovery when he was still months away from actually finding a practical filament. He had, in his words, "ransacked the world for the most suitable filament material," experimenting with "no fewer than 6,000 vegetable growths," ranging from cedar to bamboo to exotic tropical plants.

Rice's circular continued:

> In Chicago and other cities where the Great London shows have exhibited it is talked of as the most brilliant light they ever imagined possible to create, but it hurt the eyes; also many say they have not seen a well day since the exhibition. Persons predisposed to pulmonary complaints it will shorten their days and in many cases it affects the tender brain of children. Look at their street parade, but don't get near the light at night or any other time.
>
> The Public's Servant,
> Dan Rice
>
> P. S.—This is not done to impair the patronage of the London Circus. Only to put the public on their guard; this much I will say, that from reports they have a very good show.

The electric light soon ceased to be a primary worry for Rice after a fire swept through his steamboat, destroying all his show's equipment as well as its animals, save for Excelsior, a blind trick horse that managed to swim to safety.

Meanwhile, when taking over the Great London Show, Cooper & Bailey had acquired the elephants originally trained by Stewart Craven.

Bailey now hired Craven and the reunification of the trainer and the elephants resulted in a sensation worthy of the dazzling electric light.

"They are so superior to anything of the kind yet seen, having a military drill, a pyramid, a tight-rope walker, a clown elephant," Craven later said.

Craven's kind ways had succeeded in again making Hebe feel secure enough and sufficiently at ease to mate, the male being either Mandarin, as was likely before, or Basil, as Craven's son Charles would later report. Craven began to suspect the result more than a year afterward, when the elephants were performing a pyramid on soft ground after a rain. Hebe was on top and she seemed about to fall.

"The other elephants, seeing her danger, came to her aid and eased her fall to the ground so that she escaped uninjured," Craven recalled.

Craven had noted long before that elephants are highly protective of each other, but they seemed especially so with Hebe. He came to conclude that they must have sensed her particular condition, which became unmistakable even to the dimmest of humans at 2:30 a.m. on March 10, 1880.

When the moment arrived in the Cooper & Bailey show's winter quarters, the other elephants raised their trunks and began to trumpet loudly, by one written account "as though they could not make noise enough and never would get through rejoicing." Hebe broke free of her chains immediately after giving birth and newspapers described her tossing her newborn twenty yards, then charging a woodstove, "nearly demolishing" it. Another eyewitness account reported that Hebe threw the woodstove, not the newborn, and for a distance of twenty-five feet, ignoring the burns on her trunk for the sake of clearing a possible hazard for her newborn. The younger Craven said that Hebe then began to nudge the 214-pound baby with her trunk, coaxing it to stand as the other elephants tore free of their own chains and gathered protectively around, just as the herd must have at Topsy's birth. The trumpeting of this captive herd was joined by the roars and yowls of the big cats in the menagerie.

"It was the most awesome sight combined with terrific wild animal sounds that even to this time ring in my ears," Craven's son would recall years later.

The elder Craven's observation of Hebe in the immediate aftermath confirmed his view of the basic nature of elephants.

"She displayed a vast fund of motherly affection and solicitude," he said.

The baby was a girl and she was immediately named Columbia, as befitted an animal touted as the first native born, the short-lived baby Joe by the same mother apparently forgotten. A crowd of hundreds soon gathered, watching the newborn venture from under Hebe's legs and settle into a small pile of straw at the edge of a circle that the mother had made on the dirt floor with her repetitive pacing. The baby curled so that the soles of her forefeet almost met those of her hind feet and tucked her head and trunk into her chest.

"For the time being forgetful of its troubles," a reporter wrote. "The mother kept walking around and sniffing at it with her trunk until, finding it fast asleep, turned away and began to nibble at her hay. Meantime, if anyone would pass near the baby she would turn toward it and throw out her trunk as a sort of guard. The baby slept very sound for over half an hour, the only sign of life visible about it being the rising and falling of its side in its breathing. Meanwhile, the stable was full of visitors, who were anxious to see her babyship awake."

The baby began to stir, then raised her head, her mouth opening expectantly. The excited onlookers drew closer and watched as Hebe wrapped her trunk around the baby's middle and lifted her to her feet.

"As for the rest, the younger elephant seemed to understand well enough what to do. It staggered up, shook itself a little, gaped again, then waddled over and got directly under its mother's legs and began to suckle, curling its trunk up over its head and using its lips."

When the baby's hunger was abated, she broke away and started toward the keepers, evidencing "a disposition to make friends with anybody or everybody," her small black eyes "twinkling with something of the playfulness of a kitten." Had this been in the wild such as at Topsy's birth, the mother would no doubt have happily allowed the baby to play in the equally secure company of her aunts and siblings. Humans were another matter. The mother immediately reached out with her trunk and drew the baby back between her legs.

The baby made more attempts at stealing away and would be on the point of getting beyond the reach of its mother when the latter's trunk would interpose like an iron barrier and the little one would find itself unceremoniously dragged back again. Thus it was all the time during the baby's wakeful hours.

The mother was firm, but unfailingly gentle.

"In these strokes of maternal policy, the old elephant was always careful of the little one."

Craven would have been right to see a confirmation of his kindness philosophy as practiced by the elephants themselves. The reporter concluded that the mother's actions "show strikingly the strong affection this species of animal has for its young." The reporter quoted one of the keepers as saying, "If that baby elephant was to die I do believe it would kill the mother, too."

Nobody seemed to reflect on the trauma that must have resulted when a baby such as Topsy was born in the wild and was suddenly torn from its mother. What had not been forgotten about Topsy was

Barnum's offer of $100,000 for an actual American-born baby after Forepaugh's attempted fraud three years before.

Cooper & Bailey now had the genuine article and moved to make the baby an even greater triumph than the electric light. The show began by declining Barnum's offer as if it had been made to them.

"Its owner says he wouldn't take $100,000 for it," the *Chester Daily Times* reported three days after the birth.

Forepaugh must have looked on with vying measures of satisfaction, fury, and fear as Cooper & Bailey and the little Columbia followed Barnum through New England. The possessors of a genuine American-born elephant outdrew Barnum in eight cities even though he went first.

"Conventional wisdom dictated that the first show in a locale would outdraw the second, but not this time, even in Barnum's hometown of Bridgeport," the circus historian Fred Pfening III later wrote. "The infant pachyderm proved to be a tremendous money getter."

In a July interview, Barnum told a reporter that he had no doubt this American-born elephant was genuine. Barnum added, "I wish it wasn't. I should be tens of thousands of dollars better off. A full-grown elephant brings $6,000, but I offered the London Circus Company $100,000 for the mother elephant and baby and it would have been worth twice that to me. . . . It is wonderful how women flock to see that baby elephant."

Cooper & Bailey printed up a poster showing a telegram that Barnum purportedly sent saying, "Will give $100,000 for your baby elephant. Must have it." The poster also showed Cooper & Bailey's purported reply: "Will not sell at any price."

Cooper & Bailey issued a public letter declaring that the continuing competition with Barnum would be "a 'War of the Titans' that shall stir up the whole land." The newspapers carried a letter Barnum supposedly wrote to a friend after going incognito to see Cooper & Bailey's show. Barnum described it as "a clean, moral, well conducted, stunning exhibition, by far the largest and the best that ever traveled except my own."

Soon after, Barnum announced that he had signed an agreement combining his show with Cooper & Bailey. Barnum said that the idea had come to him as an epiphany while he watched his upstart competitor's show.

"Having had the godsend of a baby elephant, the only one ever born in captivity, [Cooper & Bailey] are sweeping the country like a whirlwind," Barnum said, either unaware of or discounting Hebe's prior pregnancy. "This continent can't support two such immensely expensive shows. We have been compelled, therefore, to form a grand alliance."

Later, some historians would suggest that Barnum's telegram offering the $100,000 had been a rare misstep on the public stage. They theorized that Cooper & Bailey had so successfully capitalized on the offer that Barnum decided if he could not beat them, he might as well join them.

Other historians believe the merger was planned and all but consummated prior to the supposed telegram. This theory called into question whether there ever was an actual telegram and suggested the letters to the public on both sides, along with Barnum's supposed epiphany while watching his rival's show, were all orchestrated by the Great Humbugger. His goal would have been to build up Cooper & Bailey while making Forepaugh seem not even worth mentioning.

Whatever the truth, Forepaugh was furious and issued a rant couched as an open letter to Barnum. Forepaugh declared that what Barnum had described in the newspaper interview as an epiphany was just an epic phony.

"I must exclaim with Shakespeare in *The Tempest*: 'Your tale would cure deafness.' In the falseness of its statements it out Gullivers Gulliver. . . . Perhaps, for the reason that you have so long been permitted to weave fairy tales for the press, you have become emboldened."

Forepaugh raged on, disparaging his rival professionally and personally. Forepaugh must have been all the more exasperated to find himself up against not only the Barnum name and the Barnum wiles, but also a genuine American-born elephant. And Forepaugh's mood could not have improved whenever he looked at the Asian-born elephant with which he had hoped to generate a sensation just like the sensation that had brought a windfall to Cooper & Bailey and precipitated the merger with Barnum.

Thanks to the genuine American-born baby, Forepaugh now faced what threatened to be in actual fact the greatest of shows. His Asian-born fake no longer qualified as a baby of any provenance but continued to be a reminder of the failed fraud and his accompanying failure of nerve when Barnum challenged him with the open letter and the original $100,000 offer.

On top of it all, the newspapers were reporting that Forepaugh's rival had joined with the primary heir to the Vanderbilt fortune to form the Barnum Museum Company with the purpose of constructing a monumental five-story complex on the site of the onetime railroad depot on Madison Square. Barnum had closed his hippodrome there after two years and the premises had been leased by a promoter named Patrick Gilmore, who dubbed the facility Gilmore's Garden and matched "professors" in "scientific sparring experiments," as boxing was still officially outlawed. But Barnum continued to begin each circus season there, having struck up a fast friendship with the owner, Cornelius Vanderbilt. The tycoon had died in 1877, but his son William Vanderbilt honored the arrangement even after he took over the facility with an eye toward making it the premier venue for horse shows. The Vanderbilt scion rechristened it Madison Square Garden and arranged for a Brooklyn start-up called the Fuller Electrical Company—not Edison—to install four arc electric lights whose debut on Memorial Day of 1879 was described by the *New York Times* as "the first extremely favorable test of electricity for popular uses" even though this was a month after Brush had lit up the park in Cleveland.

Now, in June of 1880, even as the birth of the genuine American-born baby elephant was prompting Barnum to combine his show with Bailey's, Barnum announced that he and young Vanderbilt would be building a new Madison Square Garden, this described by the *New York Times* as "a mammoth edifice, to be devoted to purposes of amusement." It was to have eleven acres of floor space. The entire lower floor was to be a cavernous arena, with an opera house upstairs, as well as an aquarium, a skating rink, a zoo, a palatial restaurant, and a two-floor museum "intended to exceed anything of the kind ever before attempted." The top floor was to be a "a vast tropical garden, with extensive walks, lawns, bowers, grottoes, arbors, waterfalls, palmeries, fountains, parterres, &c.," where "grand concerts will be given on every afternoon and evening of the year, and innumerable refreshment-tables will be scattered about in the European style." The building was to be fireproof and steam-heated and lit by many more than four Fuller fixtures. And the southwest corner was to feature a 250-foot observatory tower "furnished at its apex with a coronet of electric lights."

"Mr. Barnum is to have management of the entire concern," the *Times* reported.

By comparison, Forepaugh's big top could not have seemed very big at all. His winter quarters in Philadelphia could only have seemed more barnlike. And, to make it all worse, he must have known that he was now feeling exactly what Barnum surely wanted him to feel. The revived $100,000 offer. The description of Bailey's show as "moral" and "clean." The talk of a War of the Titans without mentioning Forepaugh. The plans for a new and impossibly grand Madison Square Garden. All of this could only have further stoked Forepaugh's rage. He was hardly going to fault himself and he was powerless to strike back at Barnum, but he did have a handy object on which to vent his fury.

Forepaugh beat Topsy with such abandon that he broke her tail. The elephant born of the crooked tale was henceforth known as Crooked-Tail Topsy.

THE CONTINUED
MAGIC OF KINDNESS
AND THE FIRST
BEAUTY CONTEST

Along with the genuine American-born baby, Cooper & Bailey brought to the merger with Barnum the troupe of Craven-trained elephants that was widely hailed as a true marvel, sometimes even without the instigation of a press agent. Forepaugh once more sought out Craven, privately offering to pay him what he had been paid by Cooper & Bailey if he matched what he had done for that show. Forepaugh further pledged a $1,000 bonus if Craven outdid himself.

Craven applied the magic of kindness to Forepaugh's twenty elephants. Topsy was still growing toward her full 5,000 pounds, but now was of an age to perform. The first of the rudimentary tricks she learned was likely sitting down and rearing up on her hind legs.

Craven's usual method was to use block and tackle, with two ropes attached to the forelegs, a third looped under the trunk, and perhaps a fourth tied to a leather belt around the middle. The trainer would give the verbal command and then the assistant would pull on the ropes. The routine would be repeated until the elephant understood what was expected.

Craven had indeed outdone himself with all the elephants as the 1881 season approached. The results were undeniable unless you were the miserly Forepaugh. He declared that his herd was no better than the opposition's and he flatly refused to pay the bonus.

"Forepaugh and Craven had some hot words and Craven went away without his thousand dollars," animal trainer George Conklin would later write.

Craven retained a lawyer, who sent out observers as the season commenced and the Forepaugh show moved from city to city.

"They came back and reported that the showman was boasting to the public how much better his elephants were and how much more they could do than those of Cooper & Bailey," Conklin would recall.

The lawyer himself attended a show, making sure to have some witnesses in tow when he approached Forepaugh.

"Those are pretty fine elephants you've got, Mr. Forepaugh," the lawyer said. "Their act was simply great."

"Yes, you bet they are," Forepaugh said. "They are 'nuff sight better than those things that Cooper & Bailey have got, an' they ought to be, too, for I paid good money to have them trained and I paid a thousand dollars extra to be sure they were better."

Forepaugh was subsequently confronted with his own words. The showman understood that he was sure to lose in court, where his only defense would be to publicly declare that his elephants were not better than Cooper & Bailey's elephants. The resulting publicity would be beyond his control. The controversy might even call into question the ongoing fiction that his prodigy son was the genius behind the elephants' tricks.

"It was not very long before Forepaugh was obliged to hand over the thousand dollars," Conklin noted.

That did not stop Forepaugh from crediting his son at every opportunity with the unequaled performance of the elephants. Forepaugh's press agent, Charles Day, subsequently penned a book titled *Young Adam Forepaugh, Elephant Trainer* that was sold at the show for twenty-five cents.

Day's most notable contribution was to propose to Forepaugh what would become America's first beauty contest, with a $10,000 prize supposedly going to "The Handsomest Woman in the World."

Hopefuls by the thousands applied and five finalists were announced, but of course the contest was fixed from the start. A twenty-one-year-old variety artist named Louise Montague sought out Day with a letter of introduction from a minstrel of his acquaintance. Montague told him that she had come to speak to him about the $10,000 prize. Montague was worldly enough not to be surprised when Day informed her it was really "an advertising scheme." Day said he could offer her a salary of $75 a week, which he figured was generous enough considering all she would be required to do was ride an elephant in the parade. She demanded $125 and Forepaugh made it $100.

"I'll make up the difference in the sale of photographs," Forepaugh said.

The big contest's winner was announced that April, as the 1881 season was set to open in the nation's capital.

"Miss Louise Montague, the queen of beauty who has been so fortunate as to secure Forepaugh's $10,000 offered for the handsomest woman in the world will arrive in this city from Philadelphia early this morning," the *Washington Post* reported.

Montague rode one of the larger elephants, with Topsy and the rest of the herd coming behind. Some unanticipated wagons materialized and took up the rear with signs reading "Wait for Barnum!"

Ads for the two competing shows appeared in the same issue of the *Washington Post*, Barnum reminding readers that his show would be just two weeks behind Forepaugh's. Both sides also plastered the city with thousands of "rat bills," posters disparaging the other show, Forepaugh's charging among other things that Barnum had only fourteen elephants when he claimed to have twenty.

"Fraud! Falsehood! Downright Deceit!" Forepaugh's rat bills said of the Barnum show.

On his part, Barnum denounced Forepaugh's beauty contest as the fraud it in fact was.

"The elements angry! And the populace undeceived! Oh shame! Where is thy blush? 4-Paw's Bad Day!" a Barnum rat bill said. "Who should cry aloud 'My sins are greater than I can bear'? A fraud exposed. A Swindle Laid Bare."

A blizzard of posters and bills blanketed a wide swath of the country as the shows exhibited in thirty-eight of the same cities, with Forepaugh appearing first in each instance.

"A continuous clash in all the large cities for nearly forty weeks," a Forepaugh agent later wrote. "Nothing before or since has ever compared with it."

Forepaugh proved the more thin-skinned, filing a lawsuit that charged the Barnum show with distributing "false, malicious and libelous" handbills and public advertisements aimed at persuading the populace "not to visit the exhibition of this deponent, and thereby cause him great loss and damage."

The lawsuit went on, "The defendant's further conspiring to injure the deponent caused millions of circulars to be printed and distributed in the cities of Washington and Baltimore while the deponent was exhibiting there, stating that the severe weather, together with the presence of a circus company, where hundreds have sat under a chilly canvas, has brought sickness into many households, that pneumonia has spread so rapidly for the past three days as to become almost an epidemic, and that nothing like it was ever known in Washington and that the fatality for the next forty-eight hours will be frightful."

Forepaugh soon faced a lawsuit himself, filed by his $10,000 beauty, in which she complained she had been instructed to ride a substitute elephant and was twice thrown off the creature's back "into the mud on her hands and face."

"It was the duty of the defendant to provide an elephant that was perfectly tame and free from vicious habits, so that it would be perfectly safe for the plaintiff to ride on it," the suit charged.

The litigation revealed to the public that the beauty contest had been rigged. What had been no secret from the start was Montague's discomfort while riding atop an elephant. A reporter at the *State Journal* described the Forepaugh show's parade through Madison, Wisconsin: "The chief expectancy was directed towards 'the Handsomest Woman.' When she came along bounced about on top of an elephant as though her back was being broken at every step, it rather took the romance out of the oriental Lalla Rookh, and made her look as though she was a safety valve for the elephant, and that he carried too much steam and was in momentary danger of blowing off."

Her ride became even rougher two weeks later in Woodstock, Illinois, when her usual elephant fell ill and the howdah—a rail-ringed perch—was cinched atop the substitute. The subsequent court filings accorded some insight into who in the show possessed the actual expertise regarding elephants: "Ephraim Thompson said on that day that the basket ought not to go on that elephant, that it would kill the plaintiff," the papers reported. "Addie Forepaugh, Jr., said that it must go on, that these were the governor's (his father's) orders."

Thompson did as commanded, as did Montague.

"When she got upon it, [the elephant] commenced to shake itself as if to get rid of the howdah or basket and that it reared up, and the plaintiff was thrown to the ground and fainted."

Much the same happened the next day in Waterloo, Illinois. Montague declared herself too badly injured to continue with the show. She subsequently filed the lawsuit and prevailed, though the jury awarded her only $500. Forepaugh's attorney had successfully argued that any award should be reduced because however much the show might be at fault the first time she was bucked, she was guilty of "contributory negligence" the second, "in getting upon an elephant that she knew would throw her off."

The Forepaugh show's other main attraction was an elephant nobody save perhaps Eph Thompson could safely ride. Forepaugh had bought the behemoth Bolivar at the sale of a small show and billed the elephant as "the biggest and heaviest elephant in the world." Bolivar was measured at more than eleven feet and seemed even bigger when he was angry. No doubt thanks to young Forepaugh's cruelties, he was in a foul mood so often and so dramatically that he succeeded the notorious Romeo as America's "ugliest elephant."

Bolivar did turn curiously gentle and protective when it came to one particular elephant, the juvenile female with the crooked tail. He showed an attachment to little Topsy that was altogether unusual for a big male toward another elephant of whatever gender or age.

Topsy may have been torn from her native herd before she was fully versed in its ways. She may not have learned to shun grown males. Or she may not have understood that a matriarch is necessarily female. Or her early traumas may have caused her to welcome and embrace elephants of any kind.

When it came to humans, the only trainer who could control Bolivar was Thompson. The newspapers of course gave the credit to Forepaugh's son. The *New York Times* said "the boyish looking young man" was "the most expert trainer of animals in the country, if not in the world."

"He proposes to do what no one has yet succeeded in doing—train the big elephant Bolivar to perform in the ring with other elephants," the *Times* reported.

Young Forepaugh subsequently said of Bolivar, "He is a treacherous, wicked brute, and he has to be continually watched."

To further expand his menagerie, the elder Forepaugh sent his son on an animal-buying trip to Europe. The young man evidenced an extravagance that was in keeping with his appearance.

"Among his other peculiarities young Forepaugh affected the most striking dress and make up," a Forepaugh agent later wrote. "He was always bedecked in large, flashy jewelry, never wearing a necktie and usually fastening his collar with a diamond-studded button of enormous size, while his watch and chain were of huge proportions, and an eight- or ten-carat diamond stud in his shirt front. In the winter time the richest sealskin overcoat hung to his feet."

His expenditures quickly outpaced his funds and he cabled his father saying he had come upon two gigantic monkeys and needed $2,000 immediately to acquire them. The father sent the sum only to get a cable reading, "Money received; monkeys died last night. Addie."

The son did purchase an Asian elephant nearly as big as Bolivar who had an actual royal provenance. Tip had belonged to King Vittorio Emanuele of Italy until the monarch's death. The successor, King Humbert, had sold Tip to "Mad" King Ludwig of Bavaria. Ludwig soon after sold him to "Professor" Carl Hagenbeck, the German animal dealer who had been profiting so handsomely from the rivalry between Forepaugh and Barnum.

Like Craven, but independently from that American trainer, Hagenbeck had come to conclude that rewards were more effective than fear in training animals, going so far as to say beatings were counterproductive as well as cruel. Either he did not press his philosophy upon his customers or they simply declined to embrace it. That became clear shortly after Hagenbeck made his latest elephant sale, of Tip, to the younger Forepaugh.

Rail transportation was not immediately available and Addie was required to walk his new purchase seventy-five miles to where a steamship was to take on seventy-eight other animals he had purchased. He offered some insight into his training philosophy as he described preparing Tip for the trek.

"Before I could do this I knew I should have to get acquainted with her, so I introduced myself with a pitchfork," recounted Addie, this most expert trainer of animals apparently having failed to notice that the elephant was in fact a male. "She didn't take kindly to me with being with her, and I had to be very severe."

After a rough eighteen-day crossing during which two camels perished, the steamship *Mosel* arrived in Hoboken in January of 1882. Young Forepaugh told a *New York Times* reporter who covered the arrival that his travels in Europe had taken him at one point to England, where he had sought to purchase an even bigger elephant.

"While in London, I visited the Zoological Garden and offered $10,000 for the big elephant there, the largest elephant in the world, 11 ½ feet in height, but the Britishers wouldn't part with it," young Forepaugh recalled.

He apparently forgot for a moment that his father was touting eleven-foot Bolivar as "the biggest and heaviest elephant in the world." The London elephant was an African so not surprisingly was indeed bigger than the Indian Bolivar, with outsize ears to match. This $10,000 offer was likely real, as it concerned not a beauty queen but an elephant whose name would become synonymous with bigness.

The rival Barnum show apparently got wind of the offer, though of course its official account would not mention Forepaugh. The Barnum show would say only that it made its own offer after one of its agents reported that an elephant that size was at the London Zoo.

"What is the lowest price you can take for the large African elephant?" the Barnum show's telegram to the zoo inquired.

The Barnum show would likely have also met with a rebuff had a serious case of musth not visited the elephant with a name most likely derived from Swahili, from either *jambo* (hello) or *jumbe* (chief). The once docile Jumbo turned so violent and aggressive that nobody save his trainer dared go near him. Jumbo became a problem in direct proportion to his size and the zoo's superintendent wondered if the elephant house was strong enough to hold him.

"I should be provided with, and have at hand, the means of killing this animal, should such a necessity arise," the superintendent, Abraham Bartlett, wrote the zoo's governing board.

As a boy, Bartlett had witnessed the execution of another musth-maddened elephant named Chunee, who had shrugged off a massive dose of poison and then been shot more than 120 times by a military firing squad before he finally fell dead. Bartlett was not anxious to see such a horror repeated with Jumbo. He also was less than fond of the elephant's keeper, who could not be fired as long as the otherwise uncontrollable elephant was there.

"Will sell him for 2,000 pounds," the zoo's telegraph to Barnum read.

The sum translated to roughly what Forepaugh had been willing to pay, the zoo apparently not wanting to sell for less than it had already been offered. The Barnum show immediately paid the stated price and enjoyed another stroke of luck after its agents brought a huge shipping crate to the London Zoo for the start of the trip to New York.

Jumbo repeatedly balked at entering, perhaps due to subtle prompting from his trainer, Matthew Scott. The British press decided that Jumbo was refusing to leave England and whipped up a great public clamor for him to be allowed to stay.

"Jumbo is lying in the garden and will not stir. What shall we do?" a Barnum agent telegraphed his boss.

Barnum recognized a publicity boon when one presented itself.

"Let him lie there as long as he wants to," Barnum telegraphed back.

The zoo also had an elephant named Alice whom the press now decided was Jumbo's "wife." Barnum is said to have helped spread a rumor that Jumbo was all the more determined not to leave because Alice was pregnant. All of Britain seemed possessed by "Jumbomania."

A British newspaper telegraphed Barnum, saying, "All British children are distressed at elephant's departure. Hundreds of correspondents beg us what terms will you will kindly release Jumbo."

Barnum replied, "Fifty-one millions American citizens anxiously awaiting Jumbo's arrival. My forty years invariable practice of exhibiting best that money could procure makes Jumbo's presence here imperative. Hundred thousand pounds would not be inducement to cancel purchase." He closed by wishing "long life and prosperity" to the "British nation ... and Jumbo," signing it, "the public's obedient servant, P. T. Barnum."

Barnum made sure the American newspapers got copies of the telegrams. The British clamor grew ever louder, as did the American reply.

"It seems a sad thought that a war between England and America might break out at any moment," the *New York Herald* opined. "But we must have that elephant."

The Barnum people informed Jumbo's trainer that he would no longer be needed. They were bringing in their own team to take over and make Jumbo ready for the trip—unless, of course, he wished to come to America as well, with a generous salary. Jumbo developed a sudden willingness to enter the crate and soon he and Scott were crossing the Atlantic aboard the *Assyrian Monarch*, a new steamship designed to export grain and cattle from America after delivering 1,500 emigrants at a time, fewer when carrying an elephant. The American papers gave daily updates as the ship drew ever nearer.

Jumbo was apparently not at his happiest being thus confined and Scott was said to be leery of entering the box to clean it. An American newspaper reporter noted, "It seems that during all the time he has been with Jumbo Mr. Scott has never used even a whip upon him, and that the elephant has frequently taken advantage of Mr. Scott's kindness of heart and displayed a strong disposition to do as he pleased."

A Barnum trainer, William "Elephant Bill" Newman, was on hand. The reporter recounted, "Mr. Newman, the American trainer, tried the plan adopted by elephant trainers in this country. He prodded Jumbo with a hook such as trainers use, and spoke very harshly to the animal. The astonished beast stood aside, and permitted Mr. Newman to clean the box at his pleasure."

Barnum enjoyed yet another bit of luck when U.S. Customs officials in New York notified him that he would be expected to pay the
20 percent duty imposed on the importation of all animals. The only
exceptions were those that promised to be "for the good of the United
States through an intention to improve the native stock."

Barnum immediately announced that he had every intention of
breeding Jumbo. An anonymous essay, "Home and Foreign Elephants," appeared. The unnamed writer spoke of elephants much as
others would of oil more than a century hence:

> We now depend on the Old World for our supply of these noble ani-
> mals. Were we to be engaged in a war with all the rest of the world
> lasting, say, a hundred years, we should become absolutely destitute
> of elephants, and the misery that would result therefrom would be
> appalling. What would our children do without elephants to amuse
> them? What would the sick do without the sight of elephants to
> invigorate them? What would the Nation do when the loathsome
> press of Europe would sneer at us as an elephantless people? To be
> truly patriotic we must rid ourselves of the abject dependence on other
> nations for our elephants.

The waiver was approved. More than ten thousand people cheered
the arrival of Jumbo that April. The start of the 1882 season was just
two weeks away and the chief animal trainer with the Barnum show
stepped in to get the new arrival ready. George Arstingstall had started
out as an animal trainer, then gone to hot air balloons until he fell
sixty-eight feet and decided he preferred his initial vocation. He had
worked under Craven for a time, but he operated with a very different
philosophy. He viewed elephants as innately treacherous and deceitful,
determined to take advantage of any latitude.

"Mr. Arstingstall has very fixed opinions about elephants," one reporter noted. "He has no faith in the good effects of being kind to them."

Within his first hours ashore, Jumbo repeatedly felt the sharp end of Arstingstall's always handy elephant hook, applied until the elephant cried out in pain.

Jumbo was lucky he had not arrived three years before, when the Barnum circus was still employing what it termed "the burning method," which consisted of sticking a hot poker up an elephant's trunk. That ended in 1879, after Bergh of the ASPCA ordered the arrest of a Barnum trainer for engaging in this practice. Bergh was poised to arrest Barnum himself the following year, when the show announced that Salamander the Fire Horse would be leaping through blazing hoops. Bergh sent five ASPCA agents and twenty police officers to intervene, but when the big moment came Barnum himself jumped through the hoops, followed by a dozen clowns, the flames proving to be artificial. Bergh was amused despite himself and was further placated by the numerous occasions Barnum lauded the ASPCA for its tireless efforts. Barnum went so far as to let it be known that he had made provision in his will to erect a monument in Bergh's honor. Bergh was generally so taken in that he actually defended Barnum when some tender-hearted souls protested the show's use of bull hooks. Bergh endorsed Barnum's entirely false contention that elephants do not suffer pain from the pointed prods because their hide is two inches thick. A moment's thought should have told Bergh that the hooks are persuasive only because they inflict hurt, particularly on the ears and anus and other tender places trainers liked to target. The goads were used so liberally that the word "Jumbo" may have become more synonymous with fury had the British trainer not been there to share bottles of stout with him and otherwise soothe his charge.

Jumbo drew huge crowds, becoming a bigger celebrity than the first of his kind in America, bigger even than the first American-born baby, with the press dutifully exaggerating his size in the absence of any specific measurements from Barnum. One of Jumbo's more sensational moments came when he was led over the Brooklyn Bridge. Twelve people had died there during the first week of its opening in a stampede triggered by a sudden fear it would collapse. The structure's safety was demonstrated to all by the crossing of the creature who was bigger than simply big.

"Jumbo!" people cried out wherever he went.

He had his own specially built railroad car, but that did little to change the ride itself.

"The shaking and jar of the train, the worrying noises, etc., keep him in a constant ferment of nervous excitement," his British trainer wrote.

The same conditions were suffered day after day by less celebrated elephants, including the twenty-five now with the Forepaugh show, among them Topsy, her guardian Bolivar, and the one formerly owned by three kings, now called Tip.

ELEVEN

THE WIZARD

As America's best-known showman toured the country with his bigger-than-big sensation, America's best-known inventor was preparing a sensation of his own with a half dozen twenty-seven-ton dynamos of such size they were nicknamed Jumbos. Edison's ultimate goal was literally to electrify the nation and give full luster to what would be called the Gilded Age.

Edison had finally tried a carbonized cotton thread as a filament in his lightbulb. And what had been right at hand all along proved to be the historic solution that would make him known as the father of the electric light even though at least twenty-two other inventors had preceded him with less practical systems.

"His name was synonymous with that of the incandescent lamp," his private secretary, Alfred Tate, would note. "Although many had attempted it, he alone had succeeded in converting this inventive dream into an industrial reality."

Edison had studied the gas illuminating system with an eye toward replacing it and he had created a test electrical lighting system at his lab in Menlo Park, New Jersey. A crowd worthy of a big top had taken special trains there on New Year's Eve of 1879 to see the future presaged by eight miles of wires and magically glowing bulbs. The actual system in New York was to service fifty-nine customers in a half square mile. And to run it Edison was installing the Jumbo dynamos in what was to be America's first central power station on Pearl Street in lower Manhattan.

In the meantime, Edison undertook a much smaller electrical project with William Vanderbilt, coincidentally Barnum's partner in the ongoing plans to replace Madison Square Garden with an entertainment colossus. Edison contracted to make Vanderbilt's new mansion the first private residence with electric lighting. But that baby-sized private dynamo was removed before it was put to any real use, by one account because Vanderbilt's wife refused to live with the noise, by another because the system started a small fire.

The honor then fell to the mansion of tycoon J. P. Morgan. This was more appropriate anyway, as he was a major investor in the much bigger project down on Pearl Street, not far from his financial district office. Morgan pronounced himself delighted with the revolutionary new lighting at his home uptown despite early troubles resulting in a scorched carpet as well as noxious fumes from the personal dynamo.

The six Jumbos downtown stood ready and when the big moment came on September 4, 1882, they roared into action with such a fiery fury that Edison wrote, "It was as if the gates of the infernal region were opened." Edison turned a switch that had been installed in Morgan's office a half dozen blocks away and the fury of the dynamos translated to a bright glow in each of the bulbs, what the inventor declared to be "light without flame and without danger." Edison promised that this new marvel would soon be so cheap and easily available that "only the rich will burn candles."

With a showman's flair, the Wizard dramatized the safety of his incandescent lamp by replacing what was to have been a traditional torchlight parade down Madison Avenue for presidential candidate James Blaine with some four hundred Edison employees, each wearing a helmet with a lightbulb of sixteen candlepower affixed atop. A wire ran down the back of the helmet, under the wearer's coat and out a sleeve to one of a pair of twelve-hundred-foot copper cables that extended the length of the procession. The cables were in turn connected to a dynamo and a steam engine on a wagon drawn by six powerful horses on loan from a safe company. That wagon was followed by two horse-drawn water tanks holding nine hundred and fifty gallons each and all went well until one of the hoses clogged with sediment. The avenue was plunged back into darkness, but soon the helmet lights were shining again, not saving Blaine from subsequent defeat but offering their own promise for the years to come.

"The illumination was intense and beautiful, the light flooding every nook and cranny of the streets," *Scientific American* reported.

Edison was again the showman at the Philadelphia Electrical Exhibition. The lightbulb helmets this time were worn by African-American "Edison Darkies" who distributed leaflets as they danced Juba-style. These wires ran down their pant legs to copper plates affixed to the heels of their shoes. The plates made periodic contact with electrified ribbons of copper set into the floor, each time lighting the bulb atop the helmet, translating tap dance into literal flash dance. The resulting crowd would have been the envy of any circus attraction filling the hall shoulder-to-shoulder and spilling outside.

At the Centennial in Philadelphia eight years and seemingly an age before, a gaslight chandelier had been presented as the latest advance in illumination. Edison now stood at this new exhibition before a tower festooned with some two thousand bulbs powered by another of his Jumbos. He was holding the hand of his eldest child, twelve-year-old Marion, whom he called Dot in reference to Morse code. The lights spelled out the name that he had chosen to be spelled out in lights as no name had ever been spelled out before.

"EDISON."

As any showman might, Edison subscribed to a newspaper clipping service. His private secretary, Alfred Tate, would recall him taking umbrage to a particular article that called him a scientist. Edison objected to being lumped with those such as Michael Faraday who had done pioneering work in electricity and magnetism and had famously said he did not worry about financial gain because he could not afford the time.

"I'm not a scientist, I'm an inventor," Edison said by Tate's recollection. "Faraday was a scientist. He didn't work for money. Said he hasn't time. But I do. I measure everything I do by the size of a silver dollar. If it don't come up to that standard, then I know it's no good."

Yet in the view of Tate and various ensuing biographers and historians as well as by the Wizard's own account, Edison's great desire was not to grow vastly rich but to become preeminently necessary.

"He was a utilitarian inventor, and money was the only barometer that could be employed to indicate success," Tate would write in his memoir. "If his work would sell, if the public would buy and pay their silver dollars for it, then he would know it was useful. And that was his vocation—the production of new and useful inventions."

Edison shunned even fabulous sums that did not derive directly from his work.

"The idea of incorporating under his name anything that did not represent the product of his own labors impressed him as a fraudulent device designed only to achieve wealth and he wanted no wealth that he himself did not create," Tate wrote. "Money could not tempt him. He scorned that kind of money."

At the same time, Edison was seemingly incapable of managing the sums his inventions did bring in. Tate would note that Edison had remarkable hands, "more sensitive than those of a woman," that the secretary would watch "hovering over an instrument to make delicate adjustments, with the rest of the body as rigid as a statue." But, Tate would add, "there was one thing these hands were unable to accomplish. They could not count money."

In that regard, the inventor could not have been more different than the showman Forepaugh, who continued to keep an eagle-eyed watch on his proceeds and who even in good times was known to fire employees so he could immediately hire them back at lower wages. Forepaugh had not minded expending huge sums in an effort to best Barnum, but he had begun to discern a constant amid all the historic growth and transformation as the nation entered the Gilded Age. He was coming to accept that he would never eclipse Barnum and that realization must have made the onerous expense of the competition as painful as if he were buying unnecessary butter by the ton.

On his part, Barnum seemed to understand that Forepaugh was just not going to let himself be eclipsed. Both Barnum and Forepaugh appeared ready to accept that in this booming land there was room for more than one great show just as there was room for both Ivory and Colgate soaps.

The Forepaugh and Barnum shows reached a mutual agreement that their rivalry made no business sense, whatever the emotional impetus. Each had to pay unprecedented salaries to performers and agents for fear the other show would lure them away. They also had to waste fortunes on the advertising battle, the hundreds of thousands of posters and handbills seeking to sway customers in the same cities while other cities were not visited at all.

As the 1882 season arrived, the shows signed a truce, establishing distinct territories and agreeing to tour different cities over the next two years. They seemed, for the moment anyway, as much at peace as the creatures of the Happy Family.

THE WHITE
ELEPHANT WAR

Barnum was still Barnum and he continued to search for a new sensation in his perpetual effort to top the last one, his primary rival in fact being not Forepaugh but Barnum.

"Barnum is the only man who can out-Barnum himself," the *New York Times* declared.

The question was what could be bigger, show-wise, than the elephant Jumbo? Barnum had to seek a measure other than physical size. Otherwise, he would be undercutting an attraction that by one estimate was drawing in more than $300,000 a year. He instead ventured into a realm he knew well from his museum days. The rare and exotic were, if anything, gaining more of a premium with the advent of mass production. And Barnum furthered the appeal with the assistance of a new press agent, Richard "Tody" Hamilton, who had, as the *New York Times* put it, "never been known to tell a lie when the truth would do as well." Hamilton made a point of never actually seeing the show he promoted.

"He would not allow his conception of it to be distorted by contact with the details," the *Times* noted.

With a press agent thus unfettered by fact, Barnum perpetuated a yearlong saga in the newspapers that was likely true save for when a lie served better, which it no doubt often did. The epic began in June of 1883, with a declaration from Barnum of a singular goal before he left this mortal life and passed on into eternity.

"Let thy servant depart in peace, but before I go—and I hope to remain a long time yet—I want a white elephant," the showman said.

Barnum meant a creature such as was held sacred in parts of Asia where it was believed that a white elephant had visited Buddha's mother the night before his birth, entering her side prior to arriving into the world. Barnum hoped the tallest of tales would now generate even more excitement than the biggest of elephants.

"For years Barnum's agents have been running fearful risks in Indian jungles and Siamese Courts in order to obtain one of these sacred beasts; and the tale of their adventures—as told by themselves—is as wonderful as any of Verne's romances," the *New York Times* reported.

The *Times* said that Barnum's chief agent, J. B. Gaylord, "went into the very presence of royalty itself, and actually had the audacity to offer the King of Siam, in person, seated upon his imperial throne with his regal crown upon his sovereign head, $100,000 for one of the white elephants that his Court and people worshipped."

The king was the very one who had offered America elephants with which to overcome its woeful lack of a native population. A white elephant was supposedly an entirely different matter. The king's uncles were said by the *Times* to have "implored Mr. Gaylord to flee from

Bangkok, lest the vengeance of the Court and the Siamese people overtake him for his blasphemous presumption."

Word of the supposed offer supposedly reached a "Siamese nobleman," who supposedly provided Gaylord with a white elephant only for it to be poisoned by "Buddhist fanatics." Gaylord was said to have continued on to Burma and purchased a white elephant for $200,000 from "bloody King Theebau . . . the gentleman who recently murdered his wives."

In an added twist, Theebau was said to have reconsidered two days later and dispatched men to reclaim the elephant. Gaylord reportedly managed to spirit the elephant away in the night on a steamer bound for England.

"At last the great and only Barnum has secured the prize he has coveted for half a century in the shape of a sacred white elephant, and it is expected that Jumbo will turn pale with envy," the *New York Times* announced on December 6, 1883.

An update was carried in various newspapers three weeks later.

"Bridgeport, Dec. 29—Mr. P. T. Barnum received a cable message this morning from J. H. Davis, his agent in London, stating that today's *London Telegraph* contained a column and a half announcing the arrival of the white sacred elephant in Suez in good condition."

That same day, the newspapers carried another dispatch from someone who must have felt that in trying to top himself Barnum was also trying to top everyone else, thereby breaking the truce.

"Philadelphia, Dec. 29—Adam Forepaugh, the circus proprietor, to-day received a cablegram from his agent in Algiers stating that he has been offered a white elephant for £10,000. Forepaugh, in reply, directed the agent to obtain the animal at the price mentioned."

The ship bearing Barnum's elephant arrived at Liverpool on January 15. The British press noted that the elephant was in fact largely gray save for pink splotches where pigmentation was absent. The *Times of London* reported, "It seems to be a stretch of language to call it 'white'" and suggested Barnum's latest trophy instead be called "a piebald elephant."

The British newspaper published a letter from O. P. Sanderson, official superintendent of Elephant Catching Operations in Bengal. He happened to be in London and he had inspected the creature now temporarily lodged in what was described as "Jumbo's vacant stall," attended by two supposed "Buddhist priests" who regularly performed what were supposedly religious rituals.

Sanderson said that he had seen "many thousands of elephants, wild and tame" and declared that "Mr. Barnum's so-called white and sacred elephant . . . neither in the general color of his body, in the flesh-colored blotchings on his face, ears and chest, nor in the smallest particular whatsoever, does he differ one whit from the hundreds of elephants of the Commissariat and Forest Departments which may be seen any day in India and Burmah carrying the baggage of troops, or dragging timber down to the banks of rivers."

Sanderson indicated that Barnum had himself been humbugged if he had indeed paid £40,000, when "the value of such an elephant in Burmah or India is from £150 to £200." Sanderson concluded, "We must not, however, be too hard on Mr. Barnum for not obtaining a white elephant, for the sufficient reason that such an animal does not exit."

Any suggestion that there was no such thing as a white elephant did not deter Forepaugh, who was seemingly determined not to be outdone again, as he had been with Jumbo, or to be cowed, as he had been when he tried to pass Topsy off as American born. Barnum's white elephant was still more than a week out at sea when a ship bearing what Forepaugh agents described as "a genuine white elephant from Siam" arrived in New York.

The headline in a clearly skeptical *New York Times* described Forepaugh's creature as "A Very Sea-Sick Elephant," the subhead adding, "A Beast with Brown Eyes and Gray Skin." The *Times* reported that one of the "circus men" on the pier said the elephant was in fact "a common Indian elephant from Bengal" that had been traded for three American buffalos in Calcutta and then shipped to Liverpool, where it awaited a purchaser for several months. That presented the question of how the elephant had been made paler. It was suggested that perhaps the poor creature had been rubbed with pumice stone during the voyage.

Forepaugh could only have been exasperated when the *Times* welcomed Barnum's white elephant eight days later with an article headlined "The Sacred Beast Here," the subhead reading, "From Burmah to the Great Moral Show." The reporter described how a messenger "rushed breathless" up to Barnum at Madison Square Garden with a telegram reporting that the ship bearing the "sacred white elephant" had been spotted approaching New York. Barnum set aside for the moment his continuing planning with William Vanderbilt to build a showman's ultimate venue.

"Get me my hat! Call me a cab! Notify the president!" Barnum reportedly exclaimed.

The reporter accompanied Barnum and an entourage aboard a tugboat that met the ship. A Barnum man aboard waved a white handkerchief to signal the elephant was in good condition. The two supposed Buddhist priests appeared and Barnum called up to them through cupped hands.

"How do ye do? No talkee English? Elephant! Elephant!"

The Barnum party boarded, and the elephant was described as slate-gray, with pink around the trunk and ears and chest. A purported expert inspected the creature closely.

"That's one of the finest specimens of the sacred white elephant I have seen in my life," the expert declared.

Barnum said that the elephant was named Toung Taloung, which he translated as Gem of the Sky. Barnum then intoned, "Of course we have all learned by this time that there is no such thing as a really pure white elephant. This is a sacred animal, a technical white elephant, and as white as God makes 'em. A man can paint them white but this is not one of that kind."

In response, Forepaugh retranslated his own new addition's name to mean not Tiger Killer but the Light of Asia. He somehow convinced a noted Philadelphia zoologist to confirm publicly that this was a genuine white elephant. A group of reporters took him up on an invitation for a "private viewing" at his show's winter headquarters in Philadelphia.

"We found standing in a darkened sort of stable, into which light was admitted by a very small and dirty window, the animal in question, the Light of Asia," reporter Alex Kenealy later wrote. "It struck me immediately that the elephant was a swindle."

Even in the dimness, Kenealy could make out dark spots around the elephant's watering eyes and where the elephant would place the end of his trunk into his mouth. He rubbed the skin, but no white came away on his hand. He wet his fingertips and tried again.

"I confess that I was somewhat astonished to find that a lot of white stuff . . . had come off in my hand."

That evening, Kenealy and a fellow reporter went to Forepaugh's house, threatening to report their suspicions in a Philadelphia newspaper unless the elephant were given a "thorough scrubbing" in their presence and examined by a team of experts.

"Mr. Forepaugh professed to be considerably astounded," Kenealy would later write.

Forepaugh sought for an hour to convince the reporters of "the impossibility of making a black elephant white." He finally agreed to let the reporters inspect the elephant again the following day.

"I will let you wash it with soap and water or scrub it or put ammonia on it. You can do anything you like with it," Forepaugh told them.

Kenealy returned as arranged and encountered Forepaugh's son.

"Young Forepaugh said the elephant was sick and it was doubtful if I could see it," Kenealy recalled.

The elder Forepaugh then appeared and sought to set matters right in his own way.

"I would only be too glad if you would come into my employ, Mr. Kenealy," Forepaugh said by the reporter's account.

Kenealy declined and Forepaugh went directly to the paper's publisher, seeking to stop publication. The publisher agreed to hold off, but only if Kenealy and an editor were permitted to scrub as had been promised.

"I wet the sponge and began to rub heartily on the elephant's hide," Kenealy reported. "Every moment, the hide got darker and darker until it was almost black."

Forepaugh told the newspapermen they had done enough investigating.

"It will dry white," Forepaugh said.

The authenticity of the white elephant was called further into question by a firsthand witness to the fraud at its inception, a trainer who was presently on a ship from Liverpool, apparently at Barnum's instigation. A Forepaugh agent boarded the ship the moment it docked and intercepted the trainer, George Gillespie, before he stepped ashore.

"[The Forepaugh agent] tried to induce me to accompany him immediately to Philadelphia and see Mr. Forepaugh, whom he said was a fine fellow and who would pay me treble any amount I could get in any employment in this country," Gillespie later stated in a sworn affidavit. "I replied that I had been a party to a fraud and was going to take the quickest means of clearing myself."

As detailed in the affidavit, Gillespie had most recently been employed by Liverpool animal trader William Cross, who had acquired four elephants from Ceylon, one a five-year-old named Tiny, "because he was the smallest." Tiny was purchased by a Forepaugh agent who was apparently shopping there rather than Hamburg to avoid providing Barnum with an easy refutation, as had happened with Topsy. The Forepaugh agent presented Gillespie with a packet containing "Paris white," or plaster of Paris and size.

"[The agent] told me to mix it with warm water and rub it on the elephant 'Tiny' with a brush resembling a whitewasher's brush," Gillespie recalled in the affidavit. "We gave said elephant no less than fifty applications of it, occasionally twice and frequently thrice a day."

Blisters and sores had appeared on the elephant's skin. Gillespie had applied a balm called friar's balsam, but the animal had still been suffering "pain and restlessness" as it was loaded on the steamship *City of Chester* two days later. Gillespie understood the painting had resumed after the elephant arrived in Philadelphia, with the attendant skin afflictions.

"If persisted, the coloring process will be likely to kill him," Gillespie stated.

Barnum added a grand finale to his season opener at Madison Square Garden, introducing a new attraction to go with the sacred white elephant. He declared that this other, "profane white elephant" was a fraud superior to that of his rival. The showman invited "scientific experts" to confirm that the elephant had been made actually lighter, not just whitewashed, and was indeed a genuine fake.

Barnum and an associate aptly named Phil De Spotto declined to reveal exactly what lightening agent had been employed, but suggested it could be used on more than elephants.

"There is no limit to the uses to which this solution can be applied," De Spotto said. "It will as readily and harmlessly change the black color of the Negro to that of a Caucasian or Anglo-Saxon."

The *New York Times* called "Barnum's plan of making an elephant white by artificial means in order to contrast it with the dark and genuine white elephant" an "interesting experiment."

"The inventor of the process of bleaching elephants claims that it can be applied without the slightest injury to colored people," the *Times* noted, satirically imagining a solution to America's most intractable problem. "Probably a method of straightening Ethiopian hair and repressing the exuberance of Ethiopian lips will soon follow the grand discovery of bleaching Ethiopian skin, and in that case all distinction between the two races will at once disappear, and the Negro question will vanish from our politics, never to reappear."

In truth, Barnum had used the peroxide that the city's human hair dealers employed to turn brunette to blond. The elephantine result arrived with the rest of the Barnum show in Philadelphia when Forepaugh still had two more days of his hometown season opener. The profane peroxided elephant was on prominent display as Barnum paraded through the City of Brotherly Love.

"THE WHITE FRAUD," a banner read.

The "White Elephant War" had begun. A Forepaugh poster read:

TOO WHITE FOR BARNUM
FOREPAUGH'S SACRED WHITE ELEPHANT
PROVED BY THE HIGHEST SCIENTIFIC AUTHORITY TO BE GENUINE
AND BARNUM'S "SACRED WHITE" ELEPHANT A RANK FRAUD

A Barnum poster had a drawing of "Gillespie white-washing Fore-paugh's elephant" and read:

FOREPAUGH HAS BEEN IMITATING BARNUM FOR YEARS
AND FOR ONCE BARNUM WILL IMITATE FOREPAUGH
BARNUM HAS HAD AN ELEPHANT ARTIFICIALLY COLORED
AND WILL SHOW IN HIS PARADE FREE

In a newspaper interview, Forepaugh quoted Barnum as having once said, "There's a sucker born every minute." The phrase was in fact coined by someone else, most likely an infamous con man, Joseph "Paper Collar Joe" Bessimer. But Barnum never denied Forepaugh's assertion, instead thanking him for the attendant publicity.

Meanwhile, Forepaugh got his own "Buddhist priests" in yellow and red robes to perform purported religious rites while the Light of Asia was on exhibition.

"Some observing visitor once remarked unkindly that the religious act terminated suddenly when the menagerie tent was empty and was resumed with wonderful alacrity when spectators approached," a Forepaugh aide reported.

Forepaugh said this sacred creature was too precious to include in a street parade. The more likely reason was that rain might wash away the coloring that continued to be applied despite the blisters and sores.

"It is true that the elephant was a more snowy white on Monday than at any other time of the week, although sometimes the skin had been spotted and stained on Saturday," the Forepaugh aide later wrote.

In Chicago, Forepaugh got word that the heir apparent to the Siamese throne was visiting the city while on a tour of America. Forepaugh invited him and his entourage to see the show and inspect the white elephant.

"The royal person came, accompanied by other dignitaries, looked the beast over and muttered to the interpreter something which was apparently not complimentary," the aide recalled. "The press agent saw to it, however, that the newspapers said that the prince had declared the animal the genuine article."

The prince might have been more impressed by the unpainted elephants, which were described by the show's "courier," or promotional pamphlet, as a "quarter of 100 PERFORMING ELEPHANTS! . . . 25 SAGACIOUS SCHOLASTIC ELEPHANTS. . . . A HALF-MILLION DOLLAR FEATURE THAT NO EXHIBITION IN THE WORLD CAN DUPLICATE!" The elephants included the giant said to be so fond of Topsy, the counterpart of Barnum's Jumbo, the one Forepaugh's courier called "THE KING OF ALL MASTODONS, THE LEVIATHAN MONSTER ELEPHANT 'BOLIVAR.'"

"THE GREATEST HERD OF TRAINED MASTODONS THE WORLD EVER SAW," the courier promised. "They all appear in Living Pyramids! Elephantine dances! Military evolutions! Play upon musical instruments! Stand upon their heads! Pick up needles and pins! Uncork bottles and drink their contents! Engage in racing! Walk, posture and balance upon the Tight Rope."

The elephants had indeed been trained to do all this and more, though the tightrope was really an iron beam with a halved hawser affixed along the side. The elephants had been taught to strike a drum, bells, a cymbal, a xylophone, and the keys of an organ as well as pull the slide of a trombone while a "conductor" waved a baton with her trunk. Topsy was among them and their faraway birth was now a selling point, presented as a mark of how far their training had taken them.

"ADAM FOREPAUGH, JR.'S JUNGLE BORN BAND OF MASSIVE MUSICIANS . . . THE WONDER & MARVEL OF THE AGE . . . THEY DO EVERYTHING BUT TALK."

The elder Forepaugh made a half-million-dollar pledge in the courier.

"The entire Herd, valued at the princely sum of $500,000, is introduced and performed by my son Adam Forepaugh, Jr., and I am ready to forfeit the worth of this great and costly Herd of Elephants, if his equal as an animal educator and trainer of elephants can be produced."

As both Forepaughs well knew, two men who were much more than young Adam's equal had actually taught the elephants most of their present tricks. Every performance continued to be largely a demonstration of the power of patient kindness and unflagging focus as conceived by Stewart Craven and elaborated by Eph Thompson.

"After a trick is once learned, it is never forgotten," Thompson would later say. "Ten years afterward, [an elephant] will go through the performance without a hitch."

The newer tricks were almost certainly the work of Thompson's own particular genius. His great-grandson has no doubt that Thompson actually shared Craven's view.

"He used kindness rather than cruelty and it seems to have worked," the great-grandson, Ray Perkin, would later say.

The results almost lived up to the courier's hype. The enforced secrecy of the training barn allowed young Forepaugh to take the bows.

"Forepaugh took all the credit," Perkin would add.

One of the show's hands would later offer a glimpse of the truth to the *Lewiston Evening Journal* of Maine, adding that even with

Thompson's benign and understanding approach, the elephants were subject to young Forepaugh's stringencies.

"There was 'Nigger Eph,' who was always successful in handling the animals," the hand told the newspaper. "Addie Forepaugh, son of Adam, was one of the most brutal men ever with a circus. . . . He handled his fork [bull hook] loosely, and often jabbed the animals needlessly."

The dichotomy became embodied in the big elephant Charley, who was described by the *Philadelphia Inquirer* as "perhaps the most vicious and violent and, at times, docile and affectionate elephant in captivity."

Along with the jabbing of young Forepaugh's "fork" came the perpetual and harrowing ordeal of being on the road. Such stress classically causes elephants to exhibit what is known as stereotypic behavior: repetitively rocking back and forth, swinging the trunk, bobbing the head, shuffling the feet. This phenomenon was apparently what had led the ancient Roman naturalist Pliny the elder to imagine that an elephant who had been severely punished for not performing a trick during the day practiced on his own that night. Nearly two millennia later, Thompson used the rhythms of these stress-induced stereotypies to teach the elephants to dance "quadrilles" in groups of four, with Topsy among them. The crowds marveled at the way the elephants moved to the music, though in truth the band was playing to the elephants' movements. The credit of course continued to go to the younger Forepaugh.

In the meantime, the elder Forepaugh had suddenly welcomed any opportunity to test the Light of Asia with trials by water, noting that the elephant's whiteness was undimmed despite vigorous rubbing and scrubbing.

"Suspicious onlookers sometimes said something about waterproof paint," the Forepaugh aide would recall.

The paint could not have been any less toxic than the whitewash. But the elder Forepaugh figured he had on hand a number of similarly sized elephants to become the new Light of Asia should the present one succumb to the constant whitening, with nobody being the wiser. The designated fill-ins included Topsy, despite her distinctive broken tail. She was spared the torment of perpetual repainting by the genuinely remarkable performance that she and the other unpainted elephants were now putting on twice a day. This actual marvel raised the question of why Forepaugh even needed a fraud, especially as the public's interest in the white elephant began to fade despite the waterproof whiteness.

A reporter in Syracuse, New York, wrote, "Adam Forepaugh has a white elephant on his hands," adding that the crowd was "sorely disappointed in the beast" and that the Light of Asia constituted an embarrassment in an otherwise excellent circus.

"The early death of this mooted monster would be a godsend to the show," the reporter suggested.

A month after the close of the 1884 season, the elder Forepaugh announced to the world that his Light of Asia had died at the show's winter quarters. Forepaugh reported that the elephant had caught a chill the previous week, when the keeper, apparently meaning Thompson, had carelessly left a window open overnight. Forepaugh said he had administered every medicine that seemed appropriate, but the elephant's condition only worsened, until it breathed its last.

"I will never buy another white elephant," the elder Forepaugh declared. "The people didn't appreciate the one I had."

On being told that the Light of Asia had died, Barnum replied, "More likely un-dyed."

THIRTEEN

EPH'S ESCAPE, PICKPOCKETS, AND PINK LEMONADE

The 1885 season brought a new Forepaugh attraction, named after a world-famous prizefighter.

"A dark, natural beast, in form much resembling the white elephant, appeared as 'John L. Sullivan,' the boxing elephant," recalled a Forepaugh press agent named W. C. Thompson, who was not related to the trainer. "He wore a glove on the end of his trunk and swung gently at 'Eph' Thompson, a colored trainer."

A newspaper spoke of the "boxing match between elephantine pugilist Sullivan and his trainer, Eph Thompson." The glove-tipped trunk was described as "a very lively and effective battering ram that makes a cyclone-sweep without much regard for the region of the belt." Eph Thompson was not described by his race, seemingly for the first time. He also got some actual credit as the trainer, though likely only because the younger Forepaugh would never have subjected himself to a role so close to that of a clown. The crown prince of the show could hardly be seen being struck below the belt by some elephant.

The boxing act thus allowed Eph Thompson to offer a first public glimpse of his genius. And, as the dancer Juba had already discovered, Europeans were more open to judging people of color not by their race but by their talents. The Europeans who now took notice of Thompson included Carl Hagenbeck of Hamburg, a showman as well as an animal dealer. Hagenbeck recognized who was really behind the success of the herd and hired Thompson away from Forepaugh to train six of his own elephants. Thompson subsequently appeared in Europe with Hagenbeck's circus and others, becoming a continental sensation, to pachyderms what Josephine Baker would be to dance. He soon had his own show and his own elephants, one walking a tightrope while two others held it taut. He taught an Asian elephant named Mary to somersault down a ramp.

Without the knowing and gentling hand of the true genius they had consigned to the shadows for so long, Forepaugh and his son found some of their elephants increasingly difficult to manage. Several were kept chained as too ill tempered to be in the parades. These "uglies" ate just as much as the others and Forepaugh was becoming even more aware of costs as the resumed competition with Barnum proved anew that even bloodless wars can be onerously expensive.

Louis Cooke, his new general agent, representing Forepaugh in contracts and business arrangements, later wrote, "My engagement with the new show began at the close of the season, just after the famous 'White Elephant War' that had been so disastrous to the big concerns because of the extraordinary expense of the fight as well as its demoralizing effect upon the confidence of the amusement loving public."

Cooke said of this revived rivalry between Forepaugh and Barnum, "Extraordinary salaries were offered and paid for agents, performers and everything else that might possibly be of advantage to either concern. Heated arguments often arose. Hostile sentiment prevailed. Fabulous prices were demanded and paid. Rivalry ran rampant."

Cooke noted that Forepaugh "was ambitious not only to have a show equal to any in existence, but, as he expressed it, to 'get even with Barnum.'"

The elder Forepaugh could have expected at least to match his rival had Barnum continued to ballyhoo his circus as "The Greatest Show on Earth." But with Barnum and the newspapers now calling it "The Great Moral Show," Forepaugh was hard pressed to compete. The problem was that this description had some justification. Barnum abstained from the Forepaugh ploy of keeping the ticket wagon closed until the last minute so the scalpers in the show's employ could fleece an extra dime out of anxious patrons, this followed by short-changing the more patient ones once the wagon was open. Barnum also refused to allow thieves and swindlers to operate in exchange for a cut. He actively and forcefully chased them away to such effect that a patron could actually attend the show without being swindled and robbed.

Worse for Forepaugh, the public as well as the press had begun to notice the difference. The Barnum operation was becoming known as a "Sunday School Show," to distinguish it from those such as Forepaugh's, which zestfully justified the circus business's tawdry reputation. Forepaugh continued a working relationship with the swindlers and thieves who traveled with the show, even providing them with their own railroad car, aboard which they traveled in what one thief termed "royal style." They were said to include twenty professional pickpockets headed by a fellow called Windy Dick, who paid Forepaugh $200 a day up front. A young pickpocket named George Arthur reputedly scored as many as 125 pocketbooks during a single-day stand, along with 100 watches. The watches were regularly shipped to a New York City jeweler in a soapbox along with the gang's other pilfered baubles.

During the parade that signaled the show's arrival at a new locale, the pickpockets would disperse in the crowds, operating individually but ever ready to cover each other's retreat. The best "graft" was to be found during a performance, when the thieves would deploy under the stands.

"Every man, woman, and child was in reality at their mercy," Arthur said in an interview after his retirement. "Many a woman who thought the safest place to carry valuables was in her stocking has come to grief."

The thieves were always happy when the swelter of summer turned the inside of the tent steamy.

"Many a vest was wide open, watch hanging for the picking," Arthur said.

The pickpockets' accomplices included the lads who roamed the stands selling peanuts and "pink lemonade," the latter having been invented when a vendor named Pete Conklin found himself short of water during a rush of customers and grabbed a tub in which a woman bareback rider had been soaking a pair of pink tights. The recipe, recorded by his brother, Forepaugh show veteran George Conklin, was "a tub of water, with no particular squeamishness regarding its source, tartaric acid, some sugar, enough aniline dye to give it a rich pink, and for a finish some thin slices of lemon. The slices of lemon are known as 'floaters,' and any which are left in the tub at the close of a day's business, together with those which have come back in the glasses, are carefully saved over for the next day's use. In this way the same floaters may appear before the public a considerable number of times."

When a customer flashed significant cash while purchasing a glass of the concoction, the vendor would tip off Arthur or one of the other thieves. If a patron suddenly shouted he was being robbed and ran after the thief, various members of the show would contrive to block his way. A victim who chased a pickpocket through a tent flap and then tried to return was likely to find himself confronted by a canvasman and accused of trying to sneak in. The victim would then be ejected, unless he was willing and still able to pay again.

"By this time, the grafter had gone," Arthur noted. "Nine out of ten times he was inside working again."

Through such strategies, the pickpockets went five seasons without a single arrest. Forepaugh's $200-a-day cut added up to a considerable sum, and he was a lover of even small sums. He continued the arrangement with Windy Dick even while retaining the famed Pinkerton Agency to accord at least the appearance of cleaning up. He made sure the newspapers got the story after a Pinkerton detective grabbed an interloping pickpocket called Oyster Jim, whose real sin was a failure to pay tribute. The band played the "Rogue's March" as the prisoner was trotted around the hippodrome track to hoots and jeers from the audience. Jim called out for any lawyers in the audience, saying he intended to sue.

"Whether I am a thief or not, they have no proof," he declared.

Along with his other worries, Forepaugh suffered a harrowing string of railroad accidents such as constituted a constant hazard for any circus that rode the rails. The convoy of three trains carrying the Forepaugh circus had a total of six wrecks that destroyed more than thirty cars in the course of the 1885 season. The elephants must have been shaken, if not traumatized, though none fared as badly as the prize of the Barnum show.

On September 15, near the close of the 1885 season, Jumbo was struck and killed by a locomotive that roared into a rail yard in St. Thomas, Ontario, Canada, while the circus was preparing to board another train to its next stand. Barnum concocted and some newspapers perpetuated a heart-wrenching tale that the great creature had perished attempting to save an elephant so small as to be named Tom Thumb. The truth seems to be that Jumbo was on the tracks when the locomotive suddenly appeared and the elephant tried in vain to outrun it. The locomotive was derailed by the collision.

The loss had a surprisingly profound effect on the chief Barnum trainer, George Arstingstall, who had repeatedly voiced the view that elephants were treacherous beasts on whom any kindness was wasted. He now faced the fact that his greatness was tied to Jumbo and that without the giant elephant he was just a guy with a sharp stick. He suffered an emotional collapse that was said to have been intensified by the demise of another relationship, what was described as "an affair of the heart" with a woman. A Bridgeport cop later found him sprawled across railroad tracks in an apparent suicide attempt.

Forepaugh still had big Bolivar. He also had a patriarchal advantage over his rival that, in his view, ultimately outweighed animal attractions of any kind.

"I have a boy and Mr. Barnum has none," Forepaugh declared. "My show will outlast his."

Forepaugh still could not outdo Barnum though he did now seize an opportunity to outmaneuver him.

FOURTEEN

THE TREE OF
KNOWLEDGE AND
THE FEARLESS FROGMAN

On December 8, 1885, William Vanderbilt died suddenly of a cerebral hemorrhage. The plans to replace Madison Square Garden had yet to progress beyond the drawing stage, and the old structure passed into the stewardship of an agent for the family. An agent for Forepaugh soon after offered to lease the Garden not just for a week at the start of the circus season, as had been Barnum's habit, but for a full six months. The Vanderbilt agent was either unaware of the nature of the late scion's relationship with Barnum or of a mind that money came first. Forepaugh's agent sealed the deal with five $1,000 bills before Barnum could get wind of it.

"I'm afraid it will kill Barnum," Forepaugh rejoiced.

Barnum had his agents inquire about a sublease and he could not have been surprised when Forepaugh rebuffed them. Barnum then threatened to open up at another Manhattan venue at the same time Forepaugh was opening at the Garden.

"Mr. Forepaugh hoped [he] would," the *New York Times* reported. "He liked circuses and would come and see it. He had a spare hyena to lend them if they ran short."

Bravado aside, Forepaugh had to realize that Barnum was capable of upstaging him even though his own circus now included a Wild West show. Forepaugh was also anxious for financial reasons to end the rivalry. He proposed that the two open together at the Garden. Barnum had little choice but to agree.

Forepaugh felt secure enough in his contribution to the temporary merger that he left his "uglies," including the huge Bolivar and the nearly as large Tip, behind at his show's winter quarters in Philadelphia. He did not want his triumph dimmed by having the behemoths go wild without Thompson around to control them. Anyway, he still had what he figured to be his perpetual paternal edge in the person of his son, whom he put on prominent display. Let the sonless Barnum try to match that.

The younger Forepaugh met the arriving trains at Harsimus Cove in Jersey City wearing a broad-brimmed hat and an overcoat that extended to his ankles. The *New York Times* dramatically reported that he had "slept the fitful sleep of the just who are compelled to obey duty's disagreeable calls."

The son supervised as fifty men unloaded the 205 horses and thirty-five ponies. The eighteen elephants led off the cars two by two included Topsy, no doubt sorely missed by Bolivar. Basil and Jenny were the pair that took the fore. The newspapers assumed that the male Basil was the leader but it was almost certainly Jenny, as the senior female.

Deckhands at a waiting ferryboat set up a gangplank on either side, hoping half the elephants would go up each, thereby evenly distributing the great weight. The combined power of the deckhands and the circus men proved insufficient to separate the elephants as they followed their matriarch, Jenny, up the gangplank to the left. Only a stiff wind out of the northwest saved the ferry as it listed dangerously near to the point of capsizing.

The elephants arrived at the Twenty-third Street ferry dock and were led crosstown to the most prized of venues. The elder Forepaugh arrived, as did Barnum. The two prepared to present what truly would be the greatest show on earth at what many simply called the Garden.

"Adam has tempted me and I have yielded," Barnum said, making a biblical play on his rival's given name.

"We have both eaten of the Tree of Knowledge," Forepaugh said, making a biblical play of his own.

On the night of the premiere, the combined shows had a torchlight parade down Broadway, passing along a stretch below Thirty-fourth Street now lit by arc lights installed by one of Edison's competitors and dubbed the Great White Way. Rich and poor jostled each other to glimpse what the *New York Times* described as "a combination seen but once in a lifetime. This happened to be their lifetime, and they wanted to see it."

The *Times* concluded, "The Barnum and Forepaugh combination had had their torchlight parade. Their blossoming forth at the Madison Square Garden will make the very electric lights seem pallid."

Even with a half dozen of Forepaugh's herd left behind, the Garden held more elephants than had ever been in any one place in America. The senior Forepaugh elephant trainer was still young Adam, officially anyway. Barnum had replaced the despondent George Arstingstall with Elephant Bill Newman, who had introduced Jumbo to the use of the hook, American style, on the ship from England. Newman would have represented little change for the elephants were it not for his wife, who was identified only as Mrs. William Newman. She had grown up in the circus and occasionally tried her hand at training. She took a matriarchal approach much more in keeping with the Craven philosophy, delighting not in dominating the elephants but simply in working with them, relying not on physical force but on intuition.

"A woman mastering the leviathans of the animal kingdom was one of the wonders of a circus in 1887," wrote the press agent W. C. Thompson with what seemed to be genuine admiration. "She was a matronly looking person, quite stout and pleasant-mannered, devoid withal of the masculine traits that her occupation might seem to require."

Thompson described one of her rare performances.

"At her command, the elephants, eight in number, marched, wheeled, countermarched, halted promptly and 'grounded arms' by lying on their sides. Then, like schoolboys delighted at a release from what they deemed duty, the huge beasts broke ranks and assumed different postures and occupations about the ring. One of them stood on his head, another turned a grindstone with his trunk, a third walked on a revolving barrel, and several others respectively engaged, to their own apparent amusement, in dancing on a pedestal, ringing a bell and 'clapping hands.'"

Thompson added, "Mrs. Newman gave few public exhibitions, and there has never since been a successful woman elephant trainer. For some reason, they fail in this branch of circus work, whereas in other departments they are fully the equals of the other sex."

In truth, Newman seems to have been more than the equal of her husband, as well as the other men so bent on mastering these biggest of beasts, on being the boss.

* * *

In the meantime, Forepaugh seemed to have become Barnum's equal thanks to the Madison Square ploy. Forepaugh may have even gained a little edge with his troupe of cowboys and Indians. Barnum, being Barnum, was plotting a publicity coup to restore what he viewed as the natural order.

The stunt began one hundred miles up the Hudson River with a figure in an inflatable suit made of vulcanized India rubber. Captain Paul Boyton, known as the Fearless Frogman, had achieved fame paddling feet first across the English Channel and remarkable distances of open sea, as well as along many of the world's most famous rivers, including the Thames and the Seine, and nearly the entire length of the mighty Mississippi towing behind him a floating locker containing necessities and even a little stove, so he could cook when he periodically paused to eat and sleep. He had received his captaincy from the Peruvian government, whose emissary had approached him as he strolled down Broadway and recruited him for a failed effort to paddle out to a Chilean warship and affix a torpedo. He now announced his intention to paddle down the Hudson River from Albany to New York Harbor.

That plan had to be modified when much of the river at his starting point proved to be still choked with ice. He could have waited until the spring thaw progressed, but timing was important for reasons that would soon be apparent. He instead set off from the town of Hudson thirty-seven miles downriver from what was to have been his starting point. He was cheered by big crowds as he set off, and trailed by a boatload of reporters who recorded his progress past Catskill, Germantown, and Tivoli. The reporters felt compelled to take a break from the freezing temperatures by putting in at Saugerties but caught up with him at Barrytown. Two days then passed with nothing really new to report.

"The voyage was not of unusual interest, outside of the difficulty of forging ahead through the ice floes and considerable suffering from the cold," Boyton's official biography would note.

The reporters were then told that the rubber suit had developed a leak and that the ordeal had caused Boyton to lose thirty pounds and that doctors were advising him to abandon his effort. He put in at Sing Sing three days into his voyage and one day from his destination amid speculation as to whether the Frogman would prove so fearless as to continue. The drama was accompanied by an announcement in the next morning's newspapers.

"Boyton to Travel with Barnum," read the headline in the *New York Times*.

The article reported that Boyton had agreed to tour with the Barnum show, making his first appearance early the following week at Madison Square Garden. The announcement was followed the next day by dramatic reports of what the *Times* termed "an immense crowd" gathered at the steamboat pier in Ossining to watch Boyton resolutely return to the water to complete his journey against medical advice.

An even bigger crowd, twenty thousand or more, was at the harbor's edge in New York for Boyton's arrival at the Battery the next day. Boyton reached into his floating locker. He drew cheers when he saluted the throngs by firing off rockets and blowing into a brass bugle.

Boyton seemed to make an instant recovery from the exigencies that supposedly had the doctors so alarmed. He was described as "looking none the worse for his paddle down the Hudson" when he appeared at Madison Square Garden that Monday. A water tank was conveniently on hand, having been used during the first three weeks of the Barnum/Forepaugh joint appearance by the Beckwiths, a British family of swimmers.

The man in the rubber suit now made what was ballyhooed as his very first appearance in a circus. He was said to have approached the tank "with all the frisky grace of a young hippopotamus and disported himself in its waters with the joyful levity of a light-hearted sea lion."

The newspapers reported that in the space of ten minutes, he somehow managed to paddle about, raise a small sail, shoot a handgun, launch a distress signal, cook and eat a meal, and blow his bugle anew. The accounts mentioned Barnum nearly as prominently as Boyton while Forepaugh received only passing acknowledgment as the other party in the temporary combination.

After the six-week joint appearance at Madison Square Garden, Barnum paraded over the Brooklyn Bridge with Boyton for a show on the far side. Forepaugh returned to Philadelphia and continued on with an itinerary whose fourth stop was Mount Vernon, Ohio, where he serendipitously acquired a new attraction of his own. A one-legged man appeared on the circus grounds and identified himself as Sergeant George Wagner, sole survivor of General Custer's last stand, Custer and his Seventh Cavalry having returned to Sioux lands with fatal results three years after helping to trigger the Panic of 1873. Wagner said he had lost his right leg below the knee to a poison arrow as he rode to bring a message from the doomed Custer to another detachment. Forepaugh now retained him to reenact his supposed bravery by charging around the big top on a horse to the accompaniment of blaring trumpets.

The cowboys in the Wild West show became jealous and hired a lawyer to investigate this purported hero. They reported the result to Forepaugh, telling him that Wagner had in fact lost his leg during an accidental explosion at a Fourth of July celebration and had never left Ohio before joining the show.

"What do I care whether the fellow's a fakir or not?" Forepaugh replied. "He looks the part better than any of you. He's got a wooden leg to confirm it. He's the finest liar under the tent and he's made a big hit. He stays with the troupe."

Forepaugh did make several cuts from that season's roster, simultaneously reducing his expenses and collecting a nice fee by leasing a half dozen of his uncelebrated elephants to fledgling showman Frank Robbins. They included the crooked-tailed female, Topsy, who could only have reminded Forepaugh of his first elephantine fiasco. He was resolved to have now suffered his last.

"The war of the elephants is ended," the *New York Times* correctly noted.

FIFTEEN

ANOTHER WAR BEGINS

Even as the torchlight parade down Broadway signaled the end of the war between Forepaugh and Barnum, the electric lights proliferating in the city and far beyond were marking the start of a struggle between two other would-be giants, Thomas Edison and George Westinghouse.

"The struggle for the control of the electric light and power business has never been exceeded in bitterness by any of the historical commercial controversies of a former day," Westinghouse would later say.

What would come to be called the War of Currents was for supremacy in implementing the modern marvel that now blazed not only along the Great White Way and in the mansions and offices of tycoons, but in theaters and restaurants and department stores and arenas. The ultimate outcome would add a final twist to the story of the crooked-tailed elephant presently traveling with a circus that did not even bill itself as the greatest.

In this new war, Edison was already established as one of the indisputably greatest and seemed the prohibitive favorite to prevail. He may not have actually been the father of the electric light, but he had created the most commercially viable bulb, as well as the first central power plant and the first extensive lighting system. He seemed on the way to an all-but-certain monopoly.

But Edison insisted on using only direct current, or DC, rather than alternating current, or AC. The most fundamental difference between the two is that direct current travels in only one direction, whereas alternating current continually reverses direction. The practical difference is that DC cannot easily be transmitted much farther than the square mile eventually serviced by his first plant on Pearl Street. A city using DC would require a generating plant in every neighborhood. Rural folks would be generally out of luck unless they could afford their own private plant.

Alternating current has no such limitations and can be transmitted over considerable distances economically, but Edison had been using direct current in all his systems. Either he truly believed direct current was superior or he was not about to admit that the great Wizard had been wrong. He could have been the personification of direct current, seemingly incapable by his very nature to change direction. He resisted any suggestion that he even consider switching to alternating current. He dismissed out of hand the early efforts of a would-be competitor who recognized alternating current's potential.

"None of his plans worry me in the least," Edison declared in 1886.

Edison saw himself in a far grander struggle with the divine, as evidenced when a lightning storm swept past his headquarters, suddenly illuminating his office.

"That's the opposition!" he exclaimed to Tate, his private secretary.

The merely mortal challenger was Westinghouse, who had started out as an inventor, creating the railroad air brake, without which circus train wrecks would have been even more numerous and severe. Westinghouse had gone on to become more of an entrepreneur and had a particular interest in electricity, no doubt stoked when he paid a visit to Edison's laboratory with an eye toward having a lighting system installed in his mansion. Westinghouse subsequently wrote to Edison saying he had been inspired to develop an engine to go with such a generating system that might be worth marketing. Edison is said to have responded with his usual vehemence to even the suggestion he grant his imprimatur to somebody else's invention, instructing Tate, "Tell Westinghouse to stick to air brakes. He knows all about them. He doesn't know anything about engines."

Westinghouse reportedly declared, "Well, if Edison won't use my engine perhaps I can build dynamos."

Westinghouse decided to go into the electric business himself and bankrolled a few decidedly modest DC systems before deciding he could not possibly compete with Edison's growing monopoly. He turned to AC.

One early skirmish between the predominant DC and the upstart AC came in Great Barrington, Massachusetts, the same year that Edison declared himself unworried. Westinghouse's people began work on a system that would transmit electricity at a relatively high voltage along four thousand feet of copper wire and then employ transformers to step it down to what was needed for incandescent bulbs. The system was all but ready when Edison's people installed and activated a small plant in the home of one of the local gentry just as they had at J. P. Morgan's mansion.

Edison garnered the glory of being the first to light a house in the town but the drawback to DC remained. Westinghouse signed up five times as many customers for his AC system there over the following weeks while claiming the added advantage of being able to set the smoke and noise of his power plant at a remove from homes and businesses.

With his edge, Westinghouse was able to increase his overall business fourfold between 1886 and the following year. Edison's far-flung agents reported that they were being bested everywhere by Westinghouse's marketing force, leaving them in danger of being branded what a great inventor would surely abhor: old-fashioned. Edison grumbled about Westinghouse being not so much an innovator as a marketer, a showman.

"One thing that disturbs me is the fact that Westinghouse is a great man for flooding the country with agents and travelers," Edison complained.

An energetic sales force with a superior product is a formidable business foe, as Edison himself had proven when he introduced electric lighting to replace gas. The desperate gas companies had followed Dan Rice's lead and resorted to trying to frighten the public with the supposed dangers of electricity when in fact gas was generally far more hazardous, killing hundreds every year by fires and asphyxiation. The danger of the established method of lighting was such that hotel rooms in New York had a standard sign reading "Don't blow out the gas."

"The gas was not infrequently blown out with the result that the vital flame of the occupant of the bed also went out a few hours later," noted Tate.

That had not stopped the gas companies from seeking to stoke unreasoning fear. Edison now sought to do much the same—and then some—to Westinghouse with a pamphlet that amounted to an eighty-four-page rat bill. The black lettering on the bright red cover read, "A WARNING FROM THE EDISON ELECTRIC LIGHT COMPANY."

The pages inside began by describing AC systems as both uneconomical and unreliable. A section headed "Danger" further contended that AC systems established by "advocates of cheapness" were inherently dangerous, and not just because the electricity was transmitted at higher voltages than DC.

"Any interruption of the flow of the current adds to its destructive property, whilst its complete reversal, as in the Alternating (Westinghouse) system increases this destructiveness enormously," the pamphlet said with authority but without scientific basis.

The pamphlet cited Professor Henry Smith Carhart of Northwestern University, who was as confident as he was wrong in stating, "It is absolutely certain that quite a powerful current can be taken through the body, provided it be perfectly steady, while a fluctuating current of much smaller intensity may prove fatal."

As an added caution, the pamphlet's "Danger" section was followed by a "Moral" section asking anyone who might consider investing in an AC system "whether he considers it safe to enter into business dealings and relations with men who give public expression to statements which they ought to know to be untrue. That the so-called competitors of the Edison Company have made such statements and do pursue such methods is abundantly evidenced by their own utterances."

The pamphlet ended by declaring a kind of jihad: "All electricians who believe in the future of electricity ought to unite in a war of extermination against cheapness in applied electricity, wherever they see that it involves inefficiency and danger."

And lest there be any doubt about who right-thinking people should support, the pamphlet quoted an Edison-friendly inventor, albeit from three years before, when Westinghouse was not yet a significant factor: "Mr. Edison has led the way by making his supply station in New York a practical undertaking and a commercial success.

If we wish to be successful with the future electric light supply stations in this country, we should act wisely by following in his footsteps."

But those footsteps still could lead no farther than a mile from a DC power plant even if the WARNING were not largely humbug. One actual advantage Edison did have was that the only motors capable of running on AC truly were unreliable and otherwise inferior to those that used DC. Nobody was more keenly aware of this than Westinghouse and nobody could have been more excited to hear that a brilliant Serbian immigrant named Nikola Tesla had designed an AC motor that promised to be superior to any DC counterpart.

Tesla had arrived at Castle Island in 1884 with a letter of introduction from Charles Batchelor, the head of Edison's operations in Europe. Tesla had gone to work for Edison in New York and decided to offer his idea for a revolutionary new motor despite the great inventor's feelings regarding AC.

"He was not interested in alternating current," Tesla later wrote, adding that in Edison's view, "there was no future to it and anyone who dabbled in it was wasting his time."

The problem for Tesla was finding the right opportunity to tell Edison of his breakthrough. The very high-strung Tesla was Edison's opposite on the sensory level, once noting, "I could hear the ticking of a watch with three rooms between me and the time-piece. A fly alighting on a table in the room would cause a dull thud in my ear. A carriage passing at a distance of a few miles fairly shook my whole body. The whistle of a locomotive twenty or thirty miles away made the bench or chair on which I sat vibrate so strongly that the pain was unbearable."

The opportunity finally seemed to present itself in late 1884 after Batchelor returned stateside and took Tesla on a jaunt to meet up with Edison at Coney Island. The seaside resort at the far side of Brooklyn was by then the site of several hotels, the latest of which was then under construction, a 122-foot structure in the shape of the jumbo-est of elephants. The big sensation there that year was the world's first roller coaster, the "switchback railway," opened that June by LaMarcus Thompson, who called himself "The Inventor of Gravity." The two luminaries of electricity were visiting in the off-season and there was little noise to hamper further the hearing-impaired Edison or to jangle the hypersensitive Tesla.

"The moment I was waiting for was propitious," Tesla would remember.

Of course, Edison was not likely to listen even when he could hear, but a chance however slight remained that he might have recognized Tesla's invention as an opportunity to prevail in the War of Currents. And that could have saved Topsy from becoming the one pachyderm more famous on Coney Island than the Elephant Hotel. Tesla was just working up the nerve to speak to Edison about his breakthrough when a man whom the Serb would describe as "a horrible-looking tramp" approached and made a fuss, apparently recognizing the celebrated Wizard. Tesla was jarred and Edison was distracted and the moment passed. Tesla still had not told Edison about his revolutionary motor some days later, when the two had a falling-out over a promised payment.

Much as Forepaugh had pledged to pay Craven if he could train the best elephants around, Edison had promised Tesla $50,000 if he could overhaul the Jumbo generators at his flagship plant on Pearl Street in Manhattan within a certain time. Tesla managed to do as requested, but Edison is reported to have stiffed him just as Forepaugh had Craven.

"Tesla, you don't understand our American humor," Edison supposedly told him.

Tesla set off on his own, working as a laborer for a time while establishing his own laboratory and pressing ahead with his electrical explorations. He was invited to deliver a lecture at the American Institute of Electrical Engineers in New York, which he titled "A New System of Alternate Current Motors and Transformers." The resulting buzz reached Westinghouse, who sought out Tesla and quickly came to the conclusion that the Serb's motor was superior to anything that ran on direct current. Tesla, on his part, found Westinghouse to be a distinct improvement over Edison and many other strivers he had encountered in America.

"Always smiling, affable and polite, he stood in marked contrast to the rough and ready men I met," Telsa later said of his new benefactor. "Not one word which would have been objectionable, not a gesture which might have offended—one could have imagined him as moving in the atmosphere of a court, so perfect was his bearing in manner and speech."

Yet, Tesla soon learned, this perfect gentleman was not always genteel. Telsa noted, "No fiercer adversary than Westinghouse could have been found when he was aroused. An athlete in ordinary life, he was transformed into a giant when confronted with difficulties which seemed unsurmountable [*sic*]. He enjoyed the struggle and never lost confidence. When others would have given up in despair he triumphed."

Edison said of Westinghouse, "The man has gone crazy over sudden accession of wealth or something unknown to me, and is flying a kite that will land in the mud sooner or later." And Edison dismissed Tesla as "a poet of science . . . magnificent but utterly impractical."

Even so, Edison must have understood the implications of Westinghouse acquiring the new motor. Alternating current's practical advantage was already proving to outweigh any safety concerns that Edison had managed to arouse with his WARNING pamphlet.

And under Edison's mask of unconcern there was a growing desperation and a willingness to compromise his most decent impulses for the sake of besting his rival. The proof was in an exchange of letters with a Buffalo dentist.

Back in 1881, a drunk had managed to electrocute himself after ignoring a guard's warnings to stay away from a Brush company arc light generator in Buffalo. Local dentist Alfred Porter Southwick is variously reported to have either witnessed the death or simply studied the autopsy results. He in any event declared that the drunk's demise must have been lightning quick, so fast as to be virtually painless.

Southwick then undertook a series of private experiments, electrocuting stray dogs in the name of progress and humanity. He offered his services to the City of Buffalo after a burgeoning stray population prompted it to offer a twenty-five-cent bounty for every cur, and it suddenly had many more than the pound could handle. He dispatched twenty-eight dogs using a zinc-lined wood box, with one electric wire running to an inch of water at the bottom, the other to a metal muzzle. The method was deemed more humane than the usual shooting and more efficient than the "lethal box" in which the Philadelphia branch of the ASPCA administered carbon monoxide.

Southwick thereupon decided that a variation would work just as well on his own species. He convinced a friend in the New York State legislature to introduce a measure establishing a commission to examine alternatives to hanging.

One of the commission's three members was Southwick himself. Another was Matthew Hale, grandson of Nathan Hale, who was said to have uttered the famous words "I only regret I have but one life to lose for my country" before the British hanged him as a spy during the Revolutionary War. The third and most prominent member was

Elbridge T. Gerry, grandson and namesake of a signer of the Declaration of Independence. Gerry was legal counsel to the ASPCA and had joined Henry Bergh in cofounding the New York Society for the Prevention of Cruelty to Children.

The mandate of the new commission was to "investigate and report the most humane and practical method of carrying into effect the sentence of death in capital cases." It began by diligently cataloging the various methods of execution down through history:

> Beating with clubs, beheading, blowing from a cannon, boiling, breaking on the wheel, burning, burying alive, crucifixion, defenestration, dichotomy—i.e., cutting into two parts, dismemberment, drowning, exposure to wild beasts (especially serpent's fangs), flaying alive, flogging, garrote, guillotine, hanging, hari kari, impalement, iron maiden, peine forte et dure—i.e., placing a heavy weight on the chest, which gradually reduces breathing, pounding in mortar (Proverbs 27:22), precipitation—from a lofty precipice, pressing to death, rack, running the gauntlet, shooting, stabbing, stoning or lapidation, strangling and suffocation.

Hale concurred with Southwick that electrocution was the best method, but Gerry of both the ASPCA and the SPCC leaned toward lethal injection with morphine. Southwick wrote to Thomas Edison in November of 1887, ostensibly seeking his opinion regarding "the necessary strength of current to guarantee death with a certainty in all cases and under all circumstance." He also solicited Edison's thoughts regarding the best way to administer this fatal shock.

"My own opinion has been that a chair constructed for the purpose with metal arms to which the wires were attached passing the current across the chest would be all sufficient," Southwick wrote.

Southwick's real hope in writing almost certainly was that advice from Edison would constitute an endorsement and that the de facto backing of the famous Wizard of Menlo Park would sway Gerry. But Edison replied that he had long opposed capital punishment, believing that the state should not punish killing by killing and that life behind bars was no less a deterrent.

The response did not deter Southwick from sending a second letter a month later, saying that "science and civilization demand some more humane method than the rope." Southwick fancied himself a man of modern science and was appealing to Edison as one of its deities. He was also—either knowingly or not—allowing Edison to rationalize going against a long-held and oft-stated belief.

Edison wrote back that while he would welcome any effort "to totally abolish capital punishment," he also felt that so long as it was administered, the state was indeed obligated to employ "the most humane method available."

"The best appliance in this connection is, to my mind, the one which will perform its work in the shortest space of time, and inflict the least amount of suffering upon its victim," Edison wrote. "This, I believe, can be accomplished by the use of electricity."

Edison went on, more transparent than he likely imagined as to his real motive for reconsidering his initial response to Southwick.

"The most suitable apparatus for the purpose is that class of dynamo-electric machinery which employs intermittent currents. The most effective of these are known as 'alternating machines,' manufactured principally in this country by George Westinghouse."

Edison was contriving to slow his foe's sales with a show.

Not even a circus with a real baby elephant aroused public interest like an execution. These gruesome spectacles had ended officially in

New York with the 1826 hanging of murderer Jesse Strang, who used his last moments to urge the thirty thousand spectators to purchase a pamphlet he had published about his crime. But the citizenry still continued to come by the thousands on just the chance of being admitted as a witness or catching even a glimpse of a hanging.

The Forepaugh circus visited the small upstate New York town of Fonda in 1883 on a fine day with Topsy and Bolivar and the other performing elephants, yet did only middling business. The 1878 hanging of Sam Steenburgh in Fonda drew more than fifteen thousand gawkers of both sexes and all ages even though it was held behind a high fence. Three special trains ran. Surrounding buildings nailed cleats to their pitched roofs so people could watch at one dollar a head as Steenburgh, a black man known as Nigger Sam, was put to death for killing a white farmer.

"All of the places afforded an excellent view of the scene of execution," the *New York Times* reported on its front page.

The *Times* further noted, "Acres of space were blackened with people. . . . Stands have been erected for the sale of sundaes, gingerbread, chewing gum and soda pop."

The enterprising sheriff and town clerk had paid the condemned one hundred dollars to write a supposed confession to seven murders, six of which he almost certainly did not commit. They almost lost their investment when Steenburgh twice attempted suicide the night before he was to be hung, once with a knife, once by biting into his wrist. Steenburgh survived and, on the morning of the execution, young boys went through the crowds selling twenty-five-cent copies of his "confessions."

As gawkers clambered up every tree and pole and a violinist played "The Sweet By and By," the big moment came and went. The body was placed in an open coffin afterward for public viewing in the execution yard. The corpse seemed to elicit a more primal fascination than even the greatest circus attraction.

"Men and women, boys and girls, the very aged and the very young fought and swore in the narrow entrance and trampled over each other in their efforts to be first," the *Times* reported.

An electrocution was almost certain to be held behind prison walls where no rooftop or tree would afford a view, but there seemed sure to be frenzied popular interest in an entirely new and modern means of administering the ultimate sanction. And, as two of Edison's advisers proposed, a publicist could make Mr. Westinghouse the lexiconic equivalent of Dr. Guillotin, with people speaking of a condemned criminal being strapped into the Westinghouse and being Westinghoused. Surely the public would not want that same deadly current in the home.

The new method of execution was recommended by the special commission, thanks to Edison's second letter to Southwick, which was attached to its final report to the New York State Legislature. Just as the dentist had hoped, the missive from the Wizard had convinced Gerry, the commission's blue-blood chairman. Gerry was asked during a subsequent hearing on the matter if he regarded Edison as "some sort of an oracle."

"He knows more about electricity than any other living man," Gerry replied.

"How did you come to consider [electrocution] as a means of inflicting capital punishment?" he was asked. "You never heard of its use for such a purpose by any other nation on the face of the globe, did you?"

"One of my colleagues, Mr. Southwick, who had carefully examined the subject, suggested it," Gerry replied.

Gerry's eminent opinion persuaded the legislature along with the governor. The Electrical Execution Act, largely written by Gerry, became law in June of 1888. The measure replaced hanging with electricity as the sole method of execution in New York State, though to Edison's disappointment it did not specify which type of current was to be employed.

Elephants in an Asian forest such as where Topsy thudded from womb to earth, circa the time of her birth.

A captured baby elephant, Sri Lanka, around the time of Topsy's capture.

Hachaliah Bailey's monument to Old Bet, the second elephant in America and the first to meet a violent end.

The Elephant Hotel, once headquarters of the circus in America, home of the Flatfoots.

P.T. Barnum, the one and only.

The Barnum Museum, with the world famous Egress.

Tom Thumb, giant attraction, so small he was huge.

Poster for the Greatest Show on Earth on its way to actual greatness.

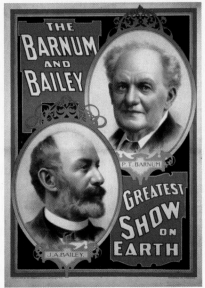

Barnum and Bailey were the bosses, but without the elephants, the showmen could not have boasted of having the greatest show.

Barnum and Bailey — a partnership forged after the first viable birth of an elephant in America.

A bigger draw than an execution. The Forepaugh elephants take to the water in 1898 before a crowd of 35,000.

The circus would arrive and up would spring a canvas realm where the laboring multitude could escape into the exotic and the fabulous.

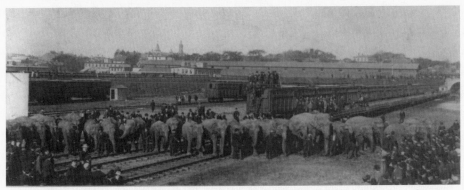

Jolted, jangled, and jarred, the lot of the elephants of any railroad circus, this one the upstart Ringling Bros., 1907.

The Peerless Prodigies of Physical Phenomena!

Jumbo and his keeper, partners in many a libation.

The great Jumbo has fallen.

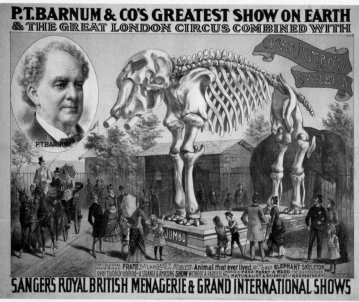

Jumbo still selling tickets in death; his bones on display.

Stewart Craven, the elephant whisperer.

Adam Forepaugh, of the crooked tale as well as Topsy's crooked tail.

Addie Forepaugh, the Crown Prince.

Mother Hebe and the first viable American-born baby elephant.

Topsy, the character who "just grow'd" and gave the baby elephant her name.

The Forepaugh & Sells Bros., keeper of Topsy's last herd, *marital, musical, clown, boxing, athletic, quadrille, polite, bicycling, equilibristic, aldermanic, mimicking, juggling, posing, mirthful elephants.*

Under the Big Top, *home of mastodonic merit in disparate droves.*

New York greets "The Glorious Paragon of All Parades."

The Fearless Frogman in action.

The Wizard in his laboratory.

Tesla, genius and lover of pigeons.

George Westinghouse, exactly himself.

Edison's electric light parade down Madison Avenue.

The electric chair, which Edison hoped would also bring the demise of Westinghouse's ambitions.

The Elephant Colossus, Coney Island: a hotel with a fabulous trunk room, then a bazaar, finally a brothel.

An elephant giving a ride at Luna Park — what was to have been Topsy's job.

The entrance to Luna Park, "The Heart of Coney Island." The elephants at Luna Park were only wonderful until they were taken to a particular deserted spot.

Bill Snyder, trainer and hater of the ill-fated Sid, with Hattie at the elephant quarters in Central Park.

Topsy's final moment, the smoke rising from the electrodes attached to her feet.

THE EXECUTIONER'S
EXPERIMENTS

A young man seeking to ingratiate himself with Edison could have done no better than did Harold Brown with his June 5, 1888, letter to the editor of the *New York Post* cautioning against the dangers of alternating current and extolling the relative safety of direct current.

"The alternating current can be described by no adjective less forceful than damnable," Brown wrote in this letter published one day after electricity became New York's official means of execution. "The only excuse for the use of the fatal alternating current is that it saves the company operating it from spending a larger sum of money for the heavier copper wires which are required by the safe incandescent systems."

Whether or not Brown was already doing Edison's bidding, Westinghouse recognized the letter as an intensification of the War of Currents. Westinghouse wrote to Edison from his home base in Pittsburgh two days later with what was essentially a peace proposal.

"I believe there has been a systematic attempt on the part of some people to do a great deal of mischief and create as great a difference as possible between the Edison Company and the Westinghouse Electrical Company when there ought to be an entirely different condition of affairs," Westinghouse wrote.

Westinghouse recalled visiting Edison's laboratory as a potential customer and now invited him as a colleague to visit his own facilities in Pittsburgh. Edison declined.

"My laboratory work consumes the whole of my time," he wrote back. "Thanking you for your kind invitation."

Edison made an invitation of his own, this to Brown. The Wizard allowed Brown to make full use of the facilities in his huge new laboratory in West Orange, New Jersey, to conduct animal experiments similar to Southwick's with the purpose of "proving" the great hazard of alternating current. Signs went up in the neighbored around Edison's lab offering twenty-five cents for stray dogs, the same bounty that had been posted in Buffalo.

Brown subsequently reported in the journal the *Electrical World* on twenty-seven experiments beginning at 10:06 p.m., July 10, 1888.

First Experiment Dog No. 1. Old black and tan bitch; low vitality; weight not taken (about ten lbs.) . . . Connection made through roll of wet cotton waste, held in place by wrappings of bare copper wire; continuous current used eight hundred volts . . . two seconds . . . Behavior of dog: Howled vigorously and made violent effort to escape, showing that it had control of muscles and that nerve functions were not destroyed. Howled loudest as circuit was broken. Continued howling and rushing about for two and a half minutes after circuit was opened, then dropped upon its side. Pulsation of heart detected until 10:21 p.m.

And then:

Second Experiment. Dog No. 2. Large half-bred St. Bernard puppy; strong and in good condition. Weight not taken (about twenty lbs.) . . . Connections made as above . . . Continuous current used . . . 290 volts . . . two seconds. Behavior of dog: Howled during time of contact and tried to escape. Easily quieted and entirely uninjured.

And then:

Third Experiment. Same dog as second experiment. Same connections. Alternating current used by introducing a circuit breaker and alternator in circuit with the dog . . . two seconds . . . Behavior of dog: Was made perfectly rigid during time of contact, unable to howl or move until current was broken, then howled and made feeble efforts to escape. Continued whining.

And then:

Fourth Experiment. Same dog and same connections. Alternating current as in previous trial . . . 800 volts . . . three seconds . . . Behavior of dog: Was turned into rigid mass during contact, no motion or tremor visible; at opening of circuit it fell with all muscles limp, howled faintly with a single expulsion of breath and died.

On it went for dog after dog. The eighth dog was hit with one thousand volts of continuous, or direct, current and Brown noted, "Dog howled and struggled violently for two minutes, then apparently died. Dog immediately dissected . . . Heart found still pulsating . . . Artificial respiration would have saved its life if resorted to immediately after moment of apparent death."

The ninth subject, a "strong and vigorous" bulldog, was hit with eight hundred volts of alternating current. Brown noted, "Dog was placed in wooden box to prevent accident in case he broke loose; slats were nailed across top of box, but these were unnecessary, as during time of contact the dog was apparently turned to stone."

The last five experiments were all on the same red setter, which was left "panting violently and perspiring copiously. Evidently dying, but to put him out of pain it was decided to give higher voltage . . . Dog died without noise or struggle."

What exactly the experiments demonstrated was not immediately clear. They were intended in part to support Brown's contention to the New York Electrical Control Board that alternating current should be restricted to less than three hundred volts. This happened to be considerably less than the voltage needed for alternating current to achieve the ease of transmission that was its great advantage over direct current.

Westinghouse refrained from conducting experiments that would have disproved his rival's contention that alternating current was inherently more deadly because the current's "impulses are given first in one direction, then in the other several thousand times a minute." He instead countered with his own letter to the editor, this to the *New York Times* and sticking largely to fact:

> It is generally understood that Harold P. Brown is conducting these experiments in the interest and pay of the Edison Electric Light Company; that the Edison Company's business can be vitally injured if the alternating current apparatus continues to be successfully introduced

and operated as it has heretofore been; and that the Edison represen-
tatives from a business point of view consider themselves justified in
resorting to any expedient to prevent the extension of this system.

Westinghouse went on, "We have no hesitation in charging that
the object of these experiments is not in the interest of science or
safety, but to endeavor to create in the mind of the public a prejudice
against the use of the alternating currents."

Westinghouse noted that the Edison Company reported expanding
its systems by forty-four thousand lights for the first three quarters
of 1888, while Westinghouse had expanded by forty-eight thousand
in the month of October alone.

Westinghouse ended by offering to send to the newspaper an impartial expert. Brown responded with a letter disputing all Westinghouse's
assertions and emphatically denying he had ever been in Edison's
employ. Brown proposed a kind of electro-duel.

"I therefore challenge Mr. Westinghouse to meet me in the presence of competent electrical experts and take through his body the
alternating current, while I take through mine a continuous current,"
Brown wrote.

Brown said they could start at one hundred volts and increase by
fifty-volt increments.

"Until either one or the other has cried enough and publicly admits
his error."

Westinghouse did not dignify the challenge with a response. Brown
conducted more experiments for the benefit of a special committee
established to determine precisely how the new method of execution
should be applied. One dog showed remarkable resistance, suffering
repeated excruciating shocks until one of the attendants could bear
it no longer and picked up the poor pooch, declaring that he was

adopting it. He named it Ajax, after the hero of Greek mythology, who was said to have defied lightning.

The supply of strays was dwindling, and Edison wrote to Henry Bergh of the ASPCA. Bergh had written to Edison some months before to ask the inventor's view about Buffalo's use of electricity to kill strays. Edison now asked Bergh to supply him with "some good-sized animals," ostensibly for experiments seeking to determine the minimum voltage required for the purpose.

Bergh may have been humbugged by Barnum into abetting the suffering of elephants but he correctly recognized that efforts to determine the least amount of electricity needed to kill an animal would necessarily inflict considerable suffering. He refused, noting that the ASPCA's goal was "instantaneous and merciful death" in every instance.

Bergh asserted that same principle when Brown and Edison's chief electrical expert mounted a public demonstration of their experiments at Columbia College. A dog was subjected to a series of painful shocks before finally being dispatched by five hundred volts of alternating current that elicited what were described as "pitiful moans." Another dog was being wired up when the ASPCA intervened and shut down the event, saying that if such tests were indeed required, they should be conducted by impartial scientists of a respected institution, not in "the interests of rival inventors."

Edison's "experiments" continued on a total of forty-four dogs that he managed to acquire. Bergh ceased to be a factor when he fell fatally ill during the big blizzard in March of 1888. The snow was so deep it was up to the hubs of the hearse's wheels as it bore Bergh's remains to St. Mark's Church in lower Manhattan, but Barnum still managed to arrive from Bridgeport and be prominent among the mourners.

He sent a big wreath despite Bergh's instructions that his funeral be kept simple.

Gerry was a pallbearer. Atop the coffin was a framed photo of a St. Bernard, though certainly not the one that had died in torment at Edison's lab.

Doubters had noted that a dog weighed considerably less than a human, and on another day Gerry traveled with the special committee to Edison's lab to witness a demonstration on larger animals, the Wizard himself presiding. Gerry was surely aware of Bergh's refusal to supply Edison with strays, but he apparently accepted these experiments as justifiable in the name of finding a more humane way of dispatching humans. Only alternating current was employed, first on two calves, one 124.5 pounds, the other 145 pounds. Both were quickly killed, the electrodes placed on the forehead and the middle of the spine.

"The meat was pronounced fit for food," the *New York Times* reported.

Next came a 1,230-pound horse, for which Edison had paid ten dollars, plus another dollar to have it led from Newark to his lab. Edison instructed that this time electrodes—which were wrapped in cloth soaked in saltwater—should be affixed to the subject's forelegs, on the theory that the electricity would travel from point to point through the chest. The horse did not react to the administration of six hundred volts, and the technicians checked the delivery system for a defective part. The second try produced no visible result other than steam curling up from the electrodes. The third try went up to seven hundred volts for twenty-five seconds. The horse pitched over dead and an "after" photo was taken to be paired with a "before" photo that documented the animal had been in good health.

Edison was left wondering if part of the problem was that bones such as in the forelegs are not good conductors. He nonetheless felt affirmed in his belief that routing the electricity through the body from one extremity to the other was most effective. He must have been delighted by the conclusion offered by the *Times*.

"The experiments proved the alternating current to be the most deadly force known to science, and that less than half the pressure used in this city for electric lighting by this system is sufficient to cause instant death. After Jan. 1 the alternating current will undoubtedly drive the hangmen out of business in this State."

An opportunity to cap off the "Westinghousing" experiments with one of the biggest of land creatures came in the form of an elephant named Chief. The owner was none other than Adam Forepaugh, who had once been as fierce a competitor in his own field as either Edison or Westinghouse. But Forepaugh seemed to have suffered a loss of competitive drive and even a general weakening of the will since his supposed victory over his rival at Madison Square Garden.

The elder Forepaugh may have indeed partaken of the Tree of Knowledge and realized that Barnum was still the great Barnum and that Forepaugh was still just Forepaugh, that it would always be so. Forepaugh could and did often draw more customers, but they generally remained of a rough sort while Barnum was still considered the class of the field, the "Sunday school show."

Perhaps, too, the elder Forepaugh was simply aging and growing weary of the road. That is what he had told his rival when the Forepaugh show passed through Bridgeport in June of 1888. The arrival of Forepaugh in Barnum's hometown initially appeared to be the direct personal challenge, a breach of the at least ostensible peace the two showmen had brokered at the time of the Madison Square Garden dual appearance. Barnum responded in his usual style, by cheerfully welcoming his rival. He made a full report in a private letter the next day to James Bailey, the partner who now handled the business end as well as day-to-day operations and was on the road with the Barnum show.

"Forepaugh seemed friendly. He will immediately stop the bills calling his 'The Greatest Show on Earth' & he says if we ever see anything wrong, he will stop it if we let him know it."

That had been surprising enough. Forepaugh had gone on to suggest he had lost faith in a son who was turning out to be more of a liability than a legacy.

"Forepaugh said when I first saw him yesterday a.m. he had directed in his will to have the show sold out when he dies."

At a second encounter with Barnum that day, Forepaugh had taken the notion a step further, suggesting he might be willing to partially sell out prior to his demise via an arrangement by which the two shows would be combined into a single entity that would then sell shares, as was the new American way of corporations.

"In the afternoon, he said, 'You and Bailey can get a million and a half of dollars or more by making the two shows in a stock company of $3,000,000 of capital.'"

Barnum reported to Bailey that Forepaugh had expressed a desire to remain involved in hiring performers, but would stay out of the business itself and "never touch a cent of money." Forepaugh had argued that a single administration would cut overhead and eliminate the need to offer competitive wages.

As for the present Forepaugh show, Barnum wrote to his partner that it had been "crammed yesterday afternoon & night. . . . He don't cater for the genteel & refined class & he don't get them, but he pleases the masses."

Forepaugh still had a Wild West show, and some customers did offer a complaint.

"The hundreds of shots by Indians and cowboys took place at the opening of the show, so the tent is so full of smoke for the first half hour that persons can't see from one ring to the other," Barnum wrote.

Barnum said he had told Forepaugh that any deal would have to meet with Bailey's approval. Forepaugh had replied that there should be no hurry in telling Bailey.

"[Forepaugh] says he likes you, knows you are an honest man & he will come & see us in the winter & thought I had better not mention it to you till then," Barnum further reported.

However Forepaugh really felt about Bailey, any regard was not mutual. Bailey's response to Forepaugh's proposal was immediate and emphatically negative. Barnum was not above trying to humbug his own partner and wrote back three days after the first letter, "I hope you did not think because I wrote you about 4-PAW'S desire to form a stock company that I favored such an idea. Far from it."

In truth, Barnum was so intrigued by the proposition that he could not just let it go. He wrote Bailey again toward the end of August to say, "I continually feel that somehow we ought to have two shows, one east and the other west & this can only be done successfully by absorbing Forepaugh's show. He is really getting more public recognition and making more and more money each year. . . . And this strengthens his name and compels us to keep up a too-expensive show."

Barnum went on to suggest a domestic factor in Forepaugh's desire to quit the road.

"Forepaugh's wife is young & wants him to stop traveling personally. He dare not trust it to his son."

Barnum made a proposal to Bailey.

"Now, perhaps if we give Forepaugh to understand that we intend to start 2 shows, he may be induced to put his son, his name & his show property into a stock company with ours, he taking say one quarter and we 3 quarters of the whole stock."

Forepaugh and his son would, of course, have to sign a paper guaranteeing they would "never again let their names be used by another enterprise." Forepaugh would be allowed to have an accountant travel with the show and keep an eye on the proceeds.

"Old Adam shall privately advise, consult, aid in buying horses or in any manner that might benefit the company, but shall not travel with it."

Barnum was doing his best to sell his partner on the idea, saying they would have "a complete monopoly which nobody would ever dare to assail." He suggested, "Then the new company could gradually establish museums and do anything else to give it strength & profit for generations."

That word "generations" suggested Barnum's ultimate goal. Forepaugh had crowed that he had a son to carry on his show, but that son had grown into a vain, profligate, and notoriously unreliable dandy who could not be entrusted with anybody's legacy. Barnum indeed had no son, but he did have a company bearing his name, a company that he envisioned still thriving when the great-grandchildren of the present audience filled the stands.

The problem was that Bailey still wanted nothing to do with Forepaugh. Barnum warned that others were certain to seize the opportunity if they did not.

"I don't like Forepaugh any better than you do," Barnum wrote, "but he is a stubborn old chap with considerable horse sense, and his show is a continual annoyance and injury to us—and also a *menace,* for in his anxiety to stop traveling personally he is almost sure to get showmen of capital to buy a share of his show."

There remained the question of young Forepaugh.

"His son, Adam, Jr., of course has his faults, but if he is managed by us he can be useful as a trainer of animals & a performer. Old Adam is determined to keep his son in the business, so if we can keep his claws cut and have him interested in making the show attractive and successful, we thus 'chain' the young tiger."

Here would be a showman's ultimate revenge: to control Forepaugh's son as if he were one of the beasts.

Bailey remained unconvinced, though as far as Forepaugh apparently knew the idea had not yet been formally presented to him. Forepaugh's hopes for a positive outcome could only have grown as he ended the 1888 season reporting record profits.

Forepaugh did encounter several setbacks, such as when the show suffered yet another major train wreck and when some pranksters fed apples stuffed with tobacco and cayenne pepper to Tip as he was being unloaded for a show. Tip had the predictable reaction in the confined space of the railroad car, crushing to death a new elephant trainer who had been hired to "assist" young Forepaugh.

More elephant trouble came as the show was arriving at its winter quarters in Philadelphia. The other animals were all off the train and caged when the younger Forepaugh gave the order to unload the two biggest elephants, Chief and Bolivar. Chief had been in an "ugly mood" of late, and had been riding chained to Bolivar to reduce both his ability to act up and his chances of escaping. Chief's disposition was not improved when his minders opened the railroad car door and sought to begin the unloading with what a reporter for the *Evening Press* called "a touch of the hook."

"Chief's eyes shot forth glares of fire and a roaring noise could be heard squares away," the reporter noted.

The minders sent for as many men as could be summoned as back-up. Chief swung his trunk and tugged at his double-linked chains as the minders sought to subdue him in a traditional way.

"The spear was applied without effect," the reporter observed.

The men waited for half an hour until Chief quieted. They began leading Bolivar and therefore Chief down a ramp that went directly into the main building. They resumed their traditional approach to encouragement, "sticking hooks in Chief's body through the car openings," the reporter noted.

Chief grew only wilder on reaching solid ground, managing to loosen the chain on his right foreleg.

"He seemed determined to escape, being aided by Bolivar, who turned troublesome," the reporter wrote.

Chief used his free leg to keep away men who sought to chain him to posts in the ground. Young Forepaugh continued with his usual approach.

"Mr. Forepaugh tried to bring Chief to bay by prodding him, but it all proved useless."

Employees who had gathered to watch began to flee even as crowds of civilians were drawn to the scene from blocks away by the trumpeting. The doors to the building were barricaded. Chief continued tugging at his fetters until he was free of Bolivar. Nobody had been injured but a good many people had been terrorized, including a squad of policemen who immediately volunteered to assist when young Forepaugh announced that the time had come to put an immediate end to it. They were joined by a number of cowboys from the show. Ten marksmen in all were armed with breech-loading rifles, likely the same ones used in the reenactments of Custer's Last Stand, only with live rounds. The building no doubt filled with gun smoke as the bullets smacked into Chief.

"At first they had no more effect than if paper balls were fired at him. Instead of quieting the beast they only enraged him the more and he tore up everything in his path."

The gunfire and Chief's bellowing incited the lions, tigers, and other animals into a roaring, screeching frenzy.

"For a time it was thought a genuine panic could not be averted."

The rifles kept firing and finally Chief went down, blood streaming from at least twenty-five bullet wounds. The men hurried to chain him to the ground.

"Nearly every part of his huge frame was punctured. . . . It was believed that he could not survive his wounds."

Yet survive he did and soon he was back on his feet. The elder Forepaugh certainly did not want any trouble to complicate his chances of achieving the merger and he had even more elephants on his hands, a total of thirty-six, after the Robbins show went bust and returned the six leased ones to him. These included the well-behaved but personally maddening Topsy as well as two persistently troublesome males, Gold Dust and Charley.

And the elder Forepaugh was weary enough of the circus life without the prospect of more aggravation from Chief during what should have been a respite.

"Owing to his growing viciousness, it was determined to kill him," the *Hartford Weekly Times* reported.

Forepaugh declared that Chief would be dispatched by a method that was being touted in the press as the most modern and humane, be it for man or beast.

"It was then decided that Chief should be killed by an electric shock."

*   *   *

Edison made clear that he welcomed the chance to provide via a five-ton elephant the ultimate demonstration of what he and Brown termed "the executioner's current." But the famously "ugly" Chief could not just be walked into the lab and wired up like some stray dog. Arrangements to do the deed at Forepaugh's winter quarters promised to take a fortnight and Chief was already growing so restless in his chains that his tenders became alarmed and alerted Addie Forepaugh.

"Word was sent to young Forepaugh who, taking in the situation at a glance, determined that Chief was set upon mischief," the *Hartford Weekly Times* reported.

Young Forepaugh declared that there was no time to wait for Edison, that Chief had to be dispatched immediately, before the beast could cause any more trouble. Basil and Bismarck were brought over from among the other elephants and positioned on either side of the condemned. Chief was not such a real and imminent threat that Adam hesitated to climb atop him and loop a fifteen-foot length of what was variously reported as either inch- or half-inch-thick rope around his neck.

"In the soft flesh behind the ears," the newspaper noted.

Even with such little notice, there was "a good-sized but quiet crowd," interestingly more subdued than at the typical execution of one of their own species. The ends of the rope were tied to chains, which then were affixed to Basil and Bismarck, who had been harnessed as if they were going to pull a wagon. Adam called out the command and Basil and Bismarck were prodded in opposite directions with elephant hooks. What was called "the death line" went taut.

"As the noose tightened, Chief's mouth flew open, his trunk shot out straight as yardstick and then, without the proverbial thud as of sheriff's gallows, the great elephant dropped in a heap," the newspaper reported.

There were no reports as to the effect on Basil and Bismarck. Elephants in the wild will surround a fallen member of the herd and stroke the body with the ends of their trunks, sometimes casting leaves and twigs in what appears to be a kind of burial ritual. They are known to return to the spot even years later, touching the bones as they sometimes touch each other in life.

In what was becoming a pattern for "ugly" elephants, newspaper reports greatly exaggerated Chief's "crimes," calling him variously "the murderer of seven men" and "killer of eleven men" and "the most vicious elephant in America," when he likely killed not even one. His demise was correctly described as "a death unlike any of its species had ever suffered," but it was still not the one that a good number of people had hoped to witness and Edison had hoped to administer.

"Many who saw or heard of the experiments made with alternating electrical light currents at the Edison laboratory, to find a substitute for hanging, will regret that the big elephant Chief, of Forepaugh's circus, sentenced to death for his viciousness, could not have been experimented with, as was promised," *Scientific American* said. "Just where the electrodes should have been placed would have been an interesting study. . . . Would the 3,000 volts current, which, we are told, will surely kill a man—they have been killed with far less than this—be enough to dull the consciousness of an elephant and then kill? It seems the circus people could not wait for the elaborate preparations necessary."

The *Electrical World* sighed, "Quite a little disappointment was caused to those who had expected to witness the killing of Forepaugh's vicious elephant 'Chief' by electricity."

Nobody could have been more disappointed than Edison, but it was reported in the *British Veterinary Journal* that "another large and vicious elephant," a "fierce brute of the Robinson's circus," was soon "to be made to serve the ends of science, by being made the test for the new system of death by electricity." The journal noted that Edison and Gerry of the capital punishment commission and the SPCA "have been experimenting this week at Edison's laboratory, to discover what amount of electric current is necessary to cause instant death."

Edison was again disappointed when the relatively small circus called the John Robinson Show changed its plans and simply donated its "fierce brute," who also happened to be named Chief, to the Cincinnati Zoo. The show, which had once punished the elephant by lowering it into a bonfire with block and tackle, now not only saved itself the bother of killing the elephant and disposing of the mountainous remains, but garnered bounteous good publicity for its supposed generosity. The move did nothing to improve this other Chief's temperament and the zoo did end up shooting the elephant to death, but that was not Robinson's problem and nobody seemed to blame the show.

The elder Forepaugh decided to follow the Robinson Show's example in ridding himself of other elephants who were periodically difficult to control, perpetually expensive to maintain, and, by his overall estimation, far more trouble than they were worth.

On December 25, 1888, Forepaugh made a Christmas present of the great Bolivar to the Philadelphia Zoo. The elephant who had shown such an unusual attachment to Topsy may have made a monumental fuss if he had known he was being led away from her for good. Bolivar arrived at his new home in a procession headed by young Forepaugh in a carriage.

"Bolivar traveled to his new home in a great state," the local press announced.

Bolivar was exalted as a magnificent addition to the city. The public reaction and the attendant publicity were so positive that Forepaugh announced he would be marking the New Year by further demonstrating his magnanimity.

Having presented the Zoological Society of Philadelphia, (my native city) with Bolivar, the largest living elephant as a Christmas gift, and feeling that I should like to present the Department of Public Parks of New York City with an elephant as a New Year's gift, I now take great pleasure in offering you Tip, the second largest of the celebrated Forepaugh herd of elephants, and one of the finest in captivity. Trusting my offer will meet with your approval and awaiting your reply, I am your obedient servant.

Adam Forepaugh
Proprietor
Forepaugh Show

The city accepted enthusiastically and on New Year's morning, 1889, young Forepaugh arrived at the Pavonia Ferry in Jersey City with Tip chained to the much smaller Jennie, who was described by one reporter as an "anchor," but who in fact led the way as the senior female. The ferryman was not at all sure what to charge for two elephants, but settled for ten dollars.

Three carriage loads of VIPs and a crowd of more than a thousand were waiting to welcome the elephant at the foot of East Twenty-third Street in Manhattan. The procession started up Tenth Avenue, Tip wearing a red blanket that announced in outsized letters, "ADAM FOREPAUGH'S GIFT TO NEW YORK CITY."

An ever-growing number of people followed, becoming what the *Times* described as "such a crowd as only the west side tenement districts could furnish." The count at East Thirty-ninth Street was three thousand, "2,000 of whom were shouting, running, and more or less dirty and ragged small boys."

The elephants set a brisk pace as they were led across town to tony Fifth Avenue.

"Then a scene occurred which will live long in the minds of the residents of that fashionable thoroughfare. . . . The advent of the two elephants and the horde of west side followers created considerable consternation. The masses have no respect for the classes and, as in this case, the masses were all moving in one direction."

The well-to-do had a choice few of them savored.

"Dignified matrons held up their hands in horror at the intrusion upon their favorite drive; promenading belles looked appealingly to their swell escorts, who looked back bewildered, but all had to make way by either turning down the side streets or going with the crowd. Probably Fifth Avenue never had such a shaking up."

Another crowd was waiting by the East Sixty-fifth Street entrance to Central Park. A captive American eagle screeched with what one reporter deemed to be envy as the elephants were photographed in the courtyard outside the zoo's executive office.

Young Forepaugh formally presented Tip to the city, pointing out the elephant's "fine points," including the two four-foot tusks, surprising intelligence, and a kind and docile nature so long as only one person sought to command him.

"He said that an elephant would obey but one master," the *Times* reported.

The head of the city parks commission, J. Hampden Robb, thanked the Forepaugh son and the absent father profusely on behalf of the city and pledged that Tip would always receive the very best of care.

SEVENTEEN

THE CHAIR

That same New Year's Day, the New York State Electrical Execution Act took effect. Harold Brown met with state prison officials and secured a contract to build three electric chairs and provide the necessary generators. He sought to bill the state $1,000 for the animal experiments, but the officials refused. The new mode of capital punishment was itself still so experimental that the contract allowed no payment at all until the equipment had been installed and then only half. The rest would be paid "upon the satisfactory and successful operation of said apparatus, at the execution of a person sentenced to death."

Brown was left short of the necessary funds to build even one chair and secure the required equipment. He went to the Edison Company for $5,000 only to be told that he would have to make his request directly to the great man himself. Brown apparently took this to mean that Edison needed convincing, when it was more likely an early sign of dissension between Edison and some of those who ran the business end of his company about the wisdom of this War of Currents. Brown wrote to Edison seeking the funds, suggesting that such a dramatic demonstration of the deadliness of alternating current was sure to inspire state authorities to outlaw its use beyond the prison walls.

"Do you not think it worth doing, as it will enable me, through the Board of Health, to shut off the alternating current circuits in the State?" Brown wrote.

Edison probably needed no convincing. He provided the $5,000, reminding Brown that only a Westinghouse dynamo should be employed in any executions. The Westinghouse forces were actively seeking to prevent Brown from obtaining one, but he was finally successful with covert assistance from Charles Coffin, a former shoe manufacturer who now ran the number-three electric firm, Thomson-Houston.

Coffin's company was an unlikely ally, as it also pegged its future largely on alternating current. By one account, Brown essentially resorted to extortion, threatening to use Thomson-Houston generators unless Coffin helped Brown acquire several from Westinghouse. Another account holds that Coffin had given up hope of prevailing over Westinghouse. Coffin was said to have at one point suggested to Westinghouse a financial scheme whereby they would both personally make money no matter how their companies fared. Westinghouse rebuffed him, saying he was "not in the habit of robbing my stockholders." Westinghouse was also said to have rebuffed Coffin's proposal that their companies merge.

"Coffin will make a man about ten different propositions in ten minutes," Westinghouse was quoted saying.

Whether as shakedown victim or as conniver or perhaps as both, Coffin now entered into a deal with Brown and managed to obtain a Westinghouse dynamo. An Edison engineer named Arthur Kennelly joined Brown in designing a wooden chair equipped with restraining straps, a metal skullcap for one electrode, and a slot in the back for a second. The criminal justice system provided a condemned man in the person of William Kemmler, who was convicted that May of killing his common-law wife with a hatchet.

Then, just as everything seemed in place, one of New York's most prominent and expensive attorneys filed suit on behalf of the indigent Kemmler, contending that death by electricity violated the constitutional prohibition against cruel and unusual punishment. The attorney, W. Bourke Cockran, had supposedly been spurred to action after his wife read of the dog experiments.

As the story went, the wife exclaimed, "Just think how terrible it would be if they would treat our dog like that." Cockran was purported to have responded, "The law providing for execution by electricity is unconstitutional. I'll beat it if I can."

In truth, Cockran was in the pay of Westinghouse, and considerable pay at that, reportedly as much as $100,000. Both Edison and Brown were witnesses at the ensuing hearing. Brown insisted he had no financial relationship with Edison and no "actual knowledge" of any ill feelings between the illustrious inventor and Westinghouse.

Edison was called to the stand for what one newspaper headline termed "Testimony of the Wizard." Edison wore black broadcloth that was said to give him a clerical air. He began by dragging his chair across the room.

"And put his best ear toward the big lawyer's mouth," the *New York Times* reported.

Cockran posed his questions at a volume that reporters felt sure could be heard by passersby in the street. He asked Edison about his great rival.

"I do not dislike Mr. Westinghouse," Edison said.

Cockran also asked about Brown. Edison stated that Brown had been a stranger to him when he showed up at the lab one day.

"Did he come up there and ask you to let him have your laboratory for the purpose of killing dogs?" Cockran asked.

"He wanted to try some experiments," Edison replied.

"Are you in the habit of giving your laboratory to everybody that asks you?"

"Yes, sometimes I let them experiment there."

"Might I entertain the hope that I might be allowed myself to go there?"

"Yes sir; you can come any time. I will be glad to see you."

"Mr. Brown evidently commended himself to your approval during these experiments?"

"He seemed to be a pretty nice kind of fellow, and it was no trouble to me and I let him do it."

"Do you know where he got his dogs from?"

"No, I think he bought them from somewhere."

Edison was apparently unconcerned that somebody might produce the note he wrote to Bergh of the ASPCA seeking to secure dogs.

"Have you ever given any jobs of any kind to Mr. Brown?" Cockran asked.

"No, sir."

A month later, a reporter from the *New York Sun* obtained a stack of letters stolen from Brown's office. The purloined trove revealed a long-standing business relationship between Edison and Brown. Here was no everyday humbug, which was always perpetrated with at least half a wink. But the blame was placed almost entirely on the upstart, not the Wizard.

Edison was further removed from the scandal by being in Paris, at the 1889 Exposition Universelle, which marked the one hundredth anniversary of the French Revolution. He and his wife, Mina, dined with Gustave Eiffel in the penthouse apartment the French engineer had incorporated into the new tower that bore his name. The composer/songwriter Charles Gounod was also present and played his "Ave Maria" on the grand piano that had been hoisted up to this aerie at what was being called the Eighth Wonder of the World.

Back down at street level, the great American inventor was hailed as a hero, greeted everywhere with shouts of "Viva Edison!" A Paris newspaper declared *"Edison est un roi,"* a king befitting the revolution, enthroned not by aristocratic lineage but by his own brilliance. Edison outshone even his countryman Buffalo Bill, who was there with his Wild West Show.

At a special performance, Buffalo Bill accorded the Edisons the honor of riding in the Deadwood stagecoach during a simulated attack by "wild Indians." Annie Oakley was there to demonstrate marksmanship that prompted the king of Suriname to offer 100,000 francs to buy her from herself. But it was Edison himself who was the greatest attraction and drew the loudest cheers, seeming to affirm the supremacy of the Wizard's very real inventions over anything a showman might conjure.

Even so, Edison shared one quality with great showmen such as Buffalo Bill as well as Forepaugh and Barnum. Edison recognized it in the man whose statue was atop the 144-foot column opposite his hotel in the Place Vendôme. Edison immediately named him when the explorer Henry Stanley asked which historical personage's voice he would most want to hear on the phonograph, which had become another of his inventions in 1877.

"Napoleon's," Edison said.

"No, no," Stanley said. "I should like to hear the voice of our Savior."

"Oh! Well," Edison replied, by his private secretary's account, fumbling for a moment before exclaiming, "You know—I like a hustler!"

Many of the hundreds of French inventors who sought out Edison were working on flying machines, and he said he had dabbled in this area but could only say that "gasbags" would not be the solution. He said he had also been working on what he called "television," theorizing that it might be possible to transmit images through the air.

"But not over long distances," he said. "The rotundity of the earth makes it impossible."

Before he departed for home, Edison received a telegram from the Cataract Construction Company, a new firm that was seeking to harness the power of Niagara Falls. The resulting electricity would be far more than would be needed for the immediate vicinity, but the city of Buffalo was twenty-four miles away.

"HAS POWER TRANSMISSION REACHED SUCH A DEVELOPMENT THAT IN YOUR JUDGEMENT SCHEME IS PRACTICABLE?" the Cataract telegram inquired.

Edison replied, "NO DIFFICULTY TRANSFERRING UNLIMITED POWER. WILL ASSIST."

In his effort to get the rest of the world to ignore his continuing inability to transmit direct current economically more than a few blocks, Edison had seemingly come to ignore it himself. He may have actually convinced himself that a current that had difficulty extending beyond an immediate neighborhood could outperform one that was easily capable of traveling many miles. Or perhaps he had simply been unable to admit that the Wizard's power as expressed by direct current could be so limited. He thought as grandly as the imperial hustler whose figure was perched atop the column outside his Paris hotel.

"When I was on shipboard coming over, I used to sit on deck by the hour and watch the waves," he told an interviewer in France. "It made me positively savage to think of all that power going to waste. But we'll chain it up one of these days along with Niagara Falls and the winds—that will be the electric millennium."

Edison's struggle to become the Napoleon of that millennium had suffered a setback with the scandal over Brown's papers, but he now saw an opportunity to advance his fortunes with the terrible misfortune of a thirty-two-year-old Western Union lineman. The lineman was named John E. F. Feeks and he had clambered up a telegraph pole at the corner of Chambers Street and Center Street in Manhattan on an October afternoon. Feeks then set to cutting away disused wires on a pole that was supposed to serve only fire and police alarms as well as telegraphs. He chanced to brush against a wire that had apparently come in contact somewhere along its length with a line from an arc light system charged with a high enough voltage of alternating current to be deadly. Feeks shuddered and began to fall, but his throat and face were caught in the wires and he dangled over the street as blue flames shot out of his mouth and nostrils and sparks exploded from the soles of his feet. Blood began dripping down to the pavement, forming a pool as the number of gawkers grew to the thousands. More citizens filled the surrounding windows, craning toward this horrifying but mesmerizing sight just behind City Hall and a block from the newspaper offices of Park Row.

Fellow linemen fearful of suffering a similar fate needed an eternal half hour to lower Feeks to the sidewalk. The crowd squeezed in for a closer look and had to be driven back by cops, who joined firemen in carrying the body away. A saloonkeeper nailed a tin box bearing the words "Remember the Victim" to the fateful pole and passersby ranging from shopgirls to laborers to businessmen to a prominent judge deposited a total of $1,873.50 for Feeks's widow and young child. The mayor ordered an immediate shutdown of the arc light system, which had by then largely replaced illuminating gas in the streets. Much of the city was plunged into darkness with no street lighting at all, prompting the *New York Times* headline: "Like a City in Mourning."

There were questions about the city's dawdling in running the lines underground as had already been mandated by the electrical control board.

"Wires are not being placed underground with a speed sufficient to insure the safety of the lives of the people of the city," the mayor declared.

But however much sympathy the populace felt for Feeks's grief-stricken family, and however much concern there was regarding the danger of the wires overhead, the ruling public passion was for the lights to go back on. The desire was too strong for there to be a widespread clamoring to outlaw alternating current, as Edison no doubt hoped. He nonetheless sought to incite such a prohibition with an article in the *North American Review* titled "The Dangers of Electric Lighting." Edison was no longer seeking to employ a proxy. He was putting the full and mighty authority of the great Wizard to the test as he called for an outright ban of alternating currents.

"They are as unnecessary as they are dangerous," he declared.

Edison described his animal experiments as a necessary effort to prevent tragedies such as befell Feeks.

"I have taken life—not human life—in the belief and full consciousness that the end justified the means. . . . I have myself seen a large healthy dog killed instantly by the alternating current."

Edison said the lineman's horrific demise now presented a challenge.

"If the martyrdom of this poor victim results in the application of stringent measures for the protection of life in the future, if the lesson taught is appreciated to the full extent of its fatal meaning, the sacrifice will not have been made in vain."

Edison correctly predicted that electricity was presently used "to a very limited extent as compared with its inevitable future use." But he went on to suggest that this also meant that "the opportunities for repetitions of the accident referred to above will be practically unlimited" unless the "facts" as set forth by his experiments were acted upon. He also said, in opposition to scientific fact, that running the lines underground would only increase the danger.

"There is no known insulation which will confine these high-tension currents for more than a limited period," he said, adding, "As the earth is approached the danger is multiplied," and declaring, "Safety will not be secured by burying these wires."

With this supposedly inevitable failure of the insulation, "a single wire carrying a current at high pressure would be a constant menace" where "other wires conducting harmless currents are liable to be rendered as deadly in effect as the former." Household electrical appliances would "be rendered at any moment dangerous to life."

Having predicted a household turned to a house of horrors, he went on to say, "I have no intention, and I am sure none will accuse me, of being an alarmist." He insisted he was simply saying that "the time has come when those in authority should adopt proper and adequate measures for the protection of life and property."

He said "the only remedy" was governmental regulation.

"There is no plea which will justify the use of high-tension and alternating currents," he concluded.

In fact, he said, alternating current could be deadly even at "exceedingly low" voltage. Its commercial appeal was still such that even "the electric-lighting company with which I am connected" had recently purchased the patents for an entire alternating current system despite "my protest against this action."

"My personal desire would be to prohibit entirely the use of alternating currents," he now wrote.

Edison had incorporated primarily to bankroll his effort to defeat Westinghouse, and for the resulting company to ignore his personal desire regarding such a crucial issue was an indicator of how much control he had lost. It was also a measure of the advantages those investors saw in alternating current, advantages that Westinghouse forcefully delineated in "A Reply to Mr. Edison," published by the *North American Review*.

"Were it a question of prohibiting the use not merely of electricity, but of all other things dangerous to life, we would no longer have fires to warm us or light to enable us to see, and, in fact, would be deprived of most of the necessaries and comforts of existence," Westinghouse wrote. "As has been the case with the utilization of all other forms of energy, the demand for the most economical methods will ultimately prevail, provided these can be made safe, as they most certainly can, by the exercise of proper precautions."

Westinghouse went on to say, "The placing of the wires underground would eliminate many of the causes of accidents from electric currents. . . . Mr. Edison's statement that the putting of the wires underground will, instead of diminishing, increase the danger to life, is little less than amazing."

Westinghouse suggested his opponent in the bitter War of Currents was concerned less with safety than supremacy. He noted that Edison had been preceded in the field of electricity by a number of inventors and quoted the Wizard telling the *New York Tribune* in 1878, "I have let the other inventors get the start of me in this matter somewhat, because I have not given much attention to electric lights, but I believe I can catch up to them now. . . . I don't care so much for a fortune as I do for getting ahead of the other fellows."

Westinghouse did engage in a little humbug of his own, suggesting that the alternating current used in the animal experiments was "not the alternating current of commerce, but was an Edison direct continuous current made alternating . . . incomparably more dangerous than the true alternating current." Westinghouse was back in the realm of fact when he pointed out that transformers reduced high voltage to low before it reached residences or businesses.

"There is not on record a solitary instance of a person having been injured or shocked from the consumers' current of an alternating system," Westinghouse contended.

Westinghouse ended by saying that the question of which current was superior was being decided in the marketplace, where alternating current systems were growing at five times the rate of direct current systems.

EIGHTEEN

WESTINGHOUSED

Even as Edison sought unsuccessfully to parlay the horrific death of the lineman Feeks into public demand for outlawing alternating current, he had to hope that this same horror did not convince the courts that execution by electrocution constituted cruel and unusual punishment. There was still a chance that Edison could get a sorely needed edge by associating Westinghouse with the new punishment said to be instantaneously deadly.

Despite Cockran's contention that if electrocution were anything but instantaneous it would involve "suffering beyond imagining," and even though the publication of Brown's letters had made clear that the electric chair was part of an Edison scheme, Judge S. Edwin Day of Cayuga County Court upheld the Electrical Execution Act of 1888. Day did so acknowledging that Brown was still tinkering with the exact particulars and that opinions regarding execution by this means were "speculative and hypothetical, for on no person has the experiment yet been tried."

Day suggested in his decision that such questions of law should really be made at the appellate level and the Westinghouse forces did indeed appeal, all the way to the top state court. They lost there and pressed on to the U.S. Supreme Court, which declined to hear the case. The victory must have been all the sweeter for Edison because the press had begun excoriating Westinghouse as Cockran's real client and accusing him of pursuing profit at the expense of due justice. The continued eminence of Edison was such that nobody seemed to consider why Westinghouse had felt compelled to step in on Kemmler's behalf in the first place. The lies Edison had told at the evidentiary hearing seemed already forgotten. The Wizard's reputation among the populace remained pristine.

By 2:00 a.m. on August 6, 1890, more than five hundred people had gathered outside Auburn Prison, squeezing around the gates to peer inside. The window to what was said to be the condemned man's cell was lit by electricity and glowed steadily as the crowd continued to grow. Figures appeared on the surrounding rooftops and in the trees and on the telegraph poles, everyone gazing as if there were something more to see than the vine-covered walls.

Just after sunrise, out of view of anybody but prison staff and the official witnesses, Kemmler was led up to the electric chair installed by Brown and an Edison electrician named Edwin Davis, who would become the state's chief executioner for the next quarter century. Brown had hoped to test the chair with a number of dogs but had been unable to schedule a time.

One observer later suggested that Kemmler was resolved to "die like a man," meaning that despite his awareness of what was to come he was calm and obliging, much like the dogs, calves, and horses of Brown's experiments.

"Gentlemen, I wish you all good luck," Kemmler said. "I believe I am going to a good place and I am ready to go. I want only to say that a great deal has been said about me that is untrue."

He had suffered a little demonizing of his own.

"I am bad enough. It is cruel to make me out worse."

He was secured to the chair with eleven leather straps and the metal skullcap was fitted over his head. Inside the cap was a wetted sponge of a species known as elephant ear.

"Warden, just make that a little tighter," Kemmler said. "We want everything all right, you know."

The cap was made snugger and salt solution from the elephant ear ran down Kemmler's cheeks. The warden uttered the prearranged signal.

"Good-bye, William."

There was a clicking sound as 1,700 volts passed between an electrode fitting into the skullcap and a second pressed against Kemmler's spine through the back of the chair. He went so rigid so instantly that witnesses were sure he would have been propelled across the room were it not for the straps. His right index finger curled up into itself with such force that its nail drew blood. A bright red rivulet trickled onto the arm of the chair.

"He is dead," a doctor pronounced after seventeen seconds.

The witnesses included Southwick, the man who had conducted the first experiments on dogs and was behind the new death-by-electricity law. He now stood ready with a pronouncement.

"We live in a greater civilization from this day," he said.

Southwick noted that Kemmler had not even cried out, though that may well have been due to the straps securing his chin and flattening his nose. What could now be heard was Kemmler's labored breathing. His chest rose and fell visibly. Witnesses called out.

"Great God, he is alive!"

"See, he breathes!"

"For God's sake, kill him and have it over!"

A press representative fainted. A prosecutor fled the room. The doctor ordered the current turned back on. Kemmler went rigid again. Blood beaded on his face like sweat. The elephant ear lost its moisture and a horrendous smell filled the room as Kemmler's scalp began to burn along with the flesh around the second electrode. An autopsy would later determine that the section of his brain underneath the skullcap was cooked medium rare. The muscles along the spine were roasted "like overdone beef."

Eight minutes after the first shock was administered, the second was ended. The definition of death at the time was based on an inability to generate warmth; the smoldering corpse remained above normal temperature for three hours before Kemmler would be pronounced dead.

In the meantime, the would-be gawkers outside heard a bell ring from within the prison and took it as an announcement that the moment had come. It was in fact just the usual signal for the civilians who supervised the prison shops to line up to enter the facility. Kemmler's death was confirmed only when the witnesses began to emerge, Southwick among them.

"This is the grandest success of the age," he said, pronouncing himself "one of the happiest men in the state of New York."

The *New York Times* reporter filed a somewhat different view.

"A sacrifice to the whims and theories of the coterie of cranks and politicians who induced the Legislature of this state to pass a law supplanting hanging by electrical execution was offered today in the person of William Kemmler, the Buffalo murderer," a dispatch read. "He died this morning under the most revolting circumstances, and with his death there was placed to the discredit of the State of New York an execution that was a disgrace to civilization."

On his part, Westinghouse denounced the execution as unconscionable savagery. He began by saying he did not want to talk about it, but then declared that Americans "are not barbarians" and that this was sure to be the last time the electric chair was employed.

"They could have done better with an axe," Westinghouse said.

Edison responded to news of the execution as if he were just an observer from afar, uninvolved in any way.

"I have merely glanced over an account of Kemmler's death and it was not pleasant reading," Edison said.

He did suggest the executioners would have done better to place the electrodes on the condemned's extremities, as he had on the horse's forelegs, though he had since decided it was better to move away from bone, to places "full of blood," such as the hands of a man.

Edison's recommendation was put to the test with the execution of nineteen-year-old Charles McElvaine for the murder of a Brooklyn grocer during a burglary. A priest took a crucifix from one of McElvaine's hands as they were secured in twin jars of solution that Edison had specifically recommended. Also in attendance was Edison's top technical man, Arthur Kennelly.

At the warden's command, the current was turned on for nearly a minute as McElvaine's face contorted and his orifices fulminated and his body bucked against the restraints with much the same violence as had Kemmler's. The current was turned off, but a check of one of McElvaine's soaking wrists determined he still had a pulse. The warden hurriedly had standby electrodes fitted to the condemned man's head and leg. A second jolt sent his body convulsing in the straps again, but he was soon after declared dead.

Edison had Kennelly report to anybody who would listen that McElvaine had died swiftly and without suffering. The Wizard's news clippings the next morning nonetheless included a *New York Times* article saying "Edison's Idea Failed." Even worse, the truth of Edison's connection to Brown was so established by then that only the most accommodating reporters employed the term "Westinghoused."

The accepted term came to be the brand-neutral, generic *electrocuted*, and the popular appeal of easily available electricity remained such that perhaps not even a humbugger as great as Barnum could have scared people away from it. Edison was left with the frustration and fury of a man who had sold his soul and gotten nothing in return. He was on his way to learning a very hard lesson about the limits of celebrity.

NINETEEN

READING YOUR
OWN OBITUARY

In the meanwhile, the patriarchal struggle in the show world was ended for all time by the smallest form of terrestrial life, which arrived in an American port just like the largest, only so tiny as to elude any initial notice at all.

This influenza virus had been reported initially in Uzbekistan and was spreading into the first global pandemic. It traveled the same American roads and railways that facilitated circus travel and had made an elephant a common sight.

This unseen visitor soon reached Philadelphia, claiming victims of all classes and stations, just as it was felling everyone from beggars to an archduke in Europe. The great showman who had made his claim to fortune and fame with captive Asian elephants fell deathly ill with what had come to be called the Asiatic flu.

On January 20, 1890, Adam Forepaugh died. His funeral was one of the biggest in Philadelphia history, the many mourners including

Frank Robbins, who had for a time leased Topsy and the other elephants. The *Buffalo Courier* sent a unique floral tribute, a throne of roses that was set beside the coffin.

"VACANT," read the inscription.

Forepaugh may have been a king, but Barnum was *the* king, as he was demonstrating with a one-hundred-performance run at the Olympia arena in London that kept him from attending his longtime rival's send-off. Barnum himself had proven to be the biggest attraction, his name as synonymous with *showman* as Jumbo's had been with *elephant*. And any hard feelings in England over the Jumbo purchase seemed not so much forgotten as incorporated into a Jumbo-size legend.

"The octogenarian showman was unique," one British scribe opined. "His name is a proverb already, and a proverb it will continue."

Barnum returned to America in what would have been triumph had his own health not failed. He had escaped the Asiatic flu but was suffering from rapidly advancing heart disease. His death seemed imminent when his press agent, Tody Hamilton, hatched a scheme to buoy the boss. Hamilton, lauded by the *New York Times* as "the greatest press agent that ever lived" and by himself for having "grabbed more space for nothing than anyone you know," went to the *Evening Sun* with some front-page news. The following day, Hamilton presented the still living boss with the latest edition. Barnum became that rarest of rare souls who are able to read their own obituary, in his case four columns, with pictures.

"It revived him after oxygen failed," the *New York Times* later reported. "His physicians agreed that the premature obituary had prolonged his life."

Four days later, on April 7, 1891, the newspapers set to preparing a second set of obituaries, having confirmed that Barnum really had died at his home in Bridgeport. The show was at Madison Square

Garden and that night's performance went on as scheduled. Both performances were canceled the day of the funeral. The Bridgeport schools closed for half a day, adding thousands of schoolchildren to the huge crowd.

"No town was ever more transformed than this city by one earthly event," a reporter wrote.

The next day, the show proceeded on schedule as if nothing had changed, now under the sole reign of a different kind of king, one who had proven to harbor no desire for fame. Bailey's passion was born of that day an orphan boy set off barefoot down a country road, determined to become his own master. He wanted control.

"He enjoyed best being the great silent power that made the show go and grow," the animal trainer Conklin wrote.

Now, with Barnum's demise, Bailey had total control of the Greatest and Most Moral Show on Earth. Bailey had also assumed control of the rival show, sweeping in with his old partner James Cooper to make the deal for the Forepaugh circus upon old Forepaugh's demise. Bailey put his brother-in-law, Joseph McCaddon, in charge, but the show continued to go by the Forepaugh name, just as the Barnum show continued to give top billing to its departed founder. The two shows alternated between the east and the west, the Forepaugh show still drawing a rougher crowd, the Barnum show still catering to the more genteel, all of it run by a lone man. The absence of Bailey's name from one show and his second billing on the other seemed to make him feel all the more the guy really in charge, all the more the patriarch. The barefoot boy had become master of the two biggest shows around.

The terms of the Forepaugh sale required Bailey to retain young Adam as a trainer just as the father had proposed, though only for two seasons. Bailey declined to extend the agreement and the erstwhile crown prince joined with some backers to launch a show as if his name were still his own. The younger Forepaugh's show was in Hyde Park, Vermont, when the local sheriff sought to arrest a member for an infraction of some kind. The other circus men moved to intervene and the sheriff summoned backup that quickly grew to a posse of deputized citizens.

"A general fight ensued, in which the circus men used bludgeons, knives, and pistols, but the officers succeeded in putting fifteen men in jail," the *New York Times* reported the next day. "All the property of the circus off the railroad track was attached. It is not certainly known whether or not Forepaugh was personally present, but officers are in pursuit of one man supposed to be him who took an early leave."

The original Forepaugh show that Bailey had purchased was far away in Topeka, Kansas, that day, but he could not have been pleased with the headline in the *Times* reading "Forepaugh's Men Arrested." Bailey posted a notice in the theatrical journals of the time:

To All Interested

JAMES A. BAILEY is the sole owner of the ADAM FORE-PAUGH SHOWS, having bought . . . the entire show property and the exclusive right to the use of the name ADAM FOREPAUGH, for all time, in connection with a circus or tented exhibition. . . .

Under the terms of the sale ADAM FOREPAUGH, JR., was employed on a salary for two years.

Since then ADAM FOREPAUGH, JR., has had no connection whatever with the shows which gave all the glory to the name of his father. . . .

In defiance of the terms of the sale, to which he consented . . . he has lent his name and services to some privilege men, who have dragged his name in the mud until patience ceases to be a virtue and this statement is prompted.

The ADAM FOREPAUGH SHOWS are and have been under the same management ever since the death of ADAM FOREPAUGH and the purchase of the shows by the undersigned.

Signed JAMES A. BAILEY, of Barnum & Bailey, Sole Owner

Young Forepaugh subsequently announced he was retiring due to ill health. He whiled away his remaining days in Philadelphia with a new female companion, having split with Lily Deacon, a British equestrienne he married back in 1882. Deacon remained officially married to Addie but distinguished herself from him when she established an animal refuge on her estate, Peaceable Hill, in Brewster, New York. She donated a water trough for horses and birds to the town, with a plaque reading "From the Society of Kindness to Dumb Creatures." The area youngsters who performed a good deed for an animal needed only visit her to receive a coin in reward.

TWENTY

THE GREAT NAME
VANISHES

An animal lover would no doubt have considered it only justice when the sponsor of the electrical experiments in New Jersey suffered an emotional shock from which he would never fully recover.

Unbeknownst to Edison, the company that still bore his name but was no longer under even his titular control had been approached about a merger with Thomson-Houston, headed by the same Charles Coffin whom Westinghouse had found so untrustworthy. The management of the Edison General Electric Company favored the proposal, but the only opinion that mattered was that of the primary investor, J. P. Morgan. And Morgan felt the Edison company was doing fine on its own. He also may have harbored a certain sentimental loyalty to Edison, having twice made history with the Wizard, once when Morgan's became the first private residence to acquire electric lighting, then with the flip of the switch that inaugurated service from the six Jumbos in the first central power station.

But any such feelings did not change the numbers on the balance sheets that the ever tenacious Coffin presented when urging Morgan to reconsider. Coffin noted that he was making twice the net return that the Edison company was and promised to bring similarly profitable management to the entire enterprise should there be a merger. Morgan agreed to the merger and offered no objection to having the resulting company named simply General Electric.

Morgan did not bother to inform Edison, much less to consult with him. Edison learned of it after the deal was sealed and then only because his private sectary, Alfred Tate, happened to hear word of it. The secretary confirmed that it was indeed so and hurried to Edison's laboratory, where he just blurted out the news, not considering the likely impact until the effect was all too apparent.

"I have always regretted the abruptness with which I broke the news to Edison but I am not sure that a milder manner and less precipitate delivery would have cushioned the shock," Tate later wrote. "I never before had seen him change color. His complexion naturally was pale, a clear healthy paleness, but following my announcement it turned as white as his collar."

Edison said nothing on the subject until some weeks later, when Tate sought him out in his library seeking technical information regarding a storage battery project. Edison responded with vehemence, such as Tate had never heard in his voice, instructing his secretary to go ask one of the technical people, the same Arthur Kennelly who had witnessed the McElvaine execution.

"He knows far more about [electricity] than I do," Edison said by Tate's recollection. "In fact, I've come to the conclusion that I never did know anything about it. I'm going to do something now so different and so much bigger than anything I've ever done before that people will forget that my name was ever connected with anything electrical."

Tate would recall, "They were bitter words spoken by a tongue in the mouth of a wound that never healed. . . . I walked silently out as though I were leaving the presence of the dead. Because I knew that something had died in Edison's heart and that it had not been replaced by the different and bigger thing to which had referred."

Tate would go on, "His pride had been wounded. There was no trace of vanity in his character, but he had a deep-seated enduring pride in his name. And that name had been violated, torn from the title of the great industry created by his genius through years of intensive planning and unremitting toil."

The writer Jill Jonnes would later note that the man who had hoped to stigmatize his rival by fostering the term *Westinghoused* had himself been what was known in the parlance of the time as *Morganized*. But ultimately Edison had put himself in position to be so badly used by refusing even to consider the merits of AC.

"The tide would not turn back at his frown," noted the trade journal *Electrical Engineer*.

Edison set his jaw and focused on his new jumbo project. He had decided that America would continue to grow so quickly that it was sure to soon run short of iron ore. He embarked on a massive project to excavate supposedly depleted mines in New Jersey, crush the rock with huge milling machines, and extract the remaining iron ore with magnets. The cost was more than the prevailing price but Edison felt sure that would change as shortages developed. The nation would have to rely on Edisoned ore and forget that he had ever been Morganized.

"All the hopes and aspirations which he had nurtured on association with [the electric] industry died within his heart, leaving only the bitter ashes of defeated ambitions, and he wanted to build above their grave an edifice of still greater achievement that forever would consign them to oblivion," Tate later wrote.

As a secondary concern, Edison became involved in a much smaller and far more genteel War of the Phonographs. Edison's device was powered by a storage battery, which could be recharged only by those who had access to electricity, which was still a relatively scant percentage of the population. He resisted the urging of Tate and others that he consider a spring mechanism.

"That a man so highly skilled in the mechanic arts should have maintained this attitude towards such a vital and obviously soluble problem is a mystery which to me will always remain a mystery," Tate later wrote.

Edison finally relented—as he never had in the current wars—when the rival Emile Berliner of the Gramophone Company produced a model powered by a hand-cranked system that had been developed by a bicycle shop repairman. Edison followed Berliner's lead and set to developing a similar mechanism.

But Berliner's gramophone further distinguished itself by dispensing with any recording capability. His was a device intended solely for playback, music in particular.

"He recognized the vast potentialities of the entertainment field and set out to conquer it," Tate wrote.

Berliner was seeking to tap into a commercial potential that had, in fact, first been suggested at Edison's lab when a child prodigy pianist named Josef Hofmann visited there and became the first well-known musician to make a recording. Edison now left a penciled note on Tate's desk making clear his feelings regarding this use of his invention.

"Tate—I don't want the phonograph sold for amusement purposes. It is not a toy. I want it sold for business purposes only."

Tate later reasoned in his memoir, "It was the old story. I knew it perfectly. He was unable to visualize the potentialities of the amusement field. Either that, or he had made up his mind to combat it."

Edison decided the phonograph should be used primarily for dictation and had the first one to be so employed installed on Tate's desk.

"I was the 'dog' on which this novel method was tried out," Tate would recall, apparently making reference to Brown's experiments. "And I cannot claim the distinction of having been a docile animal."

Tate was then tasked with marketing it. This was complicated by 1892 being a time when, in Tate's words, "young women had started to invade and subsequently to conquer the stenographic field, but as yet had displaced the male stenographer only to a degree which made him acutely and resentfully conscious of the menace."

The male stenographers viewed the phonograph as an added threat.

"Their interests were represented at the time by a stenographic journal which maintained a campaign of bitter opposition to the use of the phonograph and the whole profession combined solidly against its adoption.... The few instruments that we succeeded in installing in offices were quickly discovered to be inoperative," Tate would report.

Tate saw only one possible solution.

"I decided therefore to join the feminist movement."

Tate hired a middle-aged woman he identified only as Miss McCrae to train a dozen female phonograph/dictaphone operators at a time. Even this met with little success, though women generally continued to replace men as stenographers. Edison again gave in to financial necessity, as he had when finally forsaking the battery for the spring drive.

"Under the same influence, he reversed his decision concerning the entertainment field and began intensively the work of developing the phonograph for the reproduction of high-class musical records," Tate would recall. "He effected many improvements and refinements and raised the phonograph to a plane of perfection with respect to its fidelity in the reproduction of recorded vocal and instrumental music."

But Edison was ultimately indifferent to even the best of it.

"His heart was never in the work," Tate noted. "It required constant urging to induce him to make the various changes and adaptations demanded by the evolution of the art."

Edison continued to view the entertainment business as something for the likes of showmen, the purview of a humbugging Barnum or a loot-skimming Forepaugh, but not an Edison.

On visiting the San Francisco distributor of the phonograph, Tate saw that one of the doors was marked "C. Nestor Edison, Manager." He learned that an executive named Con Nestor was engaging in a little humbug, passing himself off as Edison's nephew.

"Edison was never aware of it," Tate would write. "I thought prudent not to tell him."

While strolling down Market Street, Tate glanced in a music shop window and also chanced to see a recording of a "Solo by Mrs. Edison" singing "Ave Maria."

"May I hear that record by Mrs. Edison?" Tate asked the clerk.

"Certainly," the clerk said. "And we have some others if you would like to hear them. They are very popular. We sell a lot of them."

The record proved to be what Tate described as "a beautiful, highly trained soprano." He inquired about it when he returned to the distributor. The reply from the supervisor for the whole West Coast could have come from Barnum.

"We found a young girl, a student who has a remarkable voice," Tate was told. "Of course her name was unknown and I thought her voice was too good to send it out without attaching some prestige to it. We had got Con fixed up all right, and as I had appropriated Edison's name I thought I might as well include Mrs. Edison. If it hadn't been such a fine voice of course I wouldn't have done it."

Tate could well imagine how Edison would react if he learned that his wife's name had been appropriated to promote the use of the phonograph, which he still felt to border on sacrilege.

"I at the time deemed it prudent to maintain silence," Tate later wrote, adding that if the real Mrs. Edison ever read his memoir, "she will be astonished to learn that in the Gay Nineties she achieved a reputation on the Pacific Coast as a vocal artist second only to that of the Swedish Nightingale."

Edison brought the same aversion regarding entertainment to an invention he described as the visual equivalent of the phonograph. He had begun work on it shortly after opening his lab in West Orange, New Jersey, and called it the kinetoscope, joining the ancient Greek *kineto* for movement and *scopos* for watch. The prototype was a four-foot-tall wooden box containing a small lone incandescent bulb before which moved a film loop thirty-five millimeters wide. The film was perforated along both edges and propelled by sprockets between the light and a pair of magnifying lenses that were viewed through a kind of peephole. The images to be viewed in the kinetoscope were captured by what Edison called a kinetograph, a motion picture camera with a sprocketed drive that engaged the same perforations in the film. He foresaw the subject matter to be primarily educational.

"I had some glowing dreams about what the camera could be made to do and ought to do in teaching the world things it needed to know, teaching it in a more vivid, direct way," Edison said.

Edison hoped to have his kinetoscope viewer ready for the up-coming World's Columbian Exposition in Chicago, which had been conceived as an American equivalent of the exposition in Paris, but marking the four hundredth anniversary of Christopher Columbus's arrival in the New World. The exposition was put off a year because of the presidential election, but Edison was still not able to get the kinetoscope ready in time. That was due partly to an assistant who was overly fond of imbibing and partly to the iron ore separation project, which had problems on a scale with its ambitions and threatened to consume all of Edison's silver dollars before it began to produce a useable product.

The exposition would proceed without a new sensation from the great Edison to soften the pain of having his name removed from the company that had been his grandest conception.

On its part, General Electric had cause to rue dropping Edison's name as it sought the contract to provide lighting for the exposition. The job promised to involve some one hundred thousand lights, the most ever. And out of its sense of its own bigness, the new General Electric conglomerate bid as if it were the only company that could possibly handle it, demanding $1.7 million, a sum that one exhibition official termed "extortionate." The bid might have been accepted as a premium for greatness if the firm had retained the name of the man still popularly recognized as the father of the electric light. Had the firm also retained some of Edison's ability to see beyond immediate profit—as he had when he sold his first lightbulbs below cost—it would have recognized the brand-building value of such a contract even at the risk of a short-term financial loss. It might not have demanded such a prohibitive sum in the first place.

Demand it did and the bid was seen for what it was, naked corporate greed. The Chicago newspapers cried robbery and cheered when a small local firm, Southside Machine and Metal Works, entered a bid for a third of what the conglomerate wanted. General Electric just scoffed, saying this so-called rival could not make good on a task of that magnitude. The local firm then sought out Westinghouse, who had just reestablished his financial stability after some corporate struggles of his own and had up to this point refrained from joining the bidding on such an ambitious project. He took up the challenge and the press hailed him as a hero.

The General Electric Company was not without influential friends and a second round of bids was held. The conglomerate bid slightly lower than the local firm's first price, but Westinghouse bid still lower. Westinghouse won the contract to illuminate the 1893 celebration of what the exhibition's official guidebook termed "the forces which move humanity and make history, the ever-shifting powers that fit new thoughts to new conditions, and shape the destinies of mankind."

Nearly one in four Americans, in excess of twenty-five million, visited the fair and thrilled at an electric blaze that offered not a tingle of danger. Westinghouse's dynamos provided the power even for the eighteen thousand miniature red, white, and blue lights on the eighty-two-foot column popularly known as the Edison Electric Tower or simply the Edison Tower. The official name was the Tower of Light, and the column was not topped by a figure of the Wizard as the similar column in Paris was topped by Napoleon. This monument culminated in an eight-foot incandescent bulb composed of thirty thousand pieces of prismatic glass. The colonnade around the base was emblazoned with the words "The General Electric Company."

In an added slight, the company that had shed Edison's name had on display its new AC system. That did not keep its press agents from seeking to maintain an association with the Wizard in the public's mind by telling reporters that Edison had approved the tower's design.

The identity of the tower's creator may have caused Edison both satisfaction and indignation. Luther Stieringer had been a top Edison assistant before striking out on his own and becoming one of America's first lighting designers. His fondness for color was seen not only in the patriotic motif of the Tower of Light but also in the multihued "electric fountains" nearby, where geysers rose up through a whole spectrum of lights, turning magically prismatic amid the fair's white blaze.

Westinghouse also had an exhibit in the center aisle. One feature was presented almost as a shrine, with a cupola whose inscription included the surname of the inventor at the heart of Westinghouse's spectacular success:

> Westinghouse Electric &
> Manufacturing Co.
> Tesla Polyphase System.

Various manufacturers displayed a vast array of electric prototypes, from household appliances to power tools to medical instruments. A view of the grounds was accorded by another new marvel powered by Westinghouse: the 250-foot, passenger-bearing wheel named after its inventor, George Ferris.

One electric device that was not wired to any power source for demonstration purposes was the contraption with which Edison had hoped to defeat his rival. The electric chair was on view along with other instruments of capital punishment in the building housing the prison exhibit. The particular form of electric current employed to dispatch the condemned in the electric chair seemed no more important than the brand of rope used for the hangman's noose. And everywhere the visitors to the fair turned was more shining proof that alternating current was a boon for all mankind, the common animating factor in a host of amazing inventions.

This teeming, incandescent exhibition was known as the White City, and it must have seemed even more dazzling amid the deepening gloom of a second national economic calamity in as many decades. The Panic of 1873 had been followed by the Panic of 1893, also triggered by hyperextended railroads and reckless speculation, seeming proof that if elephants never forget, humans never remember. Banks were folding by the hundreds. Businesses were closing by the thousands. Unemployment was tripling. Yet here was the fair's gleaming promise of better days ahead thanks to technology and industry and the power of electricity.

The White City was said to be the inspiration for the Emerald City of L. Frank Baum's *The Wizard Oz*. But for the real-life Wizard, the glow rising into the night sky from the sensation on the South Side signaled a compounded defeat both by his rival and, more stingingly, by those who now controlled the company he had founded.

"He never ceased to regret the loss of properties which abruptly terminated his direct association with the evolution of the great industry which he himself had created," Tate later wrote. "He was in the position of a parent watching the growth and prosperity of a kidnapped child."

He seems to have remained all but mute about this deep, transforming hurt.

"Beyond what he said to me Edison was silent and nursed his grievance in the solitude of his own mind," Tate recalled.

And because he would continue to silently suckle his anger for years to come, the glow that promised a brighter future for humankind portended a bitter fate for the crooked-tailed elephant appearing that very June just a short way up the city's lakefront.

TWENTY-ONE

TOPSY SOMERSAULTS;
GOLD DUST AND
DUNCAN GET A HOME

The Forepaugh show still bore the name of the deceased patriarch but was wholly owned by Bailey—and a businessman as astute as he would have been expected to skip Chicago when the competition was a mammoth fair that had the whole country abuzz. Bailey very well might have dropped Chicago from his itinerary had others not tried to force him to do so. He had previously been compelled to mount a legal fight to use Chicago's lakefront lot after the Montgomery Ward Company sought to have the show barred as a "great annoyance." Bailey had prevailed, but with the advent of the fair, local speculators offered the city $10,000 to rent the lot through November. Bailey had to fight again to hold on to it, but he had to put up $5,000 for two weeks, rather than the $2,500 he had paid the prior year for one. That landed him in Chicago for twice the usual time as even he himself fell victim to fair fever. The show's 1893 route book, a compendium such as every big circus published at the end of each season as a running historic record and memento, reported:

Chicago, Ill.   Monday, June 5th

We inaugurated our two-week stand in Chicago today.... Mr. and Mrs. James A. Bailey are on a visit to the show and will of course "take in" the world's fair as a side issue.

The show included reenactments of the American Revolution, conducted at the end so as not to blind the spectators with gun smoke as had Forepaugh of old. Bailey tried to market this feature as an extension of the Columbian extravaganza across town.

"Columbus discovered the New World for Spain. George Washington won it for America," read a big newspaper ad. "The Adam Forepaugh Show seeks to glorify the Father of Our Country without distracting from the honor due the discoverer. The most magnificent entertainment of all time. The SCENES and BATTLES of 1776—The American Revolution.... WHOSE CHILD SHOULD NOT LEARN THIS GLORIOUS LESSON SO DELIGHTFULLY TOLD?"

The ad made no mention of anything so foreign as elephants, noting only that there would be "an exhibition of AMERICAN-TRAINED WILD ANIMALS that still further upholds American superiority." A soap company ad featuring the circus did show an elephant, skipping a rope held by a tiger and a kangaroo in a big top marked 4-PAW CIRCUS.

"There are strange sights at the circus," it read. "But nothing so strange as the woman who does not know of the excellence and superiority of KIRK'S AMERICAN FAMILY SOAP."

That may or may not have sold much soap. The Forepaugh "father of our country" ad certainly did not draw crowds and in an effort to fill the seats the show held special "professional" days, offering free admittance to all thespians and then to the city's hordes of newsboys. The show also lent use of the tent to the renowned evangelist Dwight "D.L." Moody. The ad in the newspapers read:

Ha! Ha! Ha!
Three Big Shows!
Moody in the Morning!
Forepaugh in the Afternoon and Evening!

Moody drew an overflow crowd that was admitted through the menagerie tent, thousands filing past the elephants, who could be heard trumpeting as Moody delivered his sermon and voices rose in such hymns as "Rock of Ages." The hope was the faithful would return later for the circus, but more often than not, those who went anywhere chose the fair. The show's route book noted:

Chicago, Ill.   Sunday, June 18th

This is the last day in Chicago, and everybody is impatient to be on the move once more. The weather during our stay was absolutely perfect, but business by no means up to expectations. The great counter attraction of the Columbia Exposition virtually killed our afternoon business.

The show went on to visit 131 towns in 159 days, giving 312 performances in fifteen states and traveling 10,332 miles. It entered the "corn and wheat belt" that a smaller but contentious show run by the Sells brothers considered its home turf.

Marshalltown, Iowa   Friday, August 11th

Afternoon attendance very big, and at night it was up to the usual standard, notwithstanding the facts that Sells Bothers has posted notices over our paper to the effect that our date has been postponed to August 14th.

Thieves continued to trail the show with the intent of robbing patrons as if it were still the old Forepaugh days. Bailey's policy was made emphatically clear during a pause en route. Several of the show's stouter men were reported in the route book as having gone "on a hunting expedition for three disreputable followers of the 'grafting species.' They were found and after a powerful and forcible argument and a cold dip in the river as a side issue 'they never came back.'"

A grifter subsequently exacted revenge on the show's chief of security.

"Our efficient Pinkerton detective, Frank Hook, mourns the loss of an overcoat, which he has been unable to recover, not even with the assistance of the village constable."

The Forepaugh reputation for larceny lingered and when $1,600 went missing from a house while the show was in Marion, Kansas, it was held collectively to blame. The big surprise was that anybody in town had that much cash, for the area had fallen into the deep gloom of the ongoing economic downturn.

Marion, Kansas   Wednesday, August 30th

We had a beautiful day here, but as the town is in the last stages of decay, owing to financial ruin brought about by the failure of its leading bank and the general business depression, our business was very bad.

Only a meager crowd was on hand to witness what had been un-precedented for an elephant of any show.

"In the elephant races today, Topsy stumbled and fell, turning a complete and artistic somersault that almost resembled a 'flip-flap' and throwing the rider fully 15 feet. No damage."

Arstingstall's response is not reported but can well be imagined. A bit of what an elephant lover would consider justice came two days later.

Wichita, Kansas   Friday, September 1st

George Arstingstall made an aggravating mistake today in the cook tent. He saw a plate of butter in front of his plate, and thinking it to be cornstarch pudding, he sprinkled sugar over it, then gave it a liberal supply of milk, after which he took a still more liberal spoonful and placed it in his mouth. Immediately everybody was startled with a yell like a Comanche and such spitting and sputtering one never heard or saw before. It was an awful dose for the unfortunate Professor, for, confidentially, the cookhouse butter is something not to be mentioned.

Despite the trainer's harsh methods, the show ended the season with none of the elephant rampages of prior years. One reason may have been that Bailey had followed Forepaugh's example in dealing with troublesome elephants and presented the rambunctious Gold Dust along with Duncan to the Washington Zoo. The zoo had no facilities for elephants and the two were initially kept tied to a tree and led down to Rock Creek once a day to drink and bathe and exercise. The treatment here was almost certainly gentler than with the show and both elephants remained generally well behaved. "Dunc" did have a bout of ill humor, likely the result of musth. He nonetheless became a particular favorite of the capital's children.

Up at the Central Park Zoo, Tip was confined in what was called "the elephant house" but was so cramped that his back brushed the roof and he was unable to raise his head fully. He did receive daily exercise under standing orders from Superintendent William Conklin, who was inclined toward the views of Stewart Craven and Eph Thompson.

"As long as he was properly looked after, there was no danger of his doing any harm," Conklin later said of Tip.

The elephant keeper, William Snyder, did not much care for his charges and took an instant dislike to Tip in particular.

"I knew he was wicked when I first took charge of him," Snyder later said. "I guess Forepaugh was glad to get rid of the beast.... He should have been shot then, the wicked brute."

Save for the brief periods of exercise mandated over Snyder's objections, Tip was kept shackled to the floor. A "martingale" chain girded his midsection and shorter chains extended from it to his tusks, further restricting his ability to lift or even turn his head. He was continually goaded and beaten and when he grew angry he was goaded and beaten some more.

Tip was in the second year of such treatment when Snyder announced that the elephant had attempted to kill him with a swat of the trunk and an upraised foot.

"When I recovered myself, I went back, made Tip lie down, put extra chains on him, and gave him a good beating," Snyder told a reporter.

The superintendent, Conklin, remained convinced that the problem was not the elephant, but the trainer. A showdown with Snyder loomed when Conklin was suddenly swept up in scandal. A llama had died of natural causes during a show at the Academy of Music and the animal proved to belong to the zoo. It turned out that Conklin had been renting out the zoo's animals and using its facilities to his personal financial advantage.

At hearings held by the Commission of Accounts, the most damning witness was none other than Snyder. He testified that he had twice been ordered by Conklin to take elephants to theatrical shows, one in New Jersey, the other in downtown Manhattan.

"Mr. Conklin was to get fifty dollars a week," Snyder reported of the Manhattan arrangement.

Another witness alleged that Conklin's wife had gone into business as an animal dealer, using the zoo to lodge her inventory, including as many as 125 monkeys. She diverted zoo meat to feed her carnivores and was said to have actually sold pigeons to Central Park.

On the day Conklin's wife was to take the stand, her doctor informed the commission she was too ill to testify. Conklin himself was said to be "among the temporarily missing." He mailed in a one-sentence letter of resignation.

Tip was never exercised again, spending nearly three years in uninterrupted confinement. Snyder was said to look the other way when boys fed Tip apples filled with pepper. Snyder was well aware that Tip had a phobia of rodents and he sometimes left a cage filled with rats in the stall.

Snyder took the precaution of sawing off some twelve inches from each of Tip's tusks as the cycle of torment and rage escalated.

"He is the most vicious elephant I have ever seen and he has been getting worse all the time," Snyder said. "He is a treacherous beast."

In the spring of 1894, Snyder announced that Tip had again tried to kill him, this time with the sawed-off tusks.

"He ought to be killed before he does any more hurt," Snyder said. "If he isn't killed, he'll kill me."

The *New York Times* described the incident as a "treacherous attack" by an "ungrateful pachyderm" on Snyder, who "had always treated him with great kindness, although Tip has the worst temper possessed by any elephant the keeper has ever had charge of."

The paper went on, "Now that Tip is in disgrace, Snyder acts no longer as his purveyor of good things and as his valet. A rake attached to a long pole cleans out his stall and pushes in his ordinary rations."

The reporter visited the elephant house and understandably failed to recognize Tip's constant swaying as a sign of great stress. The reporter noted that Tip would go still when Snyder approached, watching the keeper intently with his "little yellow rheumy eyes."

The new superintendent, John Smith, referred the matter to the Board of Park Commissioners, whose members had received from Snyder sections of Tip's sawn-off tusks as keepsakes. Smith echoed Snyder.

"[Smith] recommended that the brute be killed at once," the *Times* noted. "Commissioner Clausen said the fact that Tip had been chained to the floor in the pen for five years might account for his vicious disposition, but Superintendent Smith said it was unsafe to release the big brute from the chains."

The *Times* further reported: "The Commissioners were disinclined to have him destroyed as he was a great attraction in the menagerie, but they also considered that his skeleton would be a great exhibit in the American Museum of Natural History."

The commissioners put off the verdict for a week, ostensibly to give Tip time to improve his behavior. The *Times* headline read, "Tip Must Reform or Die—Central Park's Big Elephant on Trial for His Life."

The board used the intervening days to consider how exactly Tip would best be killed. A colorful character known as Arizona Bill offered to kill Tip with one shot from his "unerring rifle." Another proposal came from someone described only as "a representative of a power company," almost certainly not the Westinghouse company. Westinghouse would hardly have gotten himself involved in electro-cuting animals after his adversary's notorious experiments.

And the proposal did not likely come from the company that had shed Edison's name, as it was seeking to expand into the alternating current business and dispel talk of DANGER. The proposal more likely was relayed by an emissary from Edison himself, though he surely did not imagine he could change the outcome of the War of Currents even by killing something so large, by every measure, as an elephant whose fate had been on the front page for a week.

But Edison had already been offered and then lost an opportunity to electrocute the elephant Chief back when he had imagined it might make a difference in his struggle with Westinghouse. He may have been seeking to vent via Tip the hurt and frustration and anger pent up in what Tate called "the solitude of his own mind."

And these internal roilings could only have been intensified as Westinghouse's triumph at the Chicago exposition was now being followed by a second triumph in upstate New York, one that was sure to dramatize the insurmountable shortcomings of direct current. The success of the White City had convinced the Cataract Construction Company up at Niagara Falls to use an AC system, and it announced an international competition for the best plan. Westinghouse had sus-pected that it was just a trick to get a fortune in ideas for the price of a relatively paltry award. But when the firm now just named General Electric signed up to enter the contest, he apparently felt that he had to do the same if he was to have any hope of getting the contract for actually building and installing the generating system. Edison's nem-esis Coffin apparently sought to gain General Electric an edge with some nineteenth-century industrial espionage. A raid on his office produced a number of Westinghouse blueprints and estimates. He was said to have obtained them by bribing a Westinghouse draftsman and there was talk of an indictment.

Then Cataract announced that it would not be using any of the contest entrants and would instead be doing the work itself with the help of an engineer named George Forbes. Westinghouse must have felt doubly stung for having gone against his initial instinct that he was being hustled. Edison, on his part, might have been doubly delighted.

But the Niagara project proved to be beyond Forbes's capabilities. The contract went to Westinghouse after all, the dynamos to be those designed by Tesla, who had spoken as a boy in Serbia of one day building a huge water wheel at Niagara Falls.

All this culminated shortly before the emissary most likely from Edison proposed alternating current as the best way to send Tip the behemoth to "elephant heaven."

"Electricity, it is understood, is most favored by both the commissioners and the experts," the *New York Tribune* reported.

On the appointed day, May 8, 1894, the board reconvened. The secretary had drafted what was described as an indictment. Snyder was taken at his word, including his exaggerated accounting of Tip's history of violence, saying the elephant had killed six men "(two at one time) and one boy."

The report went on to describe in detail the two supposed attempts to kill Snyder, who was termed "the best and most courageous of elephant men." Bailey offered testimony via a telegram from Washington, where the Barnum & Bailey show was performing.

"It has always been my opinion that Tip, the elephant, was dangerous to the public as well as his keeper. It seems to me the only safe way is to kill him, and the sooner the better. If he was mine, I would kill him before night."

The former superintendent, Conklin, emerged from among the temporarily missing to offer a lone authoritative voice of dissent and plead for Tip's life. Conklin said Tip had killed not seven, but at most two, both in mitigating circumstances. Conklin urged the board to replace Snyder if he was unable to manage the elephant.

"I would suggest 'Eph' Thompson, the colored animal trainer," Conklin said. "The most successful trainer of elephants ever known."

The suggestion was not even considered before the president of the board called for a vote. The other three members answered in unison.

"Kill him!"

The only remaining question was how to do it. Snyder and others had pointed out a complication regarding electrocution.

"Because we could not get near enough to him to attach the electrodes to him," a board member noted.

Snyder remained in favor of shooting, but there were worries about what might happen if Tip were only wounded. One citizen suggested affixing an explosive to his forehead.

The board's decision was reported in the morning *Times*:

Tip Tried and Convicted
   The Central Park "Rogue" Will Be Executed Tomorrow—Poison Will End His Existence.

By 5:00 a.m. the next day, more than five hundred people had gathered outside the elephant house. The crowd kept growing, extending up a hill. A sound arose that was seldom heard when the condemned was a fellow human. "The clamor of the men, women and children and many nursemaids against the sentence of death," an observer wrote.

A squad of police officers barred entrance to everyone save those who had received an official ticket.

"Admit Bearer to Execution of Tip," it read.

Just after 6:00 a.m., the assistant superintendent of the zoo handed a large, hollowed-out carrot to a curator from the American Museum of Natural History. The curator inserted what was presumed to be a fatal dose of potassium cyanide and it was presented to Tip at 6:58 a.m. The elephant tucked the carrot into his mouth and the witnesses went silent, expecting that in just moments he would collapse in a heap.

Instead, Tip let the partly chewed carrot spill from his mouth. The would-be executioners next tried a similarly poisoned apple, but Snyder had let youngsters offer him too many peppered ones. Tip cautiously sniffed the apple, rubbed it on the underside of his trunk, then set it down and stomped it. He ignored several subsequent carrots and apples as well as chunks of bread, though he did begin to show effects from however much poison he ingested in biting that first carrot. His eyes dimmed. His trunk drooped.

"Tip is a pretty sick elephant," a commissioner was heard to say.

The elephant turned away from the men as far as his chains allowed and faced the back of the pen.

"He is dying," somebody said.

A half hour later, Tip seemed to revive and he turned back with what was described as a "bland twinkle in his eye." His trunk swung back and forth with "a jaunty air" as a team of four riflemen asked for permission to chalk a target on his forehead and shoot him.

The ASPCA denied the request and the poisoning effort resumed. Snyder personally put a jumbo capsule of potassium cyanide into some wet bran and then retreated so as not to give alarm when it was presented to his nemesis.

At 4:07 p.m., Tip set to eating what would later be called "the fatal temptation." He was seized with spasms, and made a belching sound as if again trying desperately to bring up what he had just ingested.

"He writhed as much as a monster his size can writhe," the *Times* reported.

Tip lifted his trunk to the height the low ceiling allowed and trumpeted his anguish before making a wild dash toward the rear of the pen with such furious power that he snapped all of the chains save one on a foreleg. The lone remaining restraint stretched taut and he seemed sure to burst through his wooden confinement and charge free into the lush, springtime greenness of the park beyond.

The chain held. Tip suddenly seemed to lose all his strength and his legs buckled. Twelve minutes after he ate the bran and more than ten hours after being offered that first carrot, he made a final trumpeting sound that was described as faint and despairing.

A more sympathetic *Times* called Tip an "enthralled monarch of the jungle, largest and most powerful of his herd, an elephantine colossus" who "ingloriously died because he trustingly ate a pan of poisoned bran." The *Times* suggested that the outcome had been determined, as were many in the city, by who had the greater influence with the powers that be.

"He hated Snyder and Snyder hated him, and one or the other had to go," the *Times* said. "Tip was the victim. The poor fellow had no 'pull.'"

Eight men with long knives worked through the night skinning the corpse for the museum. The eyes went to the New York Eye and Ear Infirmary. The University of Chicago sought the whole brain but settled for half, "to examine the cause of the wickedness which made the killing of the animal necessary." The scientists did not seem to consider that the wickedness in question might have originated in the brains of their own species.

Word of the execution reached the Forepaugh Show as it was traveling through Kentucky. The continuing economic depression had caused the show to downsize from three rings to one and dispense with historical battle reenactments, as well as replace the thrilling but pricey trick riding of the Wild Warrior Cossacks of the Czar with an economical "example of kindness in animal education." This new money-saving feature involved only a horse and a pony supposedly trained by the methods of the late John Rarey, who had achieved worldwide fame as the original horse whisperer, applying principles similar to those of his fellow Ohioan Stewart Craven.

Next on the program were the elephants. They remained the essence of the show after financial exigencies and the dazzling, futuristic competition of the White City caused the owner to abandon the usual aspirations to greatness, for a season, anyway. The show might not have been able to afford re-creating Custer's Last Stand and it might not have set the sky aglow, but it still had Topsy leading the dance and crawling around the now single ring.

This performance was to a significant degree the residual result of kindness in animal education as practiced by Craven and Thompson, though that was not mentioned in the program or the route book. The keepers themselves no doubt continued to believe that Topsy and her herd did as bid only under the perpetual threat of the hook. The audience assumed that the elephants were simply doing what good, sagacious elephants do, what made the show the show even as hard times caused it to abandon its usual hyperbole.

"THE CIRCUS IS THE THING AFTER ALL," the 1894 route book declared.

TWENTY-TWO

THE WIZARD'S
LATEST MARVEL AND
SO MANY ELEPHANTS

That same spring, the first kinetoscope parlor was ready to open in a former shoe store on Broadway in Manhattan, within walking distance of where Tip had met his end. The Edison Manufacturing Company provided the ten machines and the film loops while the actual operation of the parlor was handled by an independent syndicate that included Alfred Tate and his brother. A plaster bust of Edison painted to look like bronze was set in the front window. A crowd formed outside even though the opening of this first kinetoscope parlor was not scheduled until the following day.

"Look here, why shouldn't we make that crowd out there pay for our dinner tonight?" Tate would recall telling his brother.

Tate sold tickets while his brother watched over the machines.

"I wish now that I had recorded the name of the person to whom I sold the first ticket," Tate later wrote. "I cannot recall even a face. I was kept too busy passing out tickets and taking in money. It was good joke all right, but the joke was on us. If we had wanted to close the place at six o'clock it would have taken a squad of policemen. We got no dinner."

The film loops at the premiere included footage of a kilted pair performing a "highland dance" and an organ grinder cranking away. A third loop, titled *Trained Bears*, had been the most demanding to make.

"The bears were divided between surly discontent and a comfortable desire to follow the bent of their own inclinations," W. K. L. Dickson, then Edison's chief filmmaker, recalled. "It was only after much persuasion that they could be induced to subserve the interests of science."

Dickson here may have been making ever so slight fun of Edison, who continued to insist that the ultimate purpose of motion pictures would be educational. The initial marvel was indeed technological— this being the machine itself, the very fact that these moving images could be recorded and replayed. But the novelty soon wore off and Edison's company sought to keep the public interested with an ever-growing variety of film loops. These were shot in the world's first movie studio, a tarpaper-covered shack erected outside the lab on tracks that enabled it to be moved during the day so the subjects inside remained in direct sunlight. The Edison name drew many illustrious figures of stage and sport to what was dubbed the Black Maria because its shape and hue were reminiscent of the police wagons known by this name. Among them were the celebrated dancer Carmencita, the contortionist Ena Bertoldi, and Eugen Sandow, the self-proclaimed strongest man in the world and pioneering proselytizer of bodybuilding. There were also purely comic scenes such as *Boxing Cats*, featuring two felines wearing miniature boxing gloves, and *The Wrestling Dog*, filmed adjacent to the site of the ghastly experiments during the War of Currents.

Annie Oakley was still with the Wild West Show and she came by the Black Maria to be filmed demonstrating her marksmanship. The filmstrip ends with her shooting glass balls tossed into the air one after another.

By then, the kinetoscope parlor was so much more a place of entertainment rather than of edification that Edison asked Tate to remove the bust from the parlor's window.

"He thought its display undignified," Tate later wrote.

Even so, Edison had an ever-growing need for silver dollars. He faced a continuing financial drain from the ore-crushing enterprise that he hoped would vanquish the memory of things electric and become the first innovation people thought of upon seeing his likeness.

"Not even so resourceful and versatile an inventor as he could at will discover something to represent the foundation of an industry so vast as that which he created when he perfected the electric incandescent lamp," Tate later wrote. "And it was these dimensions that he strove to duplicate or to surpass. Spurred by his resentment at the loss and alienation of this great industry, he poured his energies and his wealth into his iron ore milling enterprise in the belief that this would expand to the dimensions encompassed by his mind."

Edison felt sure he could top Edison because he was Edison.

"But there the Fates opposed him and forced him to develop an ephemeral though profitable industry into which his heart never entered," Tate went on. "It is a remarkable circumstance that the field which he always viewed with such pronounced aversion, which he so earnestly tried to avoid, the amusement or entertainment field, was the one in which through two of his inventions, the Phonograph and the

Kinetoscope, he recouped his fortunes and accumulated the greater part of the wealth which he left behind him."

The Barnum & Bailey circus happened to come through West Orange in May of 1895 and several performers were filmed in the Black Maria, including Princess Ali, who performed a belly dance that was quite provocative for its time, among the first stirrings of sex in the movies. The first stirrings of violence were staged in other films that year such as *The Indian Scalping* and *The Lynching* and most dramatically in *The Execution of Mary Queen of Scots*, which employed stop action. The male actor who played the ill-fated royal was substituted for a dummy whose head was lopped off.

"EXECUTION Representing the beheading of Mary, Queen of Scots," read the Edison film catalogue. "A realistic reproduction of an historic scene."

Even with gyrating hips and the tumbling head, the kinetoscope soon lost its novelty. Revenue was already dwindling when word came of a movie projector invented by two upstarts from Washington, D.C., Thomas Armat and Charles Francis Jenkins. Rather than squint through a peephole one at a time, people would be able to watch en masse images as big or even bigger than life on a screen.

The kinetoscope syndicate faced ruin and sought to position itself as a middleman, proposing an arrangement between Edison and the actual inventors of the projector whereby the Wizard would lend his name to the new device. The syndicate insisted it was not suggesting out-and-out humbug. It simply figured on allowing people to reach their own conclusions.

"We should of course not misrepresent the facts to any inquirer, but we think we can use Mr. Edison's name in such a manner as to keep within the actual truth, and yet get the benefit of his prestige," the syndicate said in its proposal.

The Edison name continued to have such commercial power that Armat and Jenkins agreed. Edison might have been expected to dismiss it out of hand. He had shown during the War of Currents that he was willing to engage in falsehoods, but he had always insisted on marketing only his own inventions, only the fruits of his own inspirations, even at the cost of losing control of the electric company he founded.

But he remained so desperate to obliterate the hurt of that loss that he now proved willing to compromise the same stubborn precept that had precipitated it. He essentially agreed to sell his name, if not some of his soul, to get the money he needed for the ore-crushing project that others were calling "Edison's folly." He remained certain it would be an all-eclipsing success.

In April of 1896, the press was invited to Edison's laboratory to see "Edison's vitascope."

"Edison's Latest Triumph," the *New York Times* headline announced.

The public got its first look later that month at Koster and Bial's Music Hall in Herald Square in New York. A clip of two dancers was followed by one of waves breaking onto a beach, and the very air was said to be charged with energy akin to that for which Edison was famous for utilizing.

"The spectator's imagination filled the atmosphere with electricity," the *New York Times* reported.

One of the two actual inventors, Armat, was present, but he went unheralded, hunched over the projector and out of view. Edison sat in an upper balcony but did not respond to cries from the audience.

"Edison! Edison!"

The big hit was screened during the second week. *The May Irwin Kiss* featured fifteen seconds of the actress kissing her leading man from the musical comedy *The Widow Jones*. The two became the first movie stars, traveling the country giving kissing demonstrations, even lessons.

In the meantime, the Edison company came up with an innovation for which it could rightly claim credit, a portable "taking machine," or movie camera that enabled filmmakers to venture into the world beyond the Black Maria and make "actuality" movies. The first such effort was *Herald Square,* which enabled the audience in the theater to see the street directly outside. The camera crew subsequently traveled north to the scene of Westinghouse's latest triumph, an electricity-generating project so big that the building housing the dynamos was called the Cathedral of Power. The crew stuck to filming Niagara Falls itself from numerous angles. The most popular clip was *Niagara Falls, Gorge,* shot from the back of a train that ran along the edge of the roaring river at the base, the white water churning with the power that Edison himself had envisioned harnessing along with the sea and the wind.

Back closer to Edison's home base, his traveling film crew shot *Bathing Scene at Coney Island* on the beach at Brooklyn's edge. There, the crew also filmed *Shooting the Chutes,* a popular ride at America's first enclosed amusement park, Captain Boyton's Sea Lion Park, operated by the same Fearless Frogman who had been such a sensation with the Barnum show.

Boyton had appeared in the Barnum show for that single season, billed below the Hairy Family as his publicity value dimmed. He had then resumed his rubber suit adventures, adding the Ohio to his list of rivers, all the while keeping an eye out for new opportunities to convert fame into fortune.

When he visited the Chicago exposition of 1893, he did not fail to note the popularity of the various amusements of the midway. The following year he opened Shoot the Chutes, a water slide toboggan ride not far from where the fair had been. He did an adequate local business but the big crowds had ended along with the exposition. He decided to relocate to Coney Island, an ocean resort so popular that it drew midway-size multitudes every summer.

On July 4, 1885, the nation's 109th birthday, Boyton opened his park, featuring performing sea lions as well as daily demonstrations of his world-famous rubber suit. The Edison crew chose to film one of the wood toboggans shooting down a huge, steep ramp and then skipping across a lagoon. The result was *Shooting the Chutes*.

Across the street from Boyton's sixteen-acre park was a big new seaside hotel built in the shape of an elephant by a Philadelphia entrepreneur named James Lafferty, who had funded the project by distributing thousands of handbills offering what were essentially time-shares in various parts of pachyderm anatomy. Not to be confused with the slightly smaller elephant-shaped hotel Lafferty built in Atlantic City, the seven-story-high Elephant Colossus in Coney Island was constructed of pine sheathed with tin. The thirty-two rooms, including the stomach room, the trunk room, and the twin eye rooms, were accessed through stairways in the rear legs, the right one up, the left down. More than fifteen thousand people had paid a dime a head to tour it when it first opened, but as the novelty wore off it became a towering white elephant. It struggled and failed first as a hotel, then as a restaurant, then as a dance hall. It remained the most iconic Coney Island landmark and the sight that first welcomed those arriving by ship into New York Harbor, but the filmmakers may have decided not to memorialize it because it had finally become a brothel, adding a wink to "seeing the elephant."

The Edison crew did film actual elephants at the Barnum & Bailey show, going to the circus in New York instead of having some of the performers come to the studio. Movies that could not have been made at the Black Maria included *Trick Elephants No. 1,* which featured a pachyderm headstand as well as a procession by a full dozen of the show's herd around the center ring, followed by a pyramid. The film was popular enough, but it offered no particular filmic magic, being shot from the perspective of a spectator and offering a sight many had seen firsthand. It was not a hit like *The Black Diamond Express,* which used perspective to give the audience the sense that a speeding train was coming right out of the screen at them only to veer at the last moment.

Live performances proved to far outdraw screened images when the Ringling Brothers Circus—a show begun by five Midwestern brothers of that name—acquired an Edison vitascope for one hundred dollars during the 1897 season and began showing movies in a "black top" adjacent to the big top. The offerings included "life-size living" images of the prizefighter James "Gentleman Jim" Corbett in action, which had an added allure because boxing was still illegal in many states, but showing moving pictures of it was not. There were also films "provided more for the entertainment of the ladies."

The Bailey-owned Forepaugh Show—which had now merged with the Sells show and reinstated the three rings—responded with its own "black tent" across from the sideshow in 1898.

"EDISON'S WONDER. THE WIZARD'S LATEST," read the banner over the main entrance.

The show also had the Corbett film, as well as a clip shot in Havana Harbor after the battleship *Maine* exploded and sank, triggering the Spanish-American War. Patriotic fervor helped pack the new tent, which the show people contemptuously nicknamed "the chamber of gloom."

Often, film programs ended with *Mr. Edison at Work in His Chemical Laboratory*, shot in the Black Maria and projected with the machine the public believed was his invention. The Wizard could be seen in a white coat, experimenting with the ingredients of some future marvel. There was no hint of the passions at work in his solitary psyche, which were so at odds with his popular persona. And nobody could have foreseen the circumstances under which this new wonder, the motion picture, would someday feature the very elephant who now led the quadrille in the main ring of the Forepaugh & Sells Brothers combined show.

In the meantime, the movies remained essentially an adjunct of the Forepaugh sideshow, to be seen before and after the performances in the big top. The show had dispensed with the money-saving example of kindness in animal education. And the hyperbole was back, as the show's promotional courier attested concerning Topsy and her now doubled herd:

> We own and everywhere exhibit in performance parade all the Adam Forepaugh elephants, all the Sells Brothers elephants, including the best performing elephants on earth . . .
> Mastodonic merit in disparate droves
> The world's wonderful exhibition of animal sagacity, proficiency, and humor
> Head stands
> Hind legs
> Elephants from Asia, Africa, Ceylon, Sumatra, and Borneo
> Elephants from everywhere and knowing almost everything
> Nearly a hundred tons of living pyramids
> Animated dancing of mountains

Martial, musical, clown, boxing, athletic, quadrille, polite, bicycling, equilibristic, aldermanic, mimicking, juggling, posing, mirthful
elephants

So many elephants.

As reported by the 1898 route book for the Forepaugh & Sells
Brothers show, the only attraction that repeatedly outdrew both the
black tent and the big top came when the circus took an ostensible
day of rest in Des Moines, Iowa.

Sunday, July 3

It was announced that the elephants would bathe in the river during
the afternoon and in anticipation thereof a tremendous crowd of at
least 35,000 gathered on the riverbank and bridges, on top of buildings
and in windows for several blocks to witness the elephantine frolic.

Other huge crowds watched the elephants hit the water at Cedar
Rapids, Iowa, on July 10 and Wichita, Kansas, on July 24. The day after
the Wichita splash, the show was in Harper, Kansas, and the diligent
Topsy was assigned to her usual post-parade duties outside the ring.

"Elephant Topsy created a little excitement while placing cages in
the menagerie after the parade," the route book reported. "She was
frightened by the appearance of a chicken under the sidewall and came
near a rampage. Our Sunday dinner had a narrow escape."

Yet Topsy as well as the other elephants remained serene when an
apocalyptic thunderstorm suddenly struck the show during a performance in Sioux City, Iowa. The equestrian act had just finished, with
the acrobats and the elephants scheduled next.

"Instead of the usual applause there broke from the audience a
smothered cry of terror and dismay as the canvas on the northwestern

side of the tent was lifted and riddled by the storm, and the exterior poles were pulled from the ground and their lashings snapped with reports like guns, and support poles were whisked to and fro among the horrified audience," the route book recounted.

The entire big top was lifted up over the reserve seats and fell upon the far side of the arena, "pummeling men, women and children with swaying tent poles, and tangling them in a labyrinth of ropes and cables, while the elements shrieked."

Hundreds ran off into the storm, halted only by the river or a row of barbed-wire fences.

"And upon it all and into it all there was deluged a torrent of rain which fell in sheets, driven edgewise by the hurricane, their surfaces illumined by monster lightning flashes."

Here was electricity at its most spectacularly elemental, not the harnessed power of modernity and the White City but untamed, wild, primal, dangerous.

"Sight was blinded by the glitter and glare and the tempestuous waters, and to the din of the elements was added the shouts of men and the hysterical lamentations of women and children. Hither and yon distracted hordes moved, blindly colliding in the tempest, many of them with all ideas of locality or direction paralyzed."

The mightiest patriarch would have been helpless before these forces of nature.

"Instantaneous havoc seemed to be loosed and puny humanity was at the mercy of powers too mighty for its insignificant resistance. Pandemonium yawned and a helpless multitude felt itself caught in the jaws of wreck and horror."

Two people had been killed and thirty-three severely injured when a procession of towering tranquillity emerged from the chaos and wreckage.

"And out of the ruin marched the herd of fourteen elephants to the train, as unconcerned as if nothing unusual had occurred."

The Forepaugh & Sells show managed to reach the next stand one hundred miles away in Manning, Iowa, by the following noon, though there was but one performance and that had to be in the menagerie tent.

"Attendance very good," noted the route book.

Business in general was on the upswing, with the economy recovering from overspeculation thanks to the production of actual wealth. The route book noted the various towns' individual contributions to the rising national prosperity. The circus proceeded in one three-day period from Wheeling, West Virginia, "a thriving city, with large iron and oil interests," to Steubenville, Ohio, "large glass and iron interests," to Beaver, Pennsylvania, which had "the largest tumbler factory in the world."

Milwaukee, Wisconsin, was even then renowned for its breweries.

"The weather is warm, but oppression is avoided by internal application of the delicious beverage for which the city is noted."

The elephants generally shared a taste for alcoholic beverages but had also come to regard the smell of it on a keeper's breath as a warning sign of a lowered threshold for punishment and a heightened penchant for brutality. That very well may have been part of the reason for an incident in the beer capital involving Topsy. She took exception to the ways of an assistant trainer.

"Frank Bloomer, an elephant man, becomes the enemy of Topsy, and is thrown to the street with great force, breaking a shoulder blade, and inflicting injuries sufficient to lay him up in the emergency hospital."

The head elephant trainer was M. J. "Patsy" Meagher, who sometimes adopted the compound surname Forepaugh-Meagher, other times simply Forepaugh. He had started out as a clown and had taken Eph Thompson's place in the boxing act with the elephant John L. Sullivan, though he adopted more of a traditional approach when he subsequently became an elephant trainer. That had predictable results after the 1899 season concluded. The show was at its winter quarters in Ohio when Meagher, aka "Patsy Forepaugh," brought the elephants into the training ring for exercise.

"Sid became unruly and the trainer jabbed the animal with his stick," a newspaper reported, a stick being a bull hook. "Sid became furious and hurled the trainer to the ground with his trunk. The elephant then fell on his victim, piercing Meagher's body with one of his tusks."

Meagher's wounds proved fatal. Sid was placed in heavy chains and his tusks were sawed to nubs, but his life was spared. That may have been due to the interim rule of the assistant elephant superintendent William Badger, who went so far as to suggest Meagher had ultimately been responsible for his own demise.

"[Meagher] was kind to [Sid] when he felt like being so, and when he was out of sorts he wasn't," Badger said. "No matter how I am feeling, I never lost my temper with Sid. I prefer to take it out of a human being."

Badger was of the Craven/Thompson school of kindness. He was also African-American, so he was not promoted to fill the superintendent spot. His tempering influence was eclipsed when the show instead brought in William Emery, who put his philosophy into action during the 1900 season's first stand, at Madison Square Garden. The Barnum & Bailey show was in Europe, so the Forepaugh & Sells show had taken over its usual opening venue.

On the last night of the two-week run, the generally well-behaved elephant Dick turned himself into an immovable object. The *New York Times* afterward reported that the sudden intransigence came when

Dick was about to be led into the ring for the night's performance and that he blocked the entrance to the pen, preventing the other elephants from being brought out. The circus route book would insist that the incident occurred after the performance, as the elephants were being led from the Garden for the trip to the next stand in Baltimore.

"He had fallen in love with the Gotham city, and framed in his brutal mind a resolution to die rather than make another trip to the one-night stands," the route book proposed.

By both accounts, Dick resisted every effort to make him budge. Rope and tackle were fetched.

"It was decided that Dick should move, alive if possible, dead if necessary," the route book said. "In a few minutes, the great rope noose was around his neck, and to the block and tackle arranged on either side of the mammoth beast were stationed several hundred men, who were the 'lord high executioners' of the occasion."

The *Times* gave the total number of men as one hundred, not hundreds. They were reported to have pulled with all their might, but their straining had no apparent effect on Dick. Two elephants were brought up and attached to either end of the rope loop, just as young Forepaugh had done twelve years before when dispatching Chief. The result was the same. The *Times* reported that a crew of sixteen men worked half a day on the carcass.

"It was found that there were 110 square feet of leather in his hide, 10 in his trunk, and 5 in his ears," the *Times* said. "The hide is worth $15 a square foot, and is used in making pocketbooks, music rolls, and similar articles, while the intestines, of which there are 1,400 pounds, and the bones are also of commercial value."

The Carnegie Museum was said to be interested in purchasing the skeleton.

"If the museum does not buy it, it will probably be sold in parts."

The *Times* suggested that Dick's death had been the unintended result of the elephant's own resistance. The headline read:

Stubborn Elephant Dead
Killed by Two Others at Madison Square Garden
Refused to Move and Resort to a Block and Tackle
Brought Him to an Untimely End.

The show proceeded north through Bridgeport, Barnum's hometown. The audience included two retired advocates of the bull hook, Arstingstall and "Elephant Bill" Newman, whose wife had employed a gentler, more matriarchal approach with remarkable results on the few occasions she was allowed in the ring.

Forepaugh & Sells had recently acquired a three-year-old "baby" elephant who was now "christened" before a crowd of twelve thousand in Boston. The show then headed on to the Midwest, arriving in Duluth, Minnesota, on July 9, 1900. The route book reported a record turnout.

"The biggest day's business in year. Every seat and all standing room sold, and a string of folks went back to town, couldn't get in."

The boomtown size of the crowd as Topsy once again led the quadrille reflected sudden prosperity brought by the discovery of astonishingly huge deposits of high-grade iron ore in northeastern Minnesota. The ore was so close to the surface that it could be scooped up and deposited directly onto a train, loading fifty tons on a car in three minutes, a single man with a steam shovel on the surface equaling the work of five hundred miners in other regions laboring with picks and shovels deep underground.

"For this revolution in mining, we have, of course, to thank Nature first," a contemporary local historian noted of this vast find in the

Missabe mountain range. "Geology has done more to make it possible than the human inventor."

A biographer would write that upon seeing that the price of iron ore had fallen considerably below what he could ever hope to achieve by milling. Edison simply gave a laugh and said, "We might as well blow the whistle and close up shop."

Edison had compromised himself and poured most of his fortune and years of effort into the New Jersey iron ore project, yet he remained as outwardly serene as an elephant in a thunderstorm. Tate would write, "He knew that his failure was not due to any technical defects in his process but to conditions beyond his power to detect or anticipate. He was defeated by Nature when she prepared a rich and vast deposit of iron which required no milling. No personal element was involved. There was no kidnapping and nothing to regret."

Edison mitigated some of his losses by adapting the ore-crushing machinery to the manufacture of cement, and there was still the revenue from his participation in entertainment, however reluctant.

The silver dollar measure indicated that the future of movies lay in storytelling spiced by violence and/or sex and many, many more kisses. Edison remained the same person who had devoured every nonfiction volume in the library as a youngster, but in his whole life claimed to have read only one novel, *Les Misérables* by Victor Hugo. He continued to say that film would become primarily an educational tool. He seems to have said nothing more about the deep hurt that could only have grown along with the ever-burgeoning electric revolution.

Some of the independent local affiliates retained the Edison name even as they moved away from direct current orthodoxy. They clearly recognized the continuing value of association with the Wizard.

One of the bigger such firms was the Edison Electric Illuminating Company of Brooklyn, which took over two smaller power firms and seemed close to securing a virtual monopoly in that borough. It was then challenged by a new firm called the Kings County Electric Light and Power Company, which had not yet finished building its first power plant but held the Brooklyn rights to Tesla's system. The *Brooklyn Daily Eagle* reported the rivalry as if the Wizard were involved and the War of Currents had not been decided in favor of Tesla and Westinghouse four years before. The paper seemed to imagine that Edison the inventor had some connection with the Brooklyn company that bore his name.

"Brooklyn will soon be the scene of one of the greatest scientific and industrial battles of the age," the paper said. "The genius of Tesla is to try conclusions with the wisdom and experience of Edison. This great struggle for supremacy in science and finance will have its seat of war right in Brooklyn."

This local struggle was in fact between two AC systems. The long-established Edison Electric Illuminating of Brooklyn appeared all but certain to prevail in January of 1898 as it put into operation a huge new plant in Bay Ridge that would produce the damnable current, the firm proving to be more adaptable than its namesake had been. But the only patents available to it were for a system less efficient and profitable than the Tesla system.

As a result, the upstart Kings County company was able to underbid the Edison company for the municipal lighting contract. The somewhat secretive syndicate backing the Kings County company then proved able to muster enough money to take over the Edison company. The upstart simply bought all the stock of the near monopoly as part of a plan to become a monopoly itself and eventually join a larger monopoly encompassing all of New York. The result was a victory for what Thomas Edison had declared to be his least favorite type.

"There was no title of reproach and contempt that he could confer on anyone more withering than that of speculator," Tate would write.

Now a vassal state rather than a kingdom, what was still called Edison Electric Illuminating of Brooklyn continued to operate the power plants it no longer owned, along with the lone one that Kings County was only now completing. Thomas Edison surely understood that the new owners were keeping his name on their subsidiary not as a testament but as a hedge against grumblings about trusts and monopolies and rates that would turn out to be not so low after all. The public would think it only natural that a company bearing the Wizard's name would be the sole source of power. This also made the company the sole recipient of the profit. Not one of those silver dollars was going to Thomas Edison as the demand for electricity in Brooklyn and everywhere else kept growing as quickly as he had envisioned it would.

As 1901 arrived, the syndicate behind the Kings County Electric Light and Power Company and therefore Edison Electric Illuminating of Brooklyn commissioned what were described as "the two biggest generating units in existence" for its Bay Ridge plant. The generators were, of course, designed by Westinghouse.

TWENTY-THREE

SID SORROWS,
TOPSY TRAIPSES

The Barnum show was still in Europe in 1901, so the Forepaugh & Sells Brothers Show again opened the season at Madison Square Garden. The elephant men were in the basement preparing the herd for the performance up in the main arena when a *New York Times* reporter appeared. The reporter asked their reaction to news that their fellow trainer Henry Huffman of the Wallace Circus had been killed by the elephant Big Charley in Peru, Indiana. Big Charley was said to have grabbed Huffman with his trunk and flung him into a stream, then held him underwater with a forefoot. Wallace Circus workers had fired on the elephant to no apparent effect before he tore through a fence into a large field, where he kept everyone at a prudent distance. Apples laced with strychnine were lobbed into his proximity and he finally ate one. An hour later, he keeled over and a rifle bullet finished him off in a coup de grâce.

"I wouldn't trust one of those damned hides," a Forepaugh & Sells assistant trainer identified only as Mike now told the reporter. "They're the trickiest beasts that live. They know more than all the rest of the animals in the circus put together. They'll fool you for a long time, by allowing you to think they love you, when they are just waiting for the chance to put you out of business with a swing of that snaky snout of theirs."

Mike went on, "I told Huff a long time ago that beast would do him in the end, but Huff laughed at me. I long ago considered the elephant as my enemy, and I will always cling to that belief. I don't ever expect to be killed by one of them for that reason. I hate them, though I'm a trainer. I rule them by brutality and fear, not by kindness."

Badger was also present and voiced a very different view, saying, "I don't believe a word of it. The elephant is one of the most knowing and kindest beasts alive. There's Big Sid, for instance. He killed poor Patsy Forepaugh a year ago. Why? Because Patsy didn't understand him."

Badger made a statement that even an elephant lover might have found dubious.

"Sid is sorry for having killed Patsy. He hasn't forgot it. I bet when that old beast is a candidate for a permanent position in some museum, carrying a ton or two of sawdust under his hide, it will be through remorse for his killing Patsy."

The other trainers scoffed. Badger led them and the reporter to where Sid was leisurely munching hay. Badger hugged the elephant's trunk, speaking to him in soothing tones. Badger then stepped back out of reach of the trunk.

"This is the only time I'm afraid of Sid," Badger told the others, "for you'll see what I say burns deep in his hide. I've never learned whether it's anger or real contrition which causes him to act so every time I mention Patsy."

The moment had come for a private demonstration that was in its own way more remarkable than all the public marvels of the circus, that surprised even the other trainers. Badger addressed the elephant.

"Where's Patsy, Sid?"

The elephant's ears perked alert.

"Where's Patsy?"

The ears began to flap and Sid shuffled his feet as much as his shackles would allow. He began swinging his trunk above his head.

"Sid killed Patsy, didn't you, Sid?"

The reporter noted that the elephant seemed to comprehend every word, straining against his chains near to the snapping point as Badger uttered the accusation again, and then again. Sid finally let out what was described as "a terrible roar that reverberated throughout the whole building." The roar came anew each time Badger repeated Patsy's name and the other elephants joined in. One of the managers hurried over from where he had been cueing performers for their entrances. He demanded the herd be hushed.

"There, don't you believe elephants have memory and that Sid is sorry for his act?" Badger asked his comrades once the elephants were finally quieted.

Badger moved to convince anybody who still harbored doubts.

"Now, wait. You'll notice when the show is over upstairs and the people come down to see the elephants that Sid won't eat," he said. "I'll bet that beast won't touch a mouthful of food for the rest of the night."

Not long afterward, the showgoers appeared and swarmed around the elephants. Sid stood as if on some deserted field and ignored the crowd's offerings of candy and peanuts. The other elephants, Topsy among them, reached with their trunks or simply opened their mouths wide to catch tossed treats.

"But they hadn't killed a man and they didn't know remorse," the reporter wrote. "Perhaps someday they will."

After a fortnight at Madison Square Garden, the show went from town to town through New England and the Midwest, finally heading south once more and arriving at Paris, Texas, at the end of September. One of the elephant keepers who was apparently more of Mike's view than Badger's aroused the ire of Topsy. She hoisted him with her trunk and dashed him to the ground. The keeper was hospitalized with three broken ribs and a battered face, but subsequent reports that the man died were apparently exaggerated. Reports that Topsy also killed a man in Waco seem to have been simply fabricated, for neither the town records nor the local newspaper seem to contain any mention of such an event when the circus passed through there.

From Texas, the show proceeded on to Louisiana. The train carrying the animals was a mile outside Baton Rouge when it rear-ended a freight train, seriously injuring three men, wrecking four cars, and setting the elephants at liberty. Topsy and the others managed to stay ahead of their pursuers for several hours. They ranged free through the countryside, a sudden escape from captivity, a taste of what might have been had they never been captured.

The reprieve ended when the elephants either chanced or were driven into Baton Rouge. A posse of citizens joined with the circus men to capture the herd. The elephants were conveniently already in the city for that night's show, and soon Topsy was once again crawling around the ring.

That summer, Edison twice visited the Pan-American Exposition in Buffalo, which was officially meant to mark the ascendency of America and became a celebration of all things electric. His host on both occasions was Luther Stieringer, the former lab aide turned lighting designer who had added a splash of color to the white blaze in Chicago. He was the chief lighting designer of the show in Buffalo, which not only outdid Chicago in sheer numbers of bulbs, but also was multihued throughout, not a White City but a Rainbow City. Edison replied with a superlative that was considerably ahead of its time.

"This is out of sight!"

Edison was equally excited by the work-in-progress he brought to the exposition, a new storage battery that would hold a charge considerably longer than those presently on the market, yet weighed half as much. He guaranteed it would revitalize the automobile industry, providing with its very use the means to transport direct current great distances.

"This new Edison battery will be the apparatus or machine to carry the power of the falls thousands of places," a local reporter rhapsodized.

The partly completed battery was displayed in the electricity pavilion. Edison could not have been happy to see a WESTINGHOUSE sign there that was so big one of the smaller companies had gone to court in an unsuccessful bid to have it reduced.

Edison also displayed his latest phonograph, refined to provide even better entertainment. He no doubt fully approved when the well-heeled overseers of the exposition declared that Rainbow City was intended to be primarily educational, a "colossal university . . . instructive of the best of the arts and trades and sciences." His roving film crew had been there to capture the opening ceremonies. The short clip *Opening, Pan-American Exposition* showed then–vice president Theodore Roosevelt leading the procession.

Among the subsequent films was *Pan-American Exposition by Night,* which opens with a daylight panorama. The sweep stops with the camera centered on the electric tower, which was being described as the exposition's "crowning centerpiece." Nobody was calling this one the Edison Tower, but the Wizard's crew was there to capture it as nightfall brought what his film catalogue would term "the coming up of the lights, an event which was deemed by all to be a great emotional climax." The culminating moment comes as the searchlights atop the tower pierce the darkness from high above the exposition's vast array of other lights.

"The effect is startling," the catalogue says, going on to sound like a circus courier. "The picture is pronounced by the photographic profession to be a marvel in photography, and by theatrical people to be the greatest winner in panoramic views ever placed before the public."

The footage did as much as black and white was able to capture the out-of-sight thrill of the Rainbow City. Another Edison film, *Panoramic View of Electric Tower from a Balloon*, begins with the gushing fountains at the foot of the tower and gradually rises until it reaches the figure the Goddess of Light at the top, then seems to descend.

"Here we have recorded a very novel scene, the camera having been placed in the basket of the captive balloon at the Pan-American Exposition," the Edison film catalogue would say. "It was then slowly elevated to the top of the Tower, a distance of 465 feet, and slowly lowered until it reached the ground, keeping the Tower in view all the time during the ascent and descent, ending with a very interesting view of the base of the Tower, with crowds of people passing to and fro."

In fact, the crew had engaged in a little humbug such as Forepaugh and Barnum might have mounted had they gone into movie making, creating the illusion of ascent and descent simply by tilting the camera slowly up and down.

*   *   *

What was missing from the initial films of the exposition was something that had been crucial to all the plans: a crowd. The exposition had everything except one essential quality, that being popular appeal. Edification was hardly proving to be a huge draw. Attendance was falling considerably short of expectations with an accompanying shortfall in revenue that resulted in it being termed a "glorious blaze of financial failure."

To the rescue came Frederic Thompson, who had been a janitor at the Chicago fair and had noted that the midway attractions there generally outdrew the main exhibits. He had put that observation to work at a smaller exposition in Omaha, when he took over a California mine exhibit that had gone defunct because, in his words, "it had nothing in it to thrill." He put a group of comely, brightly lit dancers on a rooftop stage and filled the facsimile mine shaft below with ghoulish items befitting someone who happened to have been born on Halloween. The reconceived Heaven and Hell was a big hit.

Thompson toyed with the idea of adding a fiery pit to hell at the next fair, and that raised the question of how to transport the customers across it. The answer that came to him was "airship." He then decided that an airship could be a show in itself. But where would it go?

Thompson arrived at the Pan-American Exposition planning to operate both Heaven and Hell and an elaborate virtual ride he called Trip to the Moon. He thereupon discovered that Elmer "Skip" Dundy, the son of an Omaha federal judge, had filed plans for a show identical to Heaven and Hell, having copied what he had seen at his hometown's fair. Thompson challenged him, but Dundy had grown up around lawyers and prevailed. Thompson was more impressed than angry and the two became partners in both concessions.

Trip to the Moon was now proving to be one of the most popular attractions at the Buffalo exposition's midway. The exposition's hierarchy initially dismissed Thompson's ride as a common, somewhat vulgar diversion, a barely tolerable trifling of true science. Thompson was very clear regarding his opinion of the Rainbow City.

"Architecturally and from an educational standpoint this exposition was one of the most remarkable in all the history of world's fairs," Thompson later wrote. "It was beautiful; it was tremendous; but it wasn't paying."

Thompson went to his supposed betters on the exposition's executive committee.

"[I] told them why their outlay of millions of dollars was attracting only thirty thousand people a day. I told them they were failing miserably because there wasn't a regular showman in the lot. I told them about the carnival spirit, and they came back by telling me about the educational value of the exposition."

Thompson posed a question.

"What's the use of a college if there are not students?"

Thompson made a proposal.

"I suggested that they turn over the show to me for one day, which would be sufficient to test what the executive gentlemen were pleased to call my theories."

The committee scoffed, but its president overruled them, granting Thompson a day that was less than a fortnight hence.

"The exposition was to be mine for August 3," Thompson wrote, "and I told them that it would be known as 'Midway Day.'"

He had little time and much to do.

"Within six hours after the final interview I had four printing houses at work getting out the paper with which I was going to plaster the country."

He would be promoting the exposition just as regular showmen such as Barnum and Forepaugh and Bailey promoted their shows.

"I and my sideshow associates sent ten advance men on the road to herald the coming of the big day, and within a week a large part of the eastern half of the United States was screaming: 'August third! Midway Day at the Pan-American! Don't miss it!' "

The litanies of the posters and newspaper ads could have been composed by Barnum.

"Marvels for the Millions!"

"Mirth for the Masses!"

On the appointed day, attendance jumped from thirty thousand to one hundred forty-two thousand, not counting the ten thousand who rushed in without paying before the police were able to summon reinforcements.

"How was it done?" Thompson would write. "By paying no attention to Machinery Hall, the architectural beauty of the State Building, or the interesting exhibits of Trade and Industry; and by smearing signboards of forty-five states with the carnival spirit. Instead of advertising an organ concert in Music Hall we yelled ourselves hoarse about high diving, greased poles, parades, and every other crazy thing we could think of."

At the exposition's opening, three thousand carrier pigeons had been released with invitations to world leaders. The sky now filled with ten thousand pigeons with a message to "the rest of mankind." They were joined by an actual hot air balloon that rose two thousand feet as a couple got married in its basket. Thompson stretched a long rope from the top of the electric tower and sent the renowned daredevil known by the single name Cameroni up to perch beside the Goddess of Light. Cameroni proceeded to upstage Her.

"I had a man sliding by his teeth from the top of the sky-scraping electric tower to the esplanade below. True, he had never before traveled more than thirty feet in that fashion, but we tied him on, so there was no danger. The illusion was great, and the stunt made a sensation."

The path of Cameroni's descent extended to an arena that had been modeled after the Panathenaic arena of two millennia past, in keeping with the executive committee's educational goal.

"To the stadium, which had never held a quarter of its capacity, I drew 23,000 people to see a race contested by an ostrich, a camel, an elephant, a man on a bicycle, another on a horse, an automobile, and a zebra."

At the pistol shot signaling the start of the race, the zebra bolted, followed by the camel. One observer would later say the scene looked like the wreck of a circus train. The eventual winner was the man on the horse, a cowboy. The bicycle came in second, followed by the camel and the elephant.

The elephant was Big Liz, said by her owner to be Jumbo's widow and with her husband's demise "the largest elephant in captivity." The owner, Frank Bostock, the self-proclaimed Animal King, had lost most of his menagerie earlier that year in a fire in Baltimore started by faulty insulation in an electric wire, with little else surviving beyond what he termed a "pack of hounds" and a pair of "sacred donkeys" that purportedly once wandered the Holy Land. He told the press he had hoped to display a buffalo that could walk the tightrope and do the high jump, but sadly it had died en route to the exposition. He had retained a twenty-six-inch woman, purported to be the world's smallest. Chiquita the Doll Lady, also known as the Living Doll and the Tiny Atom of Cuban Humanity, was said to be the daughter of a wealthy Cuban sugar planter who had been murdered by the dastardly Spanish along with the rest of her family. She was further said to have visited the White House to thank President McKinley personally for giving Cuba its freedom from Spain, receiving a white flower in return.

The six-ton Big Liz and the 18.5-pound Chiquita were star attractions of a Midway Day parade worthy of a great circus. There was talk that Thompson would ride Big Liz, but he was substituted atop the elephant by a cage containing a lion. The Living Doll rode in a tiny electric car, a miniature portent of Edison's promised revolution. The most curious feature of the procession, one no circus had offered, was an oblong green and white object about the size of a small steamship featuring a pair of wood and canvas wings. The "airship" *Luna* was then hung back on its guy wires inside the encompassing 34,000-square-foot building that housed the Trip to the Moon.

Every fifteen minutes there, a new batch of thirty customers paid their fifty cents and entered an auditorium where a "professor" gave them a brief lecture on "anti-gravity" such as the educationally minded executive committee would have endorsed had it been based at all on fact. The travelers then entered the *Luna*, which swayed on its wires as if floating on air. The wings began to beat. The ship was caused to vibrate. Concealed fans generated a rush of air to approximate acceleration. The cabin filled with roaring noises. Scrolled scenery flashed past the portholes to offer the illusion of ascending above the fair until all that was seen of Buffalo were the lights for which it wanted to be famous. The fantasy's flight path continued over Niagara Falls and then slipped into darkness suddenly torn by flashing lights and sounds like thunder.

"We are going through a storm," the captain announced. "We are quite safe."

The ship proceeded up into space until it soon came to the moon. The customers exited the other end to enter a lunar cavern, where they were greeted by midget barb-backed moon creatures speaking Luna-ese. Moon maidens in a green cheese room offered morsels plucked from the walls. Giants stood guard at the palace where the Man in the Moon resided.

Among the many visitors to the ride was Julian Hawthorne, son of the novelist and grandson of the ship's mate who had recorded in the log the journey that brought the first elephant to America. Hawthorne was in Buffalo to describe his journey to the moon for *Cosmopolitan* magazine.

"Elaborate illusionism ingeniously carried out instead of being a performance on a stage so that instead of viewing a performance we are participants," he would write.

Edison himself came to the ride during his second visit to the exposition, curiosity apparently having overcome his usual aversion to fantasy. He chatted with Thompson, who used electricity in powering many of the ride's special effects and who was bent on becoming the Wizard of Entertainment.

Edison may have been expected to place this would-be entertainment mogul even lower than a speculator, but the boldness and freshness of Thompson's ideas apparently aroused an improbable respect, as if indeed from one wizard to another.

"Thomas Edison expressed his wonder and delight at the electric miracles Mr. Thompson has performed," the local press reported.

After Edison's departure, the ride's highlights were memorialized by his film crew, which was also on hand during the first week of September for the arrival of one draw that almost matched the Midway Day. A crowd of 116,000 was on hand to see President McKinley, who had been urged to visit by Roosevelt. McKinley was treated to a fireworks display that featured outlines of Cuba, Puerto

Rico, and the Philippines. It culminated in a message spelled out in the night sky.

"WELCOME PRESIDENT MCKINLEY CHIEF OF OUR NATION AND OUR EMPIRE."

The Edison crew filmed McKinley addressing the crowd and reviewing troops at the stadium. The crew predictably skipped the president's visit the next morning, September 6, to the Niagara Power Project, built by Westinghouse with Tesla technology to power the whole city of Buffalo along with the exposition. McKinley pronounced the generating plant "the marvel of the electric age."

McKinley then returned to the fair and the Temple of Music, where thousands waited in line for the chance to meet him. The Edison crew set up outside, figuring on capturing the happy tumult that seemed sure to accompany the president's exit through the crowd.

McKinley was inside shaking hands when a self-proclaimed anarchist named Leon Czolgosz stepped up and shot him twice in the stomach. The gunman might have kept firing had a citizen named James Benjamin Parker not punched him and knocked the small revolver from his hand.

The Edison crew missed the assassination itself but was able to film the scene outside. The catalogue would engage in a little more humbug, saying that in *The Mob Outside the Temple of Music After the President Was Shot*, "guards are plainly seen in the background trying to check the frantic multitude as they sway backward and forward in their mad endeavor to reach the assassin," though it is not at all plain to see and the crowd seems to be too stunned to be bent on anything.

The ambulance that rushed McKinley away off-camera was electric-powered, but the operating room at the fair's hospital, being outside all public view, had not been wired. People had to hold up a mirror to catch the light of the late afternoon sun coming through the windows and deflect it onto the table as a gynecologist performed emergency surgery, both the president's personal physician and the exposition's medical director being unavailable. The operation ended with one of the two bullets still lodged somewhere in McKinley, and Edison announced from his laboratory in New Jersey that he was sending an X-ray machine he was developing. The machine arrived with a team of technicians but missing a part, and there was a great scramble to secure it. A test was then conducted and the device proved capable of locating a nickel placed under the back of a man of the same considerable girth as the president.

But McKinley seemed to be on the mend and the doctors decided to spare him the exertion of positioning himself for an X-ray. He then took a sudden turn for the worse as gangrene set in. He died eight days after being shot.

The Edison X-ray crew returned to New Jersey. The Edison movie crew made a series of short films of McKinley's body being ceremoniously transported to Washington and then on to his hometown, ending with *Funeral Cortege Entering Westlawn Cemetery at Canton, Ohio*. Edison was denied permission to film the convicted assassin being led into the execution chamber at Auburn Prison on October 29. His crew settled for a mix of reality and staging, splicing an exterior shot of the prison with a reenactment of Czolgosz being strapped into the electric chair, which Edison had helped bring into being. The resulting film was titled *Execution of Czolgosz, with Panorama of Auburn Prison*.

On returning to the Pan-American, the Edison crew nearly had an opportunity to film an actual, and exceedingly public, execution on the exposition grounds, albeit one less directly related to the assassination.

McKinley's death had turned the exposition into a murder scene and dampened the gaiety that Thompson rightly said was needed for success. Attendance fell to educational levels and Buffalo was relinquishing its dream of being the Electric City central to the American Empire.

Exhibitors clamored to display the heroic Parker on the Midway, figuring the man who had saved the president's life at least for a time could bolster sagging attendance and turn the tragedy into a tale of bravery. Parker proved actually to be as noble as he was described. He declined.

"I happened to be in a position where I could aid in the capture of the man," he said. "I do not think that the American people would like me to make capital out of the unfortunate circumstances. I am no freak anyway. I do not want to be exhibited in all kinds of shows. I am glad that I was able to be of service to the country."

Mindful of the success of Midway Day, the exposition's organizers announced a New York State Day on October 9, followed by a Buffalo Day on October 19. Business remained so bad even the Trip to the Moon cut its admission in half.

With the hope of ending on a high, or at least higher, note, the organizers proclaimed that November 2, the final day of the fair, would be Farewell Day. The big official event in the Panathenaic stadium was filmed by the Edison crew as *Sham Battle at the Pan-American Exposition*.

"On the closing day of the Pan-American Exposition, Saturday, November 2nd, 1901, a sham battle took place at the Stadium on the Pan-American Exhibition grounds, between the six tribes of American Indians and the United States Infantry stationed at Buffalo," the Edison film catalogue would report. "The scene is replete with charges and many hand-to-hand encounters. Most of the action took place close to our camera and the picture which we secured is excellent."

The event featured Geronimo, who had been performing in smaller skirmishes thrice daily at the Indian Congress, the Native American concession. The sight of the former Apache war chief prompted cries of "Geronimo!" from the audience.

"Geronimo is always sure of a recall or an encore," the local press reported.

After the battle, Geronimo and the others went about peacefully packing up for their departure. The crowd scattered into the grounds and many of the thousands who came to Farewell Day acted as if it were a mockery rather than a celebration. They grew ugly as all the Rainbow City's promises of a bright and exciting future were ending with them returning to their everyday lives. Mobs erupted into a rampage more wantonly destructive than any elephant stampede.

A local newspaper reported:

> People went mad. They were seized with the desire to destroy. Depredation and destruction were carried on in the boldest manner all along the Midway. Electric light bulbs were jerked from their posts and thousands of them were smashed on the ground. Some of the Midway restaurants were crushed into fragments under the pressure of the mob as if they were so much pasteboard. Windows were shattered and doors were kicked down. Policemen were pushed aside as if they were stuffed ornaments. The National Glass Exhibit was completely destroyed. Pabst's Café was demolished and Cleopatra's Needle was torn to the ground.

One exhibit that apparently escaped looting was a display of eleven baby incubators in actual use, premature human newborns proving to be a bigger draw than a mummified Native American papoose, and almost as big a draw as baby elephants. Also apparently untouched was the Tiffany's display, which featured 270 different uses of elephant skin, including a $1,000 handbag. There was also a $300 wastebasket made from hollowing out an elephant foot.

At midnight, after the crowd's fury was spent, the president of the exposition ceremoniously pushed a button to turn off the un-smashed lights. Then there was a residual glow and then darkness cloaked a desolate scene of destruction, disappointment, and debt.

In the middle of it all was Bostock and his menagerie, which had grown to include a large male elephant, Jumbo II, said to have fallen in love with the widowed Big Liz and to have surpassed her as the biggest in captivity. Bostock further reported that Jumbo II had served with the British army during the Abyssinian War in 1868 and had been decorated by Queen Victoria for valor, making him almost as big a hero as Parker. Bostock added that his acquisition of this distinguished pachyderm had the British people indignant "as they have not been since Barnum took the original Jumbo away from them."

But his supposed war record accorded Jumbo II little license when he was alleged to have acted as badly as the thousands of humans who rioted around him. The elephant was said in one newspaper account to have wrapped his trunk around the leg of a trainer named Henry Mullin and smashed him repeatedly to the ground. The article reported that Bostock and several helpers had come running with pitchforks. It was noted that Jumbo II had not stomped on the man because the elephant's legs were so restrictively chained he could raise his feet only inches. There was no indication why such restrictive fettering was necessary or whether it might have contributed to the elephant's ill humor. Other press accounts alleged that Jumbo II had terrified a little girl by tearing her dress and had even gone so far as to knock Bostock down. Bostock had already nearly lost an arm when he was mauled by a Bengal tiger named Rajah, but that attack had been excused as just part of being a big cat.

In the case of Jumbo II, Bostock might have been more forgiving had he not already been in a rage over another of his star attractions, the diminutive thirty-one-year-old Chiquita, who had fallen for a teenage ticket taker in his employ. Bostock had fired him, but her suitor had simply taken a new job at the nearby Indian Congress, selling tickets to the crowd that cheered Geronimo three times daily. Bostock had sought to keep the smitten Chiquita from eloping by consigning her to her trailer and nailing the windows shut.

Bostock's inability to control this tiny woman no doubt made him less able to bear defiance from the big elephant. The Animal King decided on a way to assert his supremacy and vent his rage as well as make up for declining revenue subsequent to the McKinley assassination. He announced that Jumbo II would be executed publicly in the exposition's stadium at 2:30 p.m. two days after Farewell Day.

"That is, the public will be admitted upon payment of an admission fee," a local newspaper noted.

Tickets would be going for fifty cents. There was still the question was exactly how Jumbo II would be put to death. The widely reported demise of Tip left many thinking that poison was too cruel as well as slower than an audience would desire. Bostock considered using the method that Bailey had employed so efficiently in the basement of Madison Square Garden.

"It is likely that Jumbo will be hanged, or choked to death with chains," he said.

A Bostock aide was quoted saying, "We might shoot him with an elephant gun. . . . It is improbable that anyone around here has one."

But Buffalo was the city of Southwick, the dentist who had performed the pioneering experiments dispatching dogs with electricity. Bostock finally announced that he would be employing the power of

Niagara for one final spectacle in the exposition stadium, a method more in keeping with the modern spirit of the Electric City.

As in the days when humans were executed publicly, extra trains were available to convey the spectators on the appointed day. They sat shivering in the chilly fall air only to be told that the plans had changed. Mayor Conrad Diehl had telephoned Bostock from one of the city's most exclusive clubs and said he was speaking on behalf of "society people." Diehl argued that Buffalo's reputation had suffered enough from the "financial unsuccess" of the exposition and the riot at the end of Farewell Day without such a ghoulish final note as the public electrocution of an elephant. The purpose of the exposition had been education, not eradication, particularly not as entertainment.

Bostock now announced to the paying crowd of a thousand that the public event had been canceled as the mayor asked and that they would get their money back as they exited the stadium. Some five hundred stayed, sitting in the cold and resisting repeated urgings to leave. Evening was approaching when they saw Jumbo II being led into the stadium flanked by two baby elephants whose purpose was apparently to pacify him. Jumbo II seemed the most passive and tranquil of creatures as he was guided onto a wooden platform and fettered in place. A harness was placed on him so that he had an electrode wrapped in wet cloth pressing against each shoulder.

Since the crowd was not going away, Bostock apparently figured he might as well play to it, and he made a little speech.

"He told the crowd about Jumbo's military career," an observer would recount. "He recalled the long voyage from the kingdoms of Africa to the Niagara Frontier and how hard it had been for Jumbo to adjust to life along the Midway. These events, Bostock said, had completely altered Jumbo's sanity. He had become a killer and death by electrocution was the only solution."

Bostock then signaled to an electrician named Frank Graham, who threw a switch affixed to the stadium wall that was connected via insulated copper cables to the 2,200 volts still running into the stadium. Jumbo II just continued to swing his trunk idly and flap his ears in what was described as a "a good-natured sort of way." He began to toy absently with a loose plank on the platform.

"He turned his head up and looked at the crowd as if to say, 'I wonder what all the people are looking at?'" a reporter observed.

Bostock signaled to Graham, who threw the switch again, with no more effect on Jumbo II than if the power had been shut off along with the exposition's lights. Tittering was heard in the stands and it spread until it grew to great gales of laughter, joined by catcalls and taunts aimed not at Jumbo II but at Bostock. The crowd followed as Jumbo II and the babies were led away.

"Jeering the executioner and cheering the elephant," an observer noted.

Bostock was mortified and mystified, theorizing that the electrocution had been a failure because the elephant's thick skin acted as an insulator. He allowed that he was not at all sure what to do with Jumbo II now, whether to attempt another method of execution or "try to reform him."

Bostock set that concern aside when he returned from the botched execution to discover that in his absence Chiquita had managed to escape through a gap in the trailer wall and elope with her teenage ticket taker. Bostock immediately took the matter to court, charging her with breach of contract. Bostock abandoned the Cuban fiction and told the court via his lawyer that he had come upon Chiquita in Mexico and acquired her from her widowed and impoverished father.

"He has taken as much care of her as though she had been his own," Bostock's lawyer attested.

"Yes, he has taken as much care of her as he has of his elephants," the ticket taker's lawyer replied.

The court found for the ticket taker, but Bostock refrained from venting his fury with a second attempt to execute Jumbo II. His showman's instinct no doubt told him that the electricity-resistant elephant would become a big attraction, which Jumbo II indeed proved to be when Bostock set off for other venues with his menagerie.

As for Edison's crew, if it stayed in Buffalo after the sham battle to record what was to have been Jumbo II's execution, no film was produced. Edison would not likely have distributed a film in which a jolt of alternating current failed to have the fatal effect he had predicted for even a creature as big as an elephant.

The Edison crew did film other elephants in the 1901 film *Day at the Circus*. The catalogue reports, "We present here a series of interesting pictures and show a number of scenes just as witnessed by a visitor to the Great Forepaugh & Sells Bros. combined four-ring circus. We begin by showing the complete circus parade as it takes place in the street. The first scene shows the parade coming down a broad asphalt avenue with park in background. Entire parade shows elephants, camels, band wagons, chariots, cages of animals, and full circus paraphernalia, making a most interesting subject."

The 350 feet of film proceed to show "the assembly or grand entry, and includes the entrance into the arena of the elephants, chariots, wild animals, horses, camels, etc." Topsy appears in both scenes, by now becoming known as one of the herd's premier performers. The film ends before her big moment, when she carries trainer Bill Emery from the ring at the end of the act, he standing on her head, the big top erupting into applause that for her is just part of her condition.

TWENTY-FOUR

TOPSY AND THE TORMENTOR

The Forepaugh & Sells Brothers elephants crossed the Brooklyn Bridge from Manhattan early on the morning of May 25, 1902. They were followed by the rest of the show and soon the canvas that had been taken down on Saturday night in Jersey City was raised in a lot at the corner of Halsey Street and Saratoga Avenue. The first performance of the weeklong stand was at 2:00 p.m. the next day.

Among those in attendance the following evening was James Fielding Blount. He had been a railway brakeman making use of Westinghouse's life-saving invention before he became one of those "circus-crazy" souls who quit their everyday routines to follow a show from town to town. He had been rebuffed in his efforts to secure a position as a driver, likely because of a fondness for alcohol, which he demonstrated to a habitual extreme while watching the performance. He was warned to stay away from the animals.

At five-thirty the next morning, Blount slipped under the canvas of the menagerie tent with a large glass of whiskey in one hand and a half-smoked cigar in the other. An attendant woke and sleepily asked what he was doing.

"I just came in to say good morning to the elephants," Blount replied.

"You better stay away from 'em," the attendant said before dozing off again.

"Oh, don't you bother about me," Blount reportedly said. "They all know me. I was an elephant myself once."

A staggering Blount made his way to the roped-off area at the center of the tent, where the elephants were tethered, some sleeping and still, while a few took a turn at keeping watch in the usual way of the herd. He apparently had learned to recognize the elephants by name.

"Good morning, Pete," Blount said to the first elephant in the long line, holding out the glass of whiskey. "Have a drink!"

Pete liked booze as much as did the rest of the herd. He extended his trunk only for Blount to retract the glass and laugh. Blount repeated this a few times before finally letting Pete take the glass.

"Pete lifted the glass daintily and poured it into his mouth without spilling a drop," the *Brooklyn Eagle* reported. "He then handed the glass back to Blount."

Blount continued down the line, at one point steadying himself by grabbing a trunk. The glass still smelled strongly enough of whiskey for the elephants to reach out their trunks as he repeated the teasing, which now ended not with a drink but with nothing at all, making Blount laugh that much harder.

By one account, Topsy was the tenth elephant, by another she was the unlucky thirteenth. She had apparently been sleeping and was only half awake, swaying slightly at the start of another day of stressful captivity.

"Here, Topsy, wake up," Blount said. "It's morning. Have a drink!"

Blount slapped Topsy hard on the trunk. An attendant called out a warning for Blount to cease his teasing.

"Don't bother yourself," Blount said. "I know what I'm doing."

Topsy raised her trunk slightly but did not reach out for the glass, either wise to the trick or simply sleepy. Blount apparently decided she was ignoring him and he threw sand in her face. He then stepped closer, holding out the glass. She finally reached with her trunk and he withdrew, raising the glass high. She kept reaching.

Here was this star elephant who always got a huge ovation at the end of the act while Blount sat anonymous in the crowd, unable to get even a lowly job as a driver. Blount is said to have jabbed the lit end of his half-smoked cigar into the extremely sensitive tip of Topsy's trunk. His laughter turned to a cry as Topsy seized him about the waist and hoisted him high in the air. She then dashed him to the ground with a thud that one of the keepers heard from thirty feet away.

The next sound was described as "a crushing, crunching noise." Topsy would be said to have brought her weight to bear with her forehead in one report, both knees in another, her right foot in the official coroner's finding, which noted that Blount suffered a ruptured liver and multiple fractured ribs. Topsy used the same foot to push away Blount's suddenly still form.

Superintendent William Emery was summoned and he found Blount to be beyond help. The trainer spoke sternly to Topsy for ten minutes as if she could understand every word. She made no effort to resist as he and his assistant placed double chains on all four of her feet.

"Emery says she knows just as well as a human being what she has done," the *Brooklyn Eagle* reported. "She barely tasted the hay that was given her for breakfast and when an *Eagle* reporter saw her at ten o'clock she was standing very quietly with every appearance of sorrow and dejection."

Both the *Eagle* and the *Times* reported that Topsy was slowly swaying as a photographer set up a camera but went stone still when Emery called out for her to cease. A press agent sought to prove she was no vicious beast by having her pose with three men on her back, then with Emery sitting on her head as she lay down. The press agent contrived to convey her size by standing behind her prone form. Only the top of his hat was visible.

The next day's newspapers were almost uniformly sympathetic to Topsy, the *New York Times* saying she was "amiable as elephants go and more intelligent than most," noting "she has never killed a man before." The *New York Tribune* said much the same, suggesting the blame resided not with Topsy but with Blount.

"His death was due to his foolhardiness in tormenting the elephant," the paper concluded.

Blount was identified by a $160 money order and letters from a sister found in his pocket. His body was shipped home to Indiana, and that seemed to be that as the show finished its Brooklyn run and Topsy and the other elephants walked back over the bridge. The show played Paterson, New Jersey, that Monday and then five New York State towns over the next five days, traveling 377 miles and arriving in Poughkeepsie on Sunday.

After Topsy was taken off the train, an assistant keeper had her wait for the rest of the elephants. A twenty-year-old local named Louis Dodero came out of the crowd that had gathered to watch the unloading. He had a stick in his hand and began to "tickle," more likely poke, Topsy behind the ear.

Topsy seems to have reached her limit when it came to teasing and seized Dodero around the waist with her trunk, hoisting him high in the air and just holding him there for a moment. She then threw him down and was raising her right foot in apparent preparation for finishing the job when Emery came running over and stopped her.

However understanding Emery may have been, however extenuating the circumstances, the show's owners had reached a limit of their own. They announced the same day that Topsy had been sold.

"Tops has not been a bad elephant except when teased by people," co-owner Lewis Sells said. "I have decided to sell her because she has now gained a bad reputation."

As the show continued north into New England, Topsy was transported to New York. She was led alone over the Brooklyn Bridge and across the borough to a realm whose first European settlers were governed by a matriarchy nearly as egalitarian as that of an elephant herd.

TWENTY-FIVE

FROM LADY MOODY TO
THE BILLION-DOLLAR SMILE

In 1645, the Dutch governor of New Amsterdam granted a British widow named Lady Deborah Moody and thirty-nine of her fellow religious refugees a stretch of land at the far end of Brooklyn that extended to a sandy seaside isle known to the Dutch as Konijn Hok, in English literally "rabbit hutch." The name was derived from both the area's many rabbits (*konijn*) and for the Native American women and children who sometimes sought refuge there in times of inter-tribal conflict. Konijn Hok was translated in a formal land grant to Conyen Island.

Lady Moody derived her title from her husband, Sir Henry Moody, who died in 1632. She grew weary of living alone in their country estate in Wiltshire and, in the way of many widows, experienced an urge to move out even if she could not just move on. She was living in London when the infamous Star Chamber of judges and clerics decided that the rabble might forget their betters if the betters were not in residence to remind them. There was already a provision in the penal code forbidding subjects from living away from their rightful homes for a protracted period. This was now joined by an order aimed at all gentry and singling her out by name.

"Dame Deborah Moody and the others should return to their hereditaments in forty days, in the good example necessary to the poorer class."

Moody refused and ended up going much farther from home, on a ship bound for the freedom that was said to await those who followed the Puritans into exile in New England. Moody became a member of the church in Salem, Massachusetts, during the years in which Nathaniel Hawthorne would set *The Scarlet Letter*. She came to adopt the views of the controversial Roger Williams, who had the colony abuzz with his contention that persons should be baptized only when they are of an age to knowingly make an avowal of faith. She who had come to New England as a result of one decree now found herself the subject of another. Governor John Winthrop noted in his journal that although she was a "wise and anciently religious woman," Moody had been admonished for "being taken with the error of denying baptism to infants" and, along with "many others infected with Anabaptism," had "removed thither," thither being "to the Dutch." Any hope of her returning to Massachusetts ended with her excommunication.

On Brooklyn's outer shore, Moody divided the land into forty equal plots and granted the thirty-nine other refugees an equal voice in all decisions, her added sway derived elephant-style from her peers' respect and deference to her position as senior female. The residents were able to live as freely and equally as they had hoped to live when they came to America.

This changed after Moody's death, as the men of that and the next generation began to vie for bigger portions of land. The early eighteenth century saw one settler named Thomas Stillwell eventually come to own virtually all of Coney Island, whose use heretofore had been equally shared, sensibly rotated between grazing cows and cultivating tobacco and Indian corn. His holdings were subsequently acquired by various investors who revived the Native American notion of Coney Island as a refuge, but for well-to-do city dwellers looking to escape the heat and stench of a New York summer.

In 1829, a group of what Edison would have termed speculators formed the Coney Island Road and Bridge Company and held a kind of IPO of three hundred shares at twenty dollars. They thereby funded a shell road from the mainland and the isle's first hotel, the Coney Island House. The first big crowd came after a quartet of mutineers washed ashore with a trove of stolen silver, which was promptly stolen by somebody else, who buried it in the sand but lost track of it, triggering a mass dig for buried treasure. The beach itself remained an ongoing lure, and, rather than dig, those seeking a fortune there built a second hotel, soon followed by a third and then the first bathing pavilion.

"This was the beginning," wrote the historian Peter Ross in his *A History of Long Island*. "But it is difficult to say exactly when the modern movement which resulted in making Coney Island famous fairly set in. In one sense, no date can be definitely fixed, for, like Topsy in *Uncle Tom's Cabin*, 'it just grow'd.'"

In 1846, a ferry began offering the laboring classes a summer day's escape from the teeming tenements of Manhattan. Thieves and confidence men saw much the same opportunity as offered by a circus crowd, with the added advantage of there being no police force on the beach and no show owner demanding a cut.

Numerous other bathing pavilions were joined by dance halls with singing waiters and women who hustled drinks and more. A performer known as Princess Zaza became famous for smoking a cigarette in a unique way. A "rescue house" took in a thousand "fallen" women a season. Reformers and crusading journalists railed against the rampant lawlessness and depravity of what some were calling Sodom by the Sea.

"If this advertising goes on, Coney Island won't be big enough to hold the crowd that want to go there!" said Frederick Wurster, mayor of still-independent Brooklyn.

More innocent thrills and entertainments, as well as fewer pickpockets and con men, were offered within the confines of Boyton's Sea Lion Park, where Edison's crew had filmed *Shooting the Chutes*. Boyton's success had inspired the latest owners of the Elephant Colossus just across Surf Avenue to build a kind of toboggan ride around the landmark that had failed even as a bordello.

On a September evening at the end of Boyton's second season in Coney Island, passersby noticed a gleam in the 122-foot elephant's eyes. Two minutes later, flames erupted from the howdah on top. Fire soon filled the entire structure, causing the elephant to go down on its knees with a sound eerily like a huge groan, pitch over on its side, and burn to cinders. The blaze was declared arson and there were rumors that the structure was heavily insured.

By then, a site just down Surf Avenue from Boyton's park had been taken over by George Tilyou, who had started out in Coney Island at age fourteen, selling containers of "authentic sea sand" and "authentic sea water" to tourists. Tilyou had gone on to build a Ferris wheel after seeing the original one while honeymooning at the Chicago exposition. His was half the size, but that did not deter him from posting a sign declaring it "The World's Largest." He was now inspired by

Boyton to build an amusement park of his own, in actual fact even bigger and even grander. The signature ride of his Steeplechase Park was a race in which a half dozen patrons at a time rode wooden horses on wheels along an undulating iron track, with gravity making the heavier, not the lighter jockey more likely to win.

Boyton struggled to compete, adding the Flip-Flap Railroad, the world's first loop-de-loop roller coaster. He also expanded his animal acts beyond the sea lions, and to that end he now purchased Topsy. He was apparently undeterred by her record. He figured he might even be able to teach her to shoot the chutes and give him a real edge over the wooden horses of Steeplechase.

But that season, the summer of 1902, turned out to be the worst weather-wise in memory, with rain falling on seventy of the summer's ninety-two days. Boyton had overextended himself financially in his effort to keep up with his rival and his sodden park was often all but deserted. Tilyou had the good fortune to have arranged for Trip to the Moon to relocate to Steeplechase after the Buffalo exposition. This indoor ride was self-contained and immune to the perpetual downpour and did huge business, drawing 850,000 customers even as Boyton suffered financial ruin.

Tilyou had lured Trip to the Moon's creators to his park by guaranteeing them 60 percent of the attraction's proceeds. Now that he had them there and the attraction was proving to be such a success, he sought to invert the formula, with the 60 percent going to him. He apparently figured that Thompson and Dundy would have little choice but to consent, for they could hardly just pick up and go to some other venue without exorbitant expense on top of lost revenue.

What Tilyou did not anticipate was that Boyton would announce that he was shutting Sea Lion Park and looking for somebody to take over the site. Thompson and his partner, Dundy, leased the property and secured funding from such Wall Street figures as John "Bet-a-Million" Gates to create another, permanent White *and* Rainbow City. Sodom by the Sea was to become an Electric City by the Sea. There would be an electric tower and 250,000 lights. The diversions would be as spectacular as the Buffalo exposition might have been had the duo been in charge from the start.

"A billion-dollar smile," Thompson said of the amusement business they were bringing to Coney Island, sounding like he was well on the way to being the Edison of Entertainment, the Wizard of Wow.

Along with Sea Lion Park, they leased the site of the former Elephant Hotel. Dundy was a little "circus crazy" and believed elephants were good luck. He divined only good fortune in Topsy, whom he and his partner decided to keep along with Shoot the Chutes. They figured Topsy would also come in handy when they moved Trip to the Moon three blocks down Surf Avenue from Steeplechase.

A gang of workmen set to dismantling the big building that encompassed the airship. Topsy was enlisted to assist in the latter half of October, moving the exterior structure's larger beams, which were lined up so as to constitute a pathway, then greased to facilitate dragging the *Luna* airship to the new site.

"Tops has performed his work well and he has attracted considerable attention as he made his way up Surf Avenue, drawing the big timbers," the *Brooklyn Eagle* reported, reflexively employing the masculine.

On October 29, Topsy was fitted with a harness and hitched with stout chains to the *Luna*. The perpetually inebriated handyman who had been appointed her cut-rate attendant ordered her to commence pulling. The chains grew taut as Topsy strained, but the big-winged ship did not budge. The handyman, variously identified as Frederick Ault and William Alt and known as Whitey, urged her on and she repeatedly tried anew, with no result despite her strenuous efforts.

When Topsy finally refused to continue, Whitey began poking her in the sides and between her eyes with a pitchfork. She could have stopped the abuse by this boozed-up bully simply by seizing him with her trunk. But she was apparently done with that and she continued to suffer with a forbearance for which she would get no credit.

Blood began to stream down her face and flanks and a female passerby protested. Whitey told her to mind her own business and called her "vile names." Police roundsman Bernard Clark received similar invective when he came over and ordered Whitey to cease abusing the elephant. Whitey responded by removing the harness and letting Topsy wander off into the surrounding streets. Clark arrested Whitey and the crowd of gawkers was presented with a choice. Some opted to follow the two men to the police station. The rest followed Topsy, who was eventually lassoed by other cops and brought back to her new owners. Thompson and Dundy were no doubt as sensitive as any showmen to publicity they did not control.

"Tops, the Bad Elephant, Makes Trouble at Coney," read the headline in the *Brooklyn Eagle*.

Whitey was freed on $300 bond pending a hearing in Coney Island Court two weeks hence. Whitey there argued that he was only following established and accepted practice when it came to elephants. The matter was adjourned to accord the defendant time to offer proof that his treatment of the animal was "as gentle as an elephant should receive."

Whitey remained out on bail on December 5, when an oversize wagon loaded with lumber became stuck in a monster pothole. Topsy was brought over to push the wagon out with her forehead, which she succeeded in doing despite more abuse from Whitey. The abuse continued after the job was done.

As before, a cop came over, this time patrolman Thomas Conlin, who ordered Whitey to desist. Whitey responded with characteristic obscenity, climbed onto Topsy's neck, and rode up and down Surf Avenue, drawing an ever-growing crowd. Whitey ignored Conlin's orders to come down, but when Topsy suddenly stopped at West Eleventh Street, the trainer's inebriation got the better of him. He slid off.

A furious Whitey began to stab Topsy's trunk with the pitchfork he kept handy. Conlin placed him under arrest and Whitey threatened to sic Topsy upon the crowd of onlookers. Whitey reconsidered when Conlin drew his revolver and promised to shoot Whitey if he tried to make good on his threat. Whitey fell in beside Conlin and this time the gawkers did not have to choose whom to follow. Topsy trailed along behind the trainer and the cop the three blocks to the West Eighth Street police station.

A surprise came when Conlin escorted his prisoner inside. Topsy ascended the five granite steps and sought to enter right behind them. She became wedged in the doorway and began to trumpet at full volume, causing the crowd outside to scatter in panic and the cops inside to seek refuge upstairs and in the cells. A sergeant named Levis ducked behind the front desk in terror and beseeched Whitey to get Topsy to remove herself.

Whitey eventually complied, but subjected the police to further humiliation by ordering them to get various sweets for Topsy and to keep the crowd back. That ended when the co-owner Thompson arrived. He instructed Whitey to take Topsy back to what was in the process of becoming Luna Park.

Conlin came along and once Topsy was in her quarters the officer moved to complete the arrest for disorderly conduct. Whitey sought to prevent this by wrapping his arms around the very trunk he had so viciously stabbed a short time before. Whitey challenged Conlin to go ahead and try to take him away. Conlin drew his revolver again and soon he and Whitey were walking into the station house, this time minus Topsy.

The damage to the doorway was easily repaired, but the injury to the cops' pride was more severe and made all the worse by headlines such as the one in the *New York Times*: "Elephant Terrorizes Coney Island Police."

One thing a new amusement park in rough-and-tumble Coney Island definitely needed was the goodwill of the police. Conlin and his comrades may not have been actually terrorized, but they surely did not like anybody saying they were. Sergeants in particular tend to dislike being embarrassed.

The proprietors of fledgling Luna Park could not make things right simply by firing a drunk they should not have hired in the first place. And there was also the distinct possibility that Topsy could figure in another incident involving the cops, who likely felt they had tolerated enough.

Then there was the cost. Topsy was eating about twenty-five dollars' worth of hay a week. They were paying Whitey twenty dollars a week, not counting bail. And in building their Electric City they were already extending themselves to where every penny mattered.

There was also the question of publicity. The *Brooklyn Eagle* had just run a huge feature about the construction of Luna Park and Thompson had been quoted saying, "Our motive power is furnished by steam engines, electric motors, horse, and the famous elephant Topsy, who easily does the work of a dozen horses in moving buildings or heavily loaded wagons." He had further suggested that once the work was done and the park was opened, the elephant would be among the animals available for children to ride, according "the little folks . . . no end of enjoyment." The papers were now talking about infamous Topsy, the man killer.

On the plus side, the incidents had brought Luna Park and its "bad elephant" considerable public notice. Simply killing Topsy would not necessarily generate much added attention in the newspapers. Such executions were losing their novelty. The Barnum & Bailey show had put five troublesome elephants to death during its most recent European tour and received scant attention even when it executed a sixth on board ship after docking in New York in March. The unlucky elephant had been the once-renowned Mandarin, sire of the first baby elephant actually born in America. He had been strangled with a rope hitched to a steam-powered winch called a donkey engine, after which his body had been weighted with three tons of pig iron and dumped off a seagoing tug.

And in October there had been hardly an outcry when Snyder, the keeper at the Central Park Zoo, killed another elephant who had supposedly tried to kill him. A whistling Snyder had presented a tray of poisoned bran to Big Tom such as had been presented to Tip.

"Here's your breakfast, Tom," Snyder said.

Tom collapsed after eight minutes.

"Dead," a witness announced.

But thirty seconds later Tom suddenly rose to his feet. Another dose and a total of fifty-four minutes of convulsions were required to finish the job.

"He's a hard one to kill," Snyder observed.

Snyder added without apparently intending any irony, "Anyway, I'm glad it's over, for we were good friends once."

That execution had drawn only a handful of gawkers, no more than an everyday streetcar accident. The ASPCA had not bothered to attend, much less express the kind of outrage that makes the papers.

At the same time, Thompson and Dundy surely recalled the press attention as well as the crowd at the Pan-American Exposition in Buffalo at the prospect of the public electrocution of Jumbo II. They just as surely remembered the laughter when the attempt failed, and they would not likely have risked a repeat. The one person whose advice they would have trusted was the Wizard, who had so effusively praised Thompson for his "electric miracles" in Buffalo.

Everyone save for Edison himself and a few rivals still considered Edison the foremost authority on things electric. He had presided over the electrocution of animals as large as a horse. He had sought the chance to electrocute Chief at the height of the War of Currents and perhaps Tip as well after the war was lost. His laboratory was stocked not only with a whale baleen and a hippo tooth, but also with elephant skin and a Wheatstone bridge with which to measure electrical resistance. He could have easily determined that the failure to electrocute Jumbo II was not the result of any unusual resistance pachyderm hide possessed.

A week after the incident at the police station, the *Brooklyn Daily Eagle* ran a story headlined "Tops and the Press Agent" with the subhead, "It Is Now Given Out that Coney Island's 'Bad Elephant' Is to Be Killed by Electricity." The article described "poor Tops," as "the big elephant, which has caused the police of Coney Island so much trouble of late, probably because of the alleged cruel treatment by Whitey, a blond-haired young man who has been acting as attendant to the beast." The article went on to suggest that the talk of execution was just humbug designed to drum up more publicity or, as the writer put it, "advertising," and that "it is safe to say that Tops will continue at the same old stand, where she will continue to be harmless, provided the attendant loses the fork."

The press agent was Charles Murray, lured away from Steeplechase to Luna Park with a start-up promise of a percentage of the profits rather than a salary. He certainly was as capable of humbug as any Barnum or Forepaugh press agent, particularly when he had a financial stake in the outcome. But this was not just advertising. Thompson and Dundy were deadly serious.

"Famous Baby Elephant Condemned to Death," read a subsequent headline.

The accompanying article recalled how Tospy had been "the pet of thousands of children when, as a famous 'baby elephant,' she first toured this country with Adam Forepaugh's circus twenty years ago," but made no mention of her being foisted on the public as American born. The execution was to be public and was scheduled for the following Sunday, or Monday in the event of rain.

The preparations were overseen by the press agent, Murray. He diverted some of the carpenters and laborers who were busy sawing and hammering piles of lumber into the towers and minarets of a fantasyland. A platform accessed by a bridge was built in the center of the lagoon at the foot of Shoot the Chutes. Big cloth banners were stretched across all four sides, so that a message in foot-high letters about the opening of Luna Park in May would be sure to appear in any film as well as news photos.

That Edison was sending his film crew indicates that he was almost certainly aware of this new attempt to electrocute an elephant. And the decision regarding where to place the electrodes—along with the fact that the attempt was being made at all after the disaster in Buffalo—suggests that the Wizard was considerably more involved than he had been the last time his crew visited the park, when it filmed *Shooting the Chutes*.

An elephant obviously has no hands, but there are feet with fleshy pads as removed from major bones and as "close to the blood" as human palms. The problem was that Topsy was too strong to be restrained so firmly as to keep two of her feet in jars of conducting liquid. The answer was a deadly variation on the copper-heeled lightbulb dancers at the Philadelphia exhibition where Edison's name was spelled out in lights. A twelve-inch copper electrode was affixed to each of two slabs of wood that would then be strapped to Topsy's feet as elephant-size death sandals. Her great weight would ensure the necessary contact.

The electrodes were to be connected to two wires that would be stretched the nine blocks from a plant owned by the speculator-controlled company that continued to use the Edison name but had no other connection with him except perhaps in this upcoming event. The distance from the plant was one that direct current could have managed, but this was alternating current and it was being relayed from the big new facility five miles away in Bay Ridge. That was the one whose bigger-than-jumbo generating units were manufactured by Westinghouse, a distinction that would receive no mention in the coverage of the upcoming execution but surely held some significance for Edison.

Even with the Wizard involved, the organizers did not want to risk having Topsy rise up from the apparently dead as Tom had done. They also dangled an elephant-size noose from a block and tackle atop the platform, securing the other end of the rope to a donkey engine such as was used to kill Mandarin. Topsy was to be strangled as well as poisoned at the same time the electricity was applied.

"We would have shot her with an elephant gun, too, but we weren't able to get the right kind of gun in this country and we understand they are only available in England," Murray said, echoing almost exactly what another press agent had said in Buffalo shortly before the attempted electrocution of Jumbo II.

TWENTY-SIX

"HERE I AM! HERE I AM! WHERE ARE YOU?"

On the morning of January 4, 1903, the company that was Edison in name only agreed to maximize the power available to electrocute Topsy by suspending all service in Coney Island save for the trolley cars needed to bring the expected crowds of spectators.

Thompson and Dundy were planning to collect twenty-five cents a head, but the event had received enough press attention that a whole squad of special agents from the ASPCA arrived. They announced they would not allow the elephant's death to be made into a public spectacle. They also had concerns as to the mode of execution.

"We won't allow you to hang him," the agents declared.

Thompson and Dundy explained that the motor-driven noose was only a backup in the unlikely event that the electrocution and the poison failed to speedily do the job.

"The society's agents agreed there was nothing inhumane about the plan," the *Sun* reported. "Death seemed to be pretty well arranged for."

The prohibition against a public execution remained and admission to the grounds was restricted to eight hundred nonpaying guests, these including the press and what were termed Coney Island celebrities, among them a former judge as well as a former councilman who brought his whole family as if to a midwinter picnic. The ASPCA agents were not so strict as to intervene when the owner of a saloon next to the grounds allowed spectators a perch on his roof for twenty-five cents, as had been done at America's last public official execution of a human.

More than one hundred photographers set up at the edge of the lagoon. So did the lone motion picture crew through which the Wizard's magic would make this the most public of executions. Edison had lost out on a chance to beat Westinghouse when a celebrity seeker had deterred Tesla from approaching him that day right here in Coney Island. All the subsequent experiments with animals and even the killing of his own species in the electric chair had failed to frighten people away from alternating current. In his effort to "turn back history with a frown," he had lost control of the company he founded, which shed even his name as it fell into the clutching hands of speculators. His effort to forget that defeat by topping himself with the iron ore scheme had ended in failure. And there was no hope of changing any of that now, no matter how deadly the jolt, no matter what size the subject.

Later, some historians would suggest that Edison electrocuted Topsy as part of the War of Currents. But that war had long since been lost and the execution itself and perhaps even the method were arranged by Thompson and Dundy. The participation by Edison appears to have been more akin to the rage that caused Forepaugh to leave Topsy with a crooked tail years before.

If Tate was right in believing that Edison not only harbored but also nursed his grievances "in the solitude of his own mind," then maybe this execution that his crew was filming for all the world to see was for him the culmination of an intensively personal and private drama. How apt that the wires stretched from what everybody called the Edison plant, which was operated by the Edison company but had nothing to do with Edison himself and was in fact owned by speculators. How perfect that the current would be alternating current from Westinghouse generators, but applied as Edison would recommend, with the slight modification of attaching one electrode to a forefoot, the other to a rear foot, so the deadly force would extend through the whole body, as should have been done with the horse. The film would document that Edison had not been again denied an opportunity to demonstrate the deadliness of the damnable current on the largest of land mammals, a creature so much bigger than any mere man, big enough to vent a great man's fury and frustration at being bested, to show who is truly boss.

And the Edison movie crew would be filming not just a reenactment like the execution of McKinley's assassin. This would be the real thing, the first actual death captured on film.

The execution was scheduled for noon, and as the appointed hour neared an electrician on the scene called the power plant over a telephone line that had been strung along with the wires. The plant sent out 6,600 volts for a test and Hugh Thomas, chief electrician at Luna Park, threw the switch. Smoke wafted from where the electrodes met the wood sandals.

"Working fine," a reporter noted.

The police cleared the roadway leading to the lagoon. A voice called out.

"Here it comes!"

The crowd gazed across the site to see a pair of Luna employees leading "Cupid" Langtry, a waiter known as Coney Island's fattest man outside of a sideshow. He was escorted in two big chains up to the bridge to uproarious laughter and applause.

All the while, Topsy was in her quarters, eating hay.

"Looking like any other self-regarding elephant," a reporter noted. "She didn't appear to be the least bit bad."

At a few minutes after noon, Topsy was escorted out by Skip Dundy and Carl Goliath, an elephant man who had been retained for the day. Goliath was on Topsy's left. He had a rake in his left hand, which he repeatedly employed to poke her behind the left ear even though she was ambling willingly along without so much as a tug on the harness buckled around her head and upper trunk. She continued through the construction site that would soon become the Electric Eden and passed a long row of spectators standing on a riser.

Twenty feet from the bridge leading across the lagoon, Topsy suddenly stopped. Some self-proclaimed experts would later say that elephants are leery of bridges, but in her circus travels Topsy had crossed hundreds if not thousands of them, many no doubt frailer than this one.

Whatever it was, no amount of tugging and pulling and poking could make her budge. Murray finally stepped up and tried a variation on press agentry. He held out a carrot and Topsy took a step forward to get it, seemingly as easily manipulated as public opinion.

But when Murray tried a second carrot, Topsy declined to take a second step. The press agent finally was the one to step forward. He ended up giving her a total of twenty-seven carrots but never got her to take more than that first step.

Goliath could only think to return Topsy to where they started and try it again. Topsy came back up the road as obligingly as before, and stopped at the same spot, no less resolute not to take a step farther despite a trail of grain that had been strewn before her.

"I'll bet Whitey told her what was up," a Luna employee was heard to mutter.

The would-be executioners dispatched a messenger in search of Whitey, who had been fired the day before, no doubt to save paying him for the week to come when his charge would be alive for only one more day. Whitey had apparently become upset over the impending execution despite the many times he had abused Topsy, in this way being a little like the brutal Arstingstall after Jumbo's death or, for that matter, like some abusive husbands.

By more than one account, Whitey was in tears when the messenger found him. He declined an offer of twenty-five dollars if he would come and coax Topsy over the bridge.

"Not for $1,000," he reportedly declared.

On hearing that Whitey had refused, Thompson decided there was only one thing to do before the reporters and photographers grew weary and dispersed to file stories making chumps out of Topsy's owners. The whole event was liable to end in laughter just as in Buffalo, or worse.

"We will have to kill her right here," he said.

Topsy was chained by all four feet to construction pilings so she would be kept in place even if she now decided to move. A noose was looped around her neck and attached to the donkey engine. The wires were dragged over. Topsy immediately complied when she was instructed to raise her right foot for the first death sandal.

"Not so vicious," a reporter remarked aloud.

Topsy seemed less a wild animal than a mild one. Another reporter later wrote, "She stood still in the application as quietly as could be asked, obeying all commands of the men even when telling her to get down on her knees."

After the second electrode was fitted on her rear left foot and she was again standing, Topsy did become mildly bothered. She shook off the electrode on her forefoot, but soon it was secured again and there she stood, nearly three decades after being torn from her mother and smuggled into America, where she had traveled tens of thousands of miles in perpetual servitude, endured innumerable beatings, and survived more than a dozen train wrecks. Her big dark eyes with their extravagant elephantine lashes glimmered with what a reporter discerned to be still at her core.

"There was real benevolence in her eyes and kindness in her manner," the *Tribune* reported.

Murray stepped up to act out the ultimate metaphor for his profession, feeding Topsy three carrots filled with a total of 460 grams of potassium cyanide. She took and gobbled one after another, playfully curling her trunk.

The motion picture camera had been shifted around so that Topsy was in center frame and one of the cloth banners on the platform was in full view over her left shoulder.

OPENING MAY 2ND 1903
LUNA PARK
$1,000,000 EXPOSITION
THE HEART OF CONEY ISLAND

If the gobbling of the carrots was filmed, it never made public view. The Edison crew was there to film, and the Luna Park people were there to stage, an electrocution, not a poisoning. The big worry was that the cyanide might cause her to collapse before the electricity brought her down. The third carrot was no sooner swallowed than the Edison plant got the awaited signal on the phone.

"All right!"

The camera was running and recorded Topsy again trying to shake off the electrode on her right forefoot. The electrode stayed in place. She set her foot back down and was standing motionless when the 6,600 volts coursed through the wires and the electrician, Thomas, closed the switch at the park. There were flashes and small blue flames and then smoke began to curl up from where copper met foot. Some would describe the smell as that of burning flesh, others that of burning hoof. The pain must have been excruciating and her huge form shook violently.

"Turn the current off!" a Luna employee cried out.

The smoke rose up around her flanks and she pitched forward into it, tipping to the right as her right foreleg buckled. The chain on her left leg grew taut with the fall, restraining her even in her last instant, drawing the limb straight out, displaying the electrode at the bottom of the foot. The electrode had stopped smoking. The current had been turned off after ten seconds.

Once the motion picture camera stopped filming, the donkey engine was set to work, cinching the noose tight around Topsy's neck and holding it tight for a full ten minutes. Only then, when she had been triply killed and there was not the slightest chance that she was alive, did the three veterinary surgeons approach and pronounce her dead.

From the Edison plant came word of an ironic near tragedy. The plant superintendent, Joseph Johansen, had accidentally electrocuted himself during the execution, receiving quarter-size burns oddly corresponding to Topsy's, to his right arm and left leg electro-stigmata. The doctor pronounced his survival "miraculous."

Back at Luna Park, Topsy was measured and it was recorded that she was ten feet tall and ten feet, eleven inches long. The autopsy was then performed on the spot. The heart and stomach were removed for the biology department at Princeton University. The taxidermist Hubert Vogelsang began skinning her. Some of the hide would be used to cover Thompson's office chair and two of the legs would be fashioned into umbrella holders. Thompson would tell people that the hide and leg came from the world-famous Jumbo. The head was buried in a remote, unmarked patch behind the stables.

The many witnesses to the electrocution concurred that Topsy had died without making a sound. There is no way of knowing if, in those final instants, she had made one of those cries below the level of human hearing, which a scientist of the next millennium would term a contact call and explain as a simple message elephants in the wild send to other elephants across great distances of savannah and jungle. Such a cry would have carried past the gawkers and across the grounds and the beach beyond and out over the sea, fading to an unheard whisper over the waves.

"Here I am! Here I am! Where are you?"

TWENTY-SEVEN

THE BIG SWIM

A trumpeting like Judgment Day itself blared from the predawn darkness off the shores of Staten Island on the fogbound morning of June 5, 1905. Again it came, and then again, closer, even louder through the mist. A disturbance in the glassy water began to rock the small rowboat where two fishermen were perched.

A huge form suddenly appeared off the bow, as big as a whale and preceded by what looked like a serpent spouting water. Frank Krissler and his buddy forgot their fishing lines and grabbed the oars, swinging the boat around. They began rowing back toward Staten Island as quickly as they humanly could.

The form kept coming. The fishermen kept rowing, but the form stayed right behind them the whole desperate way to shore. The moment the bow touched sand, the men scrambled onto Midland Beach. The form lumbered out of the water after them and only then did they realize what it was.

"A tame-looking, gentle-mannered creature that was neither whale nor sea serpent, but about the gentlest elephant that ever went astray in New York," the *New York Times* would report.

The men and the dripping elephant stood facing each other. Elephants had lost much of their novelty in the 109 years since the first one arrived in America on a ship sailing past this very beach on the way into New York Harbor. The larger zoos and even the more modest circuses had at least one. Audiences had grown accustomed to seeing the creatures perform tricks which were once considered marvels and made their trainers celebrities.

Here was a true marvel, apparently undertaken not at the command of a trainer, but of the elephant's own volition, a feat so inexplicable as to outdo anything performed under a big top. And it was made all the more astonishing by the mystery of where this creature had begun the big swim, with any immediate possibility seeming beyond what might be expected of so large an animal. The elephant almost could have just materialized out of the sea, spirit turned to matter.

Two other fishermen happened along and got a shock of their own. They quickly recovered their wits enough to fetch a rope, fashioning it into an outsize lasso. The elephant remained impassive on the sand as the four eventually overcame the complication of the trunk and got a loop around its neck.

The men pulled on the rope, but they had to understand that there was no forcing a creature this size. The elephant did not so much obey as acquiesce, coming along only because that was what the animal was willing to do. Krissler and the others proceeded from the beach, the latest men to discover that an elephant's amble looks slow until you try to keep up with it. They walked double-time to Adolf

Eberle's Speedway Inn, a hangout for aficionados of the new sport of automobile racing.

The elephant was in the carriage shed when the police arrived and led "it" to the mounted unit's stable in the village of New Dorp. The elephant was if anything more docile than the horses, which were put to daily service with saddles and bridles and reins.

An officer logged the elephant in the station house blotter, the chronicle of the cops' efforts to keep the local manifestations of their own species within bounds. One thing they knew for sure was that the elephant did not reside around there.

"Vagrant," the officer wrote.

As word spread, a crowd of several hundred gathered outside the station to see the swimming leviathan who had appeared so mysteriously from the sea. The officers turned giddy at hosting one of the world's wows rather than just another of its woes. They delighted in escorting into the stable all those who asked. The visitors stood mesmerized as they peered through the bars at what was pronounced "the wonderful prisoner."

The answer to the big question of where the elephant had started her swim came at 7:30 p.m., with the arrival of a delegation from Brooklyn. Pete Barlow, a onetime bareback rider who was becoming known as the Coney Island Elephant Man, was accompanied by two fellows described in news reports only as "Cingalese."

Barlow said the elephant was a female named Fanny. She was one of six Indian elephants at what had become America's new amusement sensation, Luna Park. The attractions there included a variation on Shoot the Chutes, in which the elephants whooshed down a water slide. Elephants also gave ten-cent rides to children.

A trio of heretofore docile elephants had escaped three days before, but two had been quickly recaptured. Fanny had somehow managed to remain at extra-large, making her way to the beach after midnight Saturday without raising an alarm. She had lumbered into the water with no discernible lights or shoreline before her.

Barlow would have known from the lagoon at the bottom of Shoot the Chutes that elephants are not averse to splashing around. He would have noted that they move through the water with remarkable grace and surprising ease, their lumbering bulk turned to energizing buoyancy, their legs churning with intuitive efficiency, their trunks raised as if originally meant to be snorkels.

And Barlow may have heard seafarers talk of the elephants who swim improbable distances among the Andaman Islands in the Bay of Bengal. But the Andaman elephants swim in groups from one island to another. Fanny was solitary as no female of her species seeks to be save for in the most extreme circumstances. Her destination could not have been more definite than a smudge of shoreline she had glimpsed in daytime.

She may simply have been desperate to get away, to be anywhere but there. Or perhaps she was seeking to paddle against the currents of time, through memories triggered by the scent of the sea, to before she landed in America, before the cramped and harrowing voyage, before being brought down to the docks of her native shores, before being prodded along the path leading from the forest, before the first beating, before the terror of being torn from mother and herd.

She had swum at least four miles into the darkness and fog when she heard the fishermen's voices carry across the water. She may have become so tired and lost and solitary that she headed toward anything that might lead her to land.

She would herself be a lifelong memory for all who saw her standing in the police stable, seemingly serene despite the hubbub and attention. Even with the immediate mystery solved, there remained the question of what exactly had spurred her to undertake this feat, which far outdid what even an elephant man might have expected and which topped with the force of her own, surprisingly free will anything she had ever done at someone's command. She had not likely been seeking simply to make a point about the spirit of even a long subjugated elephant, though made it she had.

She certainly had not lost her appetite. She was consuming hay and feed at such a rate that the police captain was growing progressively less gleeful to have her there. He suggested that Barlow move her immediately.

The elephant trainer prepared to lead Fanny off toward the ferry at the tip of the island, but the captain had a policeman's understanding that she could just as easily decide not to be so well behaved. He insisted that such a beast must be caged before being transported along the roads and through the villages.

No wagon of adequate size was immediately available, and Barlow had to summon one from Sheepshead Bay in Brooklyn. Fanny's appetite did not abate during the protracted wait and the captain reconsidered. He decreed that Barlow could meet the wagon on the way.

Barlow signed what was described as "an elaborate receipt" and started off with Fanny, accompanied by a big crowd.

Five miles on, Fanny suddenly stopped and refused to budge. Barlow theorized aloud that she was holding out for her favorite inducement, but vowed he would get her going without it.

"He failed entirely," noted a reporter who had come not at the urging of some press agent but because this was actual news.

The eminent trainer finally relented and gave the elephant what he termed "a highball."

"It consisted of a stiff quart of whiskey," a newspaper noted. "Fanny smacked her lips and started again."

Another mile farther on they met the wagon. A thousand onlookers watched Barlow and the Cingalese men fashion a ramp at the back by setting three planks atop a bale of hay. Fanny again refused to budge despite all cajoling.

The men finally removed the planks and sought to use just the bale as a step up. Fanny began to munch on the hay and Barlow diverted her with a quart of apples, which seemed to have a soothing effect. She finally stepped on what remained of the bale and entered the back of the wagon. Her fore and hind legs were secured with chains.

At the St. George Ferry landing, the wagon pulled up among a dozen automobiles whose sputtering engines and tooting horns clearly annoyed Fanny. She again sounded her Judgment Day trumpet, with a furious insistence. She persisted as the horses pulled the wagon to the middle of the ferry, directly behind an auto whose engine was kept running.

So many passengers pressed around the wagon to catch a glimpse of the great swimming elephant that Barlow and his helpers had to push them back. Fanny continued trumpeting and he administered "a sedative," a quart of whiskey heavily laced with cocaine. She briefly ceased to be bothered by the automobiles or the gawkers or anything else.

The jolt of the boat nosing into the slip at the tip of Manhattan roused Fanny to raise her trunk and renew her loud protests. This caused one of the horses drawing the wagon to rear and calamity threatened as it sought to bolt. The men managed to get the horse under control and the wagon carried Fanny to teeming South Street, there to await the arrival of a Brooklyn-bound ferry. Never ones to miss an advertising opportunity, the owners of Luna Park had arranged for signs to be affixed to the side of the wagon describing Fanny's feat and where she was bound.

Her continued trumpeting drew still more gawkers. Barlow and his helpers shooed away those who sought to feed her. Some lobbed in paper bags of peanuts, which Fanny quickly consumed.

The trumpeting ceased as the wagon trundled her onto a ferry. She was walked across Brooklyn, arriving without incident at Coney Island and the amusement park that exceeded the imaginings of everybody but its conceivers.

Luna Park had opened May of 1903, just as had been promised by the banner appearing in the film of Topsy's execution, when the grounds had been little more than piles of lumber and mounds of excavated dirt. The slogan from the banner was now emblazoned on a big arch over the entrance.

"The Heart of Coney Island."

Beyond the arch shone what the *New York Times* termed "a realm of fairy romance," the fantastic spires and colonnades and promenades lit with 122,000 lights powered by the big Westinghouse generators. The Russian writer Maxim Gorky had exulted, "With the advent of night, a fantastic city all of a sudden rises from the ocean into the sky."

At the lagoon where the execution platform had been built now stood a two-hundred-foot electric tower from which the great Cameroni slid down on a wire by his teeth, just as he had on Midway Day in Buffalo. Every day was Midway Day in Luna Park. It was also circus day, with two rings at the base of the tower offering twice daily what had once been the sole escape into the fantastic for much of a nation busy building a new reality. These brief performances were now almost lost in the perpetual plentitude of this whole other reality that was termed "the domain of an unknown world."

What Thompson called the Biggest Playground on Earth of course included the Trip to the Moon, though the voyage did not seem so extraordinary when starting out from so astonishing a realm. There had been one disappointing feature in this waking dream's first season, a creature described as "a sad and pensive camel" that fulfilled what was to have been one of Topsy's roles, giving rides to children.

The film of Topsy's execution was absent from the offerings on the rows of individual viewing machines arrayed beyond the Trip to the Moon. Luna Park did not have kinetoscopes but simpler and cheaper peephole viewers developed by a partnership that included an Edison engineer who had set out on his own. These coin-operated machines marketed by the American Mutoscope and Biograph Company showed individual viewers not film, but a series of photos arranged as a kind of mechanical flipbook.

No doubt some of the visitors had seen the film elsewhere on Edison devices. It had been advertised in the *New York Clipper* as "ELECTROCUTION OF AN ELEPHANT" just thirteen days after the execution and listed in a subsequent catalogue for Edison new releases. The catalogue description read:

Topsy, the famous "Baby Elephant," was electrocuted at Coney Island on January 4, 1903. We secured an excellent picture of the execution. The scene opens with keeper leading Topsy to the place of execution. After copper plates or electrodes were fastened to her feet 6,600 volts of electricity were turned on. The elephant is seen to become rigid, throwing her trunk in the air, and then is completely enveloped in smoke from the burning electrodes. The current is turned off and she falls foward to the ground dead.

When the film was screened, the opening title card read "ELECTROCUTING AN ELEPHANT," with no attempt to brand it as "Westinghousing." There was a lone name directly beneath the title, the name so all-important to the Wizard:

Thomas A. Edison

Attendance on opening day at Luna Park had been 40,000 and on that first Fourth of July it had jumped to 140,000 paying customers seeking refuge not just from the summer heat but also from workaday existence itself. Some of the profits went into acquiring four new elephants and hiring an actual trainer. Thompson and Dundy had by then become known to be "almost foolishly fond" of elephants. Thompson's office chair covered with elephant hide was seen as evidence of this fondness.

Edison's movie crew returned to make *Elephants Shooting the Chutes at Luna Park*. The film was summarized in the catalogue:

A huge elephant stands at the top of the chutes and prepares for his trip. At his back is another elephant who starts his companion. The huge animal assumes a sitting position as he leaves the top and like a flash slides down the steep incline into the water. He strikes the water with a tremendous splash, remains under the water for a short time, enjoying his cool bath. It takes considerable coaxing on the part of his Arabian keeper to get him to come out of the water.

That film was followed by *Elephants Shooting the Chutes Luna Park No. 2*. These exhibitions by living elephants appear to have been more popular in the movie houses and with the kinetoscopes than the execution, which did not seem to rouse the same morbid fascination as the prospect of actually seeing a killing live. None of the "actuality" films were as big a hit as some of the fictional narratives, which offered another kind of escape that was in some ways more complete than that offered by Luna Park. The Wizard's big hits included such entertainments as *The Great Train Robbery*. That and *Uncle Tom's Cabin*, the seventh scene of which featured the character for whom the crooked-tailed elephant had been named.

On the wintry night of February 10, 1904, Anthony Pucciani awoke in the workmen's quarters at the wildly successful Luna Park to behold what he would describe as the ghost of the elephant who had been electrocuted the year before. The immigrant laborer would report that the big astral form stood over him with her feet set wide apart, sparks issuing from her trunk, her eyes glowing brightly like blown coals. His response was to faint.

Another laborer would say that he also saw the ghost of Topsy and was temporarily paralyzed by the sight. He said the fiery eyes dimmed as the elephant departed, her shrill trumpeting fading into the sounds made by the wind whistling through the dark and deserted park.

A third man, a frankfurter vendor, would report seeing the ghost doing acrobatics on a tightrope stretched between the Shoot the Chutes ride and the electric tower. He insisted that the phantasmagoric pachyderm hung by her trunk and wiggled her toes.

"Not to be believed," a newspaper opined.

The following day, Pucciani led a group of six laborers to see Hugh Thomas, the electrician who had thrown the switch on Topsy and who also served as a work foreman at Luna. The laborers announced they were quitting and demanded their pay. Thomas dismissed the talk of a ghost as "hocus pocus" but gave them their wages. He hired a new crew that may have known little or nothing of Topsy's sad end.

Then, at the advent of the 1905 season, Barlow brought six of his herd to Luna Park from the Hippodrome, the cavernous theater that Thompson and Dundy had opened near Times Square. The elephants had been showing no signs of stress as they performed on stage before capacity crowds of five thousand in such mega-productions as *Yankee Circus on Mars*, in which they at least appeared to drive automobiles stocked with chorus girls. They seemed equally unbothered by the blazing lights and the throngs of fun seekers at Luna Park. Barlow described his generally docile and obedient charges as "the best elephants on earth."

And that made Barlow all the more puzzled on seeing his elephants become so uncharacteristically restive whenever they were near a quiet and remote back corner at the western end of the twenty-two-acre lot, behind the stables where they were lodged in the off-hours. Any time the elephants were brought near this particular spot where fantasyland became bare dirt, they would halt and visibly shiver as they raised their trunks and trumpeted. Whatever the cause of the agitation, it had almost certainly spurred the triple escape and Fanny's swim.

As Barlow now brought Fanny back to Luna Park, Fanny had become almost as big an aquatic star as the site's previous owner, the Fearless Frogman, but the mystery of what prompted her to bolt remained unsolved. The agitation continued into early August and Barlow finally remarked on the persistent trouble to Thompson. The "Amuser of Millions" went silent, and then suddenly erupted in laughter.

Thompson told Barlow to take him to the patch that had this seemingly inexplicable effect on the elephants. The new work crew was summoned with shovels. These laborers were the replacements of those who had quit en masse over what was ridiculed as superstitious nonsense involving a gargantuan ghost.

"Dig," Thompson now commanded.

Fanny, along with Alice and Jennie, stood nearby, watching intently as the men began digging on this hot summer day in 1905. The work stopped and the trio raised their trunks and trumpeted mournfully as Barlow peered down. He did not need his long experience with elephants to recognize immediately that what lay in the hole was the answer to the mystery.

The three elephants at the edge of the unmarked grave trumpeted mournfully as Topsy's head was removed. Barlow had the three-hundred-pound skull carted away, to be delivered to his home in Huntington, Long Island. The crew filled in the hole and the elephants returned silently to their stalls. They offered no more trouble and continued to thrill the crowds.

AFTERWORD

The following year, 1906, the big news in the show world was the death in April of James Bailey, who had fallen ill after overseeing the opening of another season at Madison Square Garden. The initial reports were that he caught a chill after removing his coat to help unload snow-heavy soil for the ring. Subsequent, more likely accounts suggested that the control-obsessed patriarch who had ordered the killings of at least seven elephants had suffered a tiny insect's bite that developed into acute erysipelas, colloquially known as holy fire.

The Ringling Brothers bought the Barnum & Bailey operation after his death. The Ringling Brothers, Barnum & Bailey Circus continued in seeming perpetuity, billing itself as the Greatest Show on Earth, the name and the superlative eventually covering two shows, one trans-ported by train, the other, smaller one by truck. Both carried Barnum's name into the future, just as he had hoped, complete with publicity stunts as if he were still alive to pull them. That included having the elephant John L. Sullivan, once the Light of Asia and now just Old John, carry a wreath fifty-three miles from Madison Square Garden to the monument in Somers, New York, that Hachaliah Bailey had built a century before to Old Bet, the second elephant in America and the first of her species to be murdered here. The newspapers dutifully reported Old John's progress as he trudged up the length of Manhattan and through the Bronx and into Westchester. He finally arrived at the granite pillar that the original Bailey had erected outside the original Elephant Hotel, which was shaped like a hotel, not an elephant, but had been the headquarters of the circus in America and was now destined to become the town hall and a museum. The crowd that gathered likely included the younger Forepaugh's ex-wife, the humane Lily Deacon, who still lived nearby on an estate turned animal refuge.

The elephant John L. Sullivan's former boxing partner Eph Thompson died in 1909 in the Egyptian city of Alexandria and was buried in England, where he left a family. Thompson was able before his death to make a return visit to his hometown of Ypsilanti, Michigan, which he had left as a young teen after going circus crazy. He brought his four elephants, who did "all new and original tricks, no copy from anyone," including "Mary, the only somersaulting elephant in the world." He was described in the local *Daily Press* as the man "who ran away from Ypsilanti and become one of the most renowned elephant trainers in the world." He must have proven what he needed to prove, for not long afterward he put the elephants up for sale.

His mentor, Stewart Craven, had died at age 56 in 1890, but his widow lived long enough to celebrate her 102nd birthday by dancing as her son played the harmonica. The tricks pioneered by Craven and Thompson were approximated if not quite equaled over the years, though the general approach remained rougher than either man favored. That began to change as the public started to show actual concern, occasionally even outrage.

In 1995, two private citizens founded a 2,700-acre sanctuary in Tennessee for "sick, old, and needy elephants," exclusively female save for the occasional male admitted only in extreme circumstances. That gave the U.S. Department of Agriculture a suitable place to lodge elephants whom the agency found to have been mistreated, usually by animal dealers or the smaller circuses. The humans there of course had their rivalries, and the cofounder Carol Buckley was ousted by the board of directors. Buckley sued, saying, "I don't believe I could live" if she continued to be barred from seeing the elephants.

The same year the sanctuary was founded, the Greatest Show on Earth sought to better its image by establishing the Ringling Brothers Elephant Conservation Center, "in the interest of the species' present and future well being." The stated purpose was "reproduction, research, and retirement," and by 2010 the center had reported the successful birth of twenty-three calves.

The ASPCA was not to be mollified. The organization founded by Bergh brought suit in federal court against Ringling Brothers, Barnum & Bailey Circus accusing it of cruelty to its elephants in violation of the Endangered Species Act. The case was filed in 2000 and finally came to trial in 2009. Judge Emmet Sullivan found for the defendant, ruling that the plaintiff's star witness, former Ringling trainer Tom Rider, had lied about receiving payment from animal activists.

Trainers continued to use bull hooks, but the ones employed by the Ringling show have hooks so small as to be barely visible from even a few feet away. There have been no recent reports of beatings anything like those of old, though the elephants continue to display stereotypic behavior that suggests significant stress. The Ringling show visits Madison Square Garden at its present location farther uptown, arriving by train in Queens, then walking the elephants through the Midtown Tunnel and across West Thirty-fourth Street, to the surprise and delight of late-night pedestrians. The elephants turn just before they come to the Hotel New Yorker, where Tesla ended his days in hopeless love with a white pigeon, saying after it died, "Yes, I loved that pigeon. I loved her as a man loves a woman and she loved me. As long as I had her, there was purpose in my life."

As for the elephants, one of the Garden's security staff in 2009 marveled at how they took turns keeping watch while the others slept. He wondered aloud why they swayed back and forth, back and forth.

In the summer of 2010, the smaller Ringling show, the truck show, made a prolonged appearance in Coney Island. The Internet age had not changed the fundamentals of publicity and it was arranged for the show's star elephant, Susie, to lead the Mermaid Parade that now marks the start of the summer season there.

With the easy elephantine amble that forces humans to scurry if they want to keep pace, Susie came up Surf Avenue, a magician and his girlfriend straddling her neck. Tenders armed with tiny but no doubt sharp hooks surrounded her, a muttered instruction from one of them enough to prompt Susie to raise and curl her trunk, a supposed sign of luck. A half dozen cops also scurried alongside as Susie passed the former site of Steeplechase Park. It had been torn down in 1966 by Donald Trump's real estate developer father, Fred, who held a party at which people were invited to throw bricks through the facade bearing George Tilyou's famous trademark, a smiling face.

"Do we have to stop at the stop light?" a tender now asked.

"No," a cop said.

Susie and her escorts continued on past the very spot where the cops' predecessor Roundsman Clark had ordered Whitey to desist with the pitchfork as Topsy struggled to budge the Trip to the Moon. The curbs on both sides of the street were now packed with people who smiled and cheered on seeing the elephant.

Susie crossed Stillwell Avenue, named for the acquisitive male who secured ownership of all of Coney Island after the demise of

Lady Moody and her egalitarian matriarchy. A block ahead and on the seaward side was the Coney Island Museum, where an artist had fashioned a memorial to Topsy featuring a hand-cranked Mutoscope viewer, but one whose workings were more like those of a kinetoscope and loaded with the film clip of her final moments. The viewer stands safely on copper plates while watching what can be seen on YouTube by searching for "Topsy" and "Coney Island." The clip begins with a card bearing the title and a lone credit that some now consider a condemnation.

Electrocuting an Elephant
Thomas A. Edison

The company that so obligingly provided the deadly volts was still serving Coney Island, along with the rest of the New York, though the Edison Electric Illuminating Company had become Brooklyn Edison and then joined with the city's other power companies into Consolidated Edison. The company's name had been shortened on vehicles, such as one now parked on the street, to Con Edison. People now generally shortened the Wizard's name as well and spoke of Con Ed with little thought of the Wizard who for all his bitterness regarding his name had been so revered upon his death in 1931 that the nation observed a minute of darkness the night of his burial, by chance the fifty-second anniversary of the first successful test of a practical incandescent bulb.

No such honors had accompanied the passing of George Westinghouse in 1914, despite his victory in the War of Currents. He, too, had suffered the humiliation of losing control of the company he founded in 1909, though his name remained even as the company began selling off pieces of itself. It then bought CBS and named itself CBS

Corporation and, in turn, was acquired by Viacom, which subsequently divided itself into Viacom and CBS Corporation.

As this was Mermaid Parade Day, there was a reviewing stand, just down the street from a collection of carnival rides that calls itself Luna Park and just across from the western edge of where the original Luna Park stood before the great fire of 1944. The Electric Eden's owners had long since died, both of natural causes, Dundy just four years after Topsy, Thompson in 1919, having lost control of his Billion-Dollar Smile and so broke his grave went without a tombstone for three years before some show world cronies kicked in to buy one.

The reviewing stand judges now watched the parade participants pass them in the eminently imaginative, ocean-themed costumes that make the Mermaid procession an annual escape from the ordinary. There was, of course, no escape for Susie, who had on a red leather version of the harness worn by her predecessor in the Edison film. Susie's included a medallion that fitted on her forehead reading "Greatest Show on Earth."

"Here comes Susie!" a woman on the reviewing stand announced over the public address system. "Hello, Susie!"

As compliant as her predecessor up to the very end, Susie stopped on command and raised her left foot in what could be taken as a salute but was just another learned trick. The voice again came over the PA system.

"Do not refer to Susie as Topsy, whatever you do."

Only a few people seemed to understand the reference, but that was still more than your average long dead elephant could expect. Susie was ordered to continue on up to West Tenth Street, once the far end of Luna Park, now where she was supposed to swing back around. A police supervisor cleared a large area, as if for some monster tractor-trailer to make a U-turn. The elephant pivoted about almost in place and returned down Surf Avenue at the same easy pace that now had some of the escorts huffing, the cops in particular.

A dozen blocks down, Susie and her escort turned into a parking lot. The magician and his girlfriend slid off her neck and Susie stood at the side entrance to the circus grounds while a truck that had pulled in ahead of her was unloaded. She could have tossed and trampled any of the people around her. Nothing was immediately stopping her from just ambling away, across the beach and into the sea for a long swim of her own if she so desired.

She stayed where she was, the trunk that could kill anybody in reach seeming harmless, her size not the least threatening, her whole manner conveying the same kindliness the witnesses had seen in Topsy in those final moments just up Surf Avenue. Her huge eyes shimmered with that same benevolence, now as then not in response to anything, more likely despite almost everything.

What was conveyed by Susie's manner and eyes was simply what was in her, what had always been in her, what makes elephants giants by measures that are ultimately even more remarkable than their height and weight.

The truck pulled away. Susie went in through the gate.

ACKNOWLEDGMENTS

I set out to tell the story of Topsy after seeing Edison's *Electrocuting an Elephant* on YouTube. I soon discovered that because of the subterfuge accompanying Topsy's arrival in America and her subsequent status as just a member of the herd, there was relatively little documentary material directly concerning her. I was left feeling all the more that the tale of how she came to meet such a cruel end so far from her native land deserved to be told. I have sought to do so largely by recounting the history through which her life progressed. In that effort, I relied on the work of many other writers, ranging from underpaid reporters to underpaid historians to underpaid scientists, who together produced a wealth of knowledge and insight.

Among the newspaper writers, I owed a particular debt to scribes at the *New York Times*. I am no less indebted to the authors of numerous books. Tom McNichol's *AC/DC: The Savage Tale of the First Standards War* is a masterful work and served as a template for my delineation of the War of Currents. William Slout's *Clowns and Cannons* was hugely helpful and a fine resource in every way, most particularly regarding another war, the Battle of the Dwarfs. Jill Jonnes's *Empires of Light* is another masterwork and a fine guide to the interplay of Edison, Tesla, and Westinghouse. Richard Moran's *Executioner's Current* was a

347

clear-eyed guide to the genesis of the electric chair. Also very helpful in that regard was Mark Essig's *Edison and the Electric Chair*. Alfred O. Tate's *Edison's Open Door* accorded me intimate insight into the mind of the Wizard. Charles Musser's *Before the Nickelodeon* is an able history of early Edison movie making. W. C. Thompson's *On the Road with a Circus* is an invaluable firsthand account of traveling with a show. Woody Register's *The Kid of Coney Island* is a remarkable biography of another Thompson, Fred, cofounder of Luna Park. I am only the latest of many writers to use Oliver Pilat and Jo Ranson's classic *Sodom by the Sea* as a guide to the history and buoyant spirit of Coney Island. Eric Scigliano's *Love, War, and Circuses* was a particular help to me and offers much wisdom about elephants and shows. M. H. Dunlop's *Gilded City* was a great resource about the fate of the elephant Tip. Paul Chambers's excellent *Jumbo* was a jumbo-sized resource and showed me all that can be done with a story about an elephant. Stephen Alter's *Elephas Maximus* was of great assistance regarding Asian elephants. Among the more remarkable scientific works were Caitlin O'Connell's *The Elephant's Secret Sense* and Katy Payne's classic *Silent Thunder*, as well as Cynthia Moss's *Elephant Memories*. Nikola Tesla's autobiographical *My Inventions* offered a genius's own words to complement Marc J. Seifer's *The Life and Times of Nikola Tesla*.

Other invaluable books include S. L. Kotar and J. E. Gessler's *The Rise of the American Circus 1716–1899*, Silvio Bedini's *The Pope's Elephant*, Erik Larson's *The Devil in the White City*, Eric Ames's *Carl Hagenbeck's Empire of Entertainments*, and Wyn Wachhorst's *Thomas Alva Edison*.

I am greatly indebted to such circus historians as Stuart Thayer, Fred Dahlinger, Bob Cline, and Bob Parkinson. I also wish to thank Erin Foley and Peter Shrake at the Robert L. Parkinson Library and

Research Center at the Circus World Museum, a big top of scholarly devotion. I owe an equal debt to Margaret Kieckhefer of the Library of Congress as well as AnnaLee Pauls and her colleagues at the Special Collections office at the Princeton University Library.

I further wish to thank all the people at Grove/Atlantic, notably the big boss who bought the book, Morgan Entrekin, and my editor, Jamison Stoltz, who debunked many myths about the decline of publishing. I received further editorial assistance from the ever-wise Nancy Cardozo and my brilliant brother, Doulas Daly. I also wish to thank my agent, Flip Brophy, and my friend Gali Hagel, who kindly read the manuscript with the eye of someone with a long interest in elelphants.

Without my day job, there would be no book, so I thank my former employer, Mort Zuckerman, and my present employer, Tina Brown. The days off and nights would have been too bleak for writing were it not for the Daly girls of Brooklyn, just up Ocean Parkway from where Topsy met her end and Fanny made her great swim.

INDEX

of animals during tests, 189, 196–98, 199–200, 201–2, 211
by electric chair
  Electrical Execution Act and, 189–91, 193
  Kemmler, 226–28, 229
  McElvaine, 229
as public spectacles, 191–93, 319
traditional methods, 190

Fanny
  big swim, 326, 329
  encounters fishermen, 326–27
  escape attempt of, 9
  moved back to Luna Park, 330–32
  at police station, 328–30
  restiveness of at Luna Park, 336–37
"Father of the American circus," 53. *See also* Howes, Seth B.
Feeks, John E. F.
  death of, 220–21
  Edison's response to, 221–23
  Westinghouse's response to Edison, 223–24
Fire Annihilator project, 54–55
Flatfoots, The, 31, 53
Foot, Commodore, 84–85
Forbach, Adam, 87. *See also* Forepaugh, Adam
  acquires Mabie Menagerie and Show assets with O'Brien, 87–89
  changes name to Forepaugh, 89
  early career of, 87, 88
  purchases Romeo, 87
  retains Rice, 88

Forepaugh
  Adam, 89 (*See also* Forbach, Adam; Forepaugh's Circus; Mabie Menagerie and Show)
  "American-born" elephant and, 13–15, 115
  America's first beauty contest and, 135
  background of, 10–11
  Barnum and Cooper & Bailey merger and, 129–30
  Barnum competition, 11–12, 104–5
  Bolivar given to Philadelphia Zoo, 211–12
  Centennial Year and, 12–13, 112–13
  changes name from Forbach, 89
  circus-oriented crimes and, 92, 169–71
  competition with Barnum, 11–12
  considers selling to Barnam & Bailey, 202–6
  Cooper & Bailey's electrical innovations and, 122–24
  Craven and, 108, 110–11, 133, 134–35 (*See also* Craven, Stewart)
  death of, 231–32
  dishonesty of, 92, 169–71
  dissolves O'Brien partnership, 93
  electricity and, 122–24